LIVING THE WORD

**Scripture Reflections and Commentaries
for Sundays and Holy Days**

אנכי
יהוה
אלהיך

Εν αρχη ην
ο Λογος
και ο λογος
ην πρός
τον θεον
και θεος
ην ο λογος

Auch werdet
werdet - das Wort
des Christus
wohne reichlich
unter euch mit
aller Weisheit

YEAR A

**1 DECEMBER 2019
22 NOVEMBER 2020**

JOHN R. BARKER OFM • **KARLA J. BELLINGER**

LIVING THE WORD

Scripture Reflections and Commentaries
for Sundays and Holy Days

Vol. 35   December 1, 2019–November 22, 2020

Published annually

Individual copy: $14.95
2-9 copies: $10.95 per copy;
10-24 copies: $9.95 per copy;
25-99 copies: $8.95 per copy;
100 or more copies: $6.95 per copy

Editor: Alan J. Hommerding
Copy and Production Editor: Marcia T. Lucey
Cover Design and Typesetting: Tejal Patel
Cover Image: Tony Ward • tonywardarts.com

Director of Publications: Mary Beth Kunde-Anderson

In accordance with c. 827, permission to publish is granted on June 17, 2019, by Most Reverend Ronald A. Hicks, Vicar General of the Archdiocese of Chicago. Permission to publish is an official declaration of ecclesiastical authority that the material is free from doctrinal and moral error. No legal responsibility is assumed by the grant of this permission.

World Library Publications,
the music and liturgy division of J. S. Paluch Company, Inc.
3708 River Road, Suite 400, Franklin Park, IL 60131-2158
800 566-6150 • fax 888 957-3291
wlpcs@jspaluch.com • www.wlpmusic.com

Printed in the United States of America
WLP 006772 • (ISSN) 1079-4670 • (ISBN) 978-1-58459-974-6

INTRODUCTION

Our liturgy presumes that those who gather for Eucharist, as members of the Body of Christ, are already familiar with the word that they hear proclaimed every Sunday. *Living the Word* is designed to assist individuals, homilists, catechumens, candidates, discussion groups, religious education classes, and similar gatherings to deepen that familiarity with the Sunday scriptures.

Inside this book you will find the readings for each Sunday and holy day from Year A of the liturgical cycle. Each day's readings are preceded by a brief passage intended to suggest a focus or approach to consider while reading these particular scriptures. The readings are followed by a commentary that provides a context for understanding them, making use of biblical scholarship and the Church's longstanding traditions. Then a reflection is offered that expands upon the initial focus and incorporates the fuller understanding from the commentary section. The discussion questions and suggestions for responses that follow are provided as helps to move from reflection to action, inviting those who use this volume to go about truly "living the word."

When reflecting on the scriptures in a group setting or individually, it is best to do so in the context of prayer. Users of this book are encouraged to create an atmosphere that will foster prayerful reflection: in a quiet space, perhaps with lit candle and simple seasonal decoration (incense or soft music may also be appropriate), begin with a prayer and reading of the scriptures aloud for that day, even if you are alone. In a group, encourage members to focus on one word or idea that especially strikes them. Continue with each reading the same way, perhaps taking time to share these ideas with one another.

After you spend some quiet time with the readings, ask yourself how they have changed you, enlightened you, moved you. Move on to the commentary, reflection, and prayer response. Allow the discussion questions to shape your conversation, and try the prayer response on for size. Will you rise to its challenge? Does it give you an idea of something to try in your own life? Share your ideas with someone else, even if you have been preparing alone.

Once you have spent a suitable time in reflection or discussion, you may wish to make a prayerful response to the readings by means of a song or a blessing of someone or something. Pray spontaneously as you think about the texts' meaning for you, or invite people in the group to offer prayers informally.

Finally, challenge yourself, or each other in your group, to take action this week based on your understanding of the readings. You may propose your own prayer for help to undertake this mission or simply stand in a circle and pray the Lord's Prayer. If you are in a group, offer one another a sign of peace before departing. If alone, surprise someone with a sign of peace, either in person, by making a phone call, or offering a simple prayer.

As you repeat this pattern over time, your prayerful reflection can deepen your appreciation of God's word and enable you to live it more fully every day.

Repeating this pattern over time can help your prayerful reflection to deepen your appreciation for and commitment to God's word every day of your life.

Table of Contents

Individual Prayers Before and After Reading Scripture

Speak to me as I read your word, O Lord,
and send your Spirit into my heart.
Guide me today and each day in your service,
for you are the way, the truth, and the life. Amen!

or

May the words of my mouth, and the meditations of my heart
be acceptable to you, O Lord, my rock and my redeemer. Amen!

God of all graciousness,
I thank you for speaking to me
through your holy word.

Let me put your word into action
today and every day. Amen!

or

Blessed are you, Lord God,
maker of heaven and earth,
for sending your Holy Spirit today
to teach me your truth. Amen!

Group Prayers Before and After Reading Scripture

Blessed are you, Lord God,
you teach your people by your word.
Open our hearts to your Spirit,
and lead us in the ways of Christ your Son.
All praise and glory be yours for ever. Amen!

or

Speak, Lord,
your servants are listening:
You alone have the words of everlasting life. Amen!

We praise you, loving God, for sending us your word today.

Grant that we may continue to think and pray on these words,
and to share them with others throughout this day. Amen!

or

May this word of life
fill our hearts, be on our lips,
and guide our every thought and deed. Amen!

ADVENT/CHRISTMAS

The first readings for Advent are clear–eyed about the state of the world as it currently stands—engulfed in chaos, violence, sin, and infirmity—yet they assure us that God firmly intends to heal our wounds, no matter how severe or deeply entrenched. Isaiah foretells a day when the universal recognition of the sovereignty of the God of Israel will bring an end to war (Isaiah 2:1–5), and offers a vision of God's peaceful reign, overseen by the ideal Davidic king, that is so unlike what we now consider normal that even "natural enemies" will live in harmony (Isaiah 11:1–10). God's repair of the world will include overcoming the infirmities of human sin (Genesis 3:9–15) and illness (Isaiah 35:1–6a). Nothing, in short, will be impossible with God. In the Christmas season, we continue to see the divine intention to bless and enable human flourishing, from the individual (Numbers 6:22–27) to the family (Sirach 3:2–6) to the whole world (Isaiah 42:1–4; 60:1–6).

The second readings emphasize the universal scope of salvation offered through Christ, as well as our appropriate response to this divine gift. In Advent we are exhorted to strive for holiness and allow ourselves to be transformed as we await Christ's return in glory (Romans 13:11–14; 15:4–9). Both our commitment to renewal and our hope of Christ's return require us to have faith in the mysterious, unseen work of God deep within the world (James 5:7–10). The Christmas readings focus on the person of Jesus as the Son, imprint, and heir of God (Hebrews 1:1–6). Those who have been baptized into Christ now have a place in the divine household and a share of the inheritance. As foretold by the prophets, this inheritance and the salvation it brings now extend, in Christ, beyond the ethnic bounds of Israel to include all nations (Ephesians 3:2–3a, 5–6; Acts 10:34–38).

Early in Advent the Gospel reminds us to "Stay awake!" lest we be caught unprepared for Christ's return (Matthew 24:37–44). The theme of preparation continues with the appearance of the Baptist, calling for repentance (Matthew 3:1–12). John's role as messenger and "Preparer" is emphasized also in the third Sunday of Advent, now in conjunction with Jesus' role as "the One who is to come," bringing with him the healing promised through the prophets. Beginning with the Fourth Sunday of Advent we encounter several iconic scenes that remind us of the humility of the Incarnation, the depth of which can only be appreciated with a consideration of John's Prologue and the grand vision of the Word of God made flesh (John 1:1–18). The Christmas season ends with the Baptism of God's beloved Son, now ready to bring the Kingdom to a broken and troubled world.

FIRST SUNDAY OF ADVENT

Today's Focus: Living on the Edge—of Time

Every moment of our lives is a moment with the potential for things to shift, to change. In Advent, we stand on this edge, looking for Christ's coming.

FIRST READING   *Isaiah 2:1–5*

This is what Isaiah, son of Amoz,
saw concerning Judah and Jerusalem.
  In days to come,
the mountain of the LORD's house
  shall be established as the highest mountain
  and raised above the hills.
All nations shall stream toward it;
  many peoples shall come and say:
"Come, let us climb the LORD's mountain,
  to the house of the God of Jacob,
that he may instruct us in his ways,
  and we may walk in his paths."
For from Zion shall go forth instruction,
  and the word of the LORD from Jerusalem.
He shall judge between the nations,
  and impose terms on many peoples.
They shall beat their swords into plowshares
  and their spears into pruning hooks;
one nation shall not raise the sword against another,
  nor shall they train for war again.
O house of Jacob, come,
  let us walk in the light of the LORD!

PSALM READING   *Psalm 122:1*

Let us go rejoicing to the house of the Lord.

SECOND READING   *Romans 13:11–14*

Brothers and sisters: You know the time; it is the hour now for you to awake from sleep. For our salvation is nearer now than when we first believed; the night is advanced, the day is at hand. Let us then throw off the works of darkness and put on the armor of light; let us conduct ourselves properly as in the day, not in orgies and drunkenness, not in promiscuity and lust, not in rivalry and jealousy. But put on the Lord Jesus Christ, and make no provision for the desires of the flesh.

Jesus said to his disciples: "As it was in the days of Noah, so it will be at the coming of the Son of Man. In those days before the flood, they were eating and drinking, marrying and giving in marriage, up to the day that Noah entered the ark. They did not know until the flood came and carried them all away. So will it be also at the coming of the Son of Man. Two men will be out in the field; one will be taken, and one will be left. Two women will be grinding at the mill; one will be taken, and one will be left. Therefore, stay awake! For you do not know on which day your Lord will come. Be sure of this: if the master of the house had known the hour of night when the thief was coming, he would have stayed awake and not let his house be broken into. So too, you also must be prepared, for at an hour you do not expect, the Son of Man will come."

Understanding the Word

The reading from Isaiah focuses on future, universal recognition of the sovereignty of the God of Israel. God's mountain refers to the site of the temple, yet the image evokes more than location. Not only God's dwelling place, but also as the place from which the divine King exercises dominion through law-giving and judgment, the mountain represents God's sovereign rule. In time, the kingship of God will extend beyond Israel as other nations receive both instructions previously reserved for Israel and the benefit of God's just judgment. Enlightened by God's instruction and obedient to God's judgment of conflicts, the nations will have no need to resort to war.

Having exhorted the Roman Christians not to conform themselves to the present age, but to allow their minds to be transformed (Romans 12:2), Paul has insisted they must love one another, for "love is the fulfillment of the law" (13:10). Paul now places his plea within the context of God's plan: moral transformation is both necessary and urgent, for the dawn of salvation has begun. To remain in former ways is to be caught "asleep" as the sun rises. Transformation comes about by putting on the "armor of light," Christ himself ("put on the Lord Jesus Christ"), who protects against the seductions of the flesh, physical or social. Thus, it is Christ who brings about in the believer this saving transformation.

Jesus' speech picks up this same idea of not being caught off guard when he returns. Just as the flood brought with it a sudden change from life as usual to judgment, so it will be when the Son of Man comes back. Now is the time to make whatever changes need to be made in one's life. As in the Pauline passage, there is a union of eschatology and ethics—one must live in a way that is fitting for the reign of God. There will come a time when it will be "too late," when the time of preparation will have passed.

Reflecting on the Word

When you stand at the lip of the Grand Canyon, you can see into a vast distance. You know that you are at the edge of something. Today, we are on the edge of something, too—the edge of time. That is a little harder to see. A pregnant mother breathes with the contractions of her womb; she is on the edge of the moment of birth. The family of a dying man waits by his hospital bed, attentive to his breathing, on the brink of the time of his death. Time has edges. Time has moments when something is about to shift.

At the time of First Isaiah, bloodthirsty Assyria hovered over Israel. The prophet sensed that time was about to change. Now we know that it was the total destruction of Israel's northern kingdom and the loss of the ten northern tribes. Only Isaiah felt it coming. His people didn't know. They were on an edge when history was about to shift.

Jesus alerts us to this edginess: we do not know our own time or hour. We do not know the time or the hour for our loved ones. Each moment of the present is a shifting point between past and future. We live on the edge of time.

Today, we are on the edge of Advent. Advent is the liturgical time that alerts us: Stay awake! Be ready! We know that Christmas is coming. We do not know when Jesus will come again in glory. With Isaiah, we pray that swords will be turned into plowshares. Are we on the edge of a shift in history? We do not know. But with God's help, we hold onto this quiet Advent hope: Our God is timeless, but is also the Lord of time. Jesus is here, now and always.

Consider/Discuss

❖ Think of your own moments of transition and change, the edginess of time in your own life. How has God been with you in those moments?

❖ As we look toward the unfolding of Advent, how can we use this season of preparation purposefully to grow spiritually stronger for the next "something" that is coming our way?

Living and Praying with the Word

Lord, as we begin our Advent preparation, we wait for you. We listen for you in the stillness. We wait for you as in the quiet darkness before the dawn. We do not know what is ahead, but in this moment, breathe within us and strengthen us. Abide with us. Cleanse our hearts and let us be ready to receive you, no matter what may swirl around us. Come, Lord Jesus! Come and be born in our hearts.

SECOND SUNDAY OF ADVENT

Today's Focus: Seeing Differently, through God's Eyes

Our mortal eyes mostly see the here and now.
When we immerse ourselves in the life of God,
our vision also sees what may be, what may come.

FIRST READING   *Isaiah 11:1–10*

On that day, a shoot shall sprout from the stump of Jesse,
    and from his roots a bud shall blossom.
The spirit of the Lord shall rest upon him:
    a spirit of wisdom and of understanding,
a spirit of counsel and of strength,
    a spirit of knowledge and of fear of the LORD,
    and his delight shall be the fear of the LORD.
Not by appearance shall he judge,
    nor by hearsay shall he decide,
but he shall judge the poor with justice,
    and decide aright for the land's afflicted.
He shall strike the ruthless with the rod of his mouth,
    and with the breath of his lips he shall slay the wicked.
Justice shall be the band around his waist,
    and faithfulness a belt upon his hips.
Then the wolf shall be a guest of the lamb,
    and the leopard shall lie down with the kid;
the calf and the young lion shall browse together,
    with a little child to guide them.
The cow and the bear shall be neighbors,
    together their young shall rest;
    the lion shall eat hay like the ox.
The baby shall play by the cobra's den,
    and the child lay his hand on the adder's lair.
There shall be no harm or ruin on all my holy mountain;
    for the earth shall be filled with knowledge of the LORD,
    as water covers the sea.
On that day, the root of Jesse,
    set up as a signal for the nations,
the Gentiles shall seek out,
    for his dwelling shall be glorious.

PSALM RESPONSE   *Psalm 72:7*

Justice shall flourish in his time, and fullness of peace for ever.

SECOND READING

Brothers and sisters: Whatever was written previously was written for our instruction, that by endurance and by the encouragement of the Scriptures we might have hope. May the God of endurance and encouragement grant you to think in harmony with one another, in keeping with Christ Jesus, that with one accord you may with one voice glorify the God and Father of our Lord Jesus Christ.

Welcome one another, then, as Christ welcomed you, for the glory of God. For I say that Christ became a minister of the circumcised to show God's truthfulness, to confirm the promises to the patriarchs, but so that the Gentiles might glorify God for his mercy. As it is written:

Therefore, I will praise you among the Gentiles
and sing praises to your name.

GOSPEL

John the Baptist appeared, preaching in the desert of Judea and saying, "Repent, for the kingdom of heaven is at hand!" It was of him that the prophet Isaiah had spoken when he said:

A voice of one crying out in the desert,
Prepare the way of the Lord,
  make straight his paths.

John wore clothing made of camel's hair and had a leather belt around his waist. His food was locusts and wild honey. At that time Jerusalem, all Judea, and the whole region around the Jordan were going out to him and were being baptized by him in the Jordan River as they acknowledged their sins.

When he saw many of the Pharisees and Sadducees coming to his baptism, he said to them, "You brood of vipers! Who warned you to flee from the coming wrath? Produce good fruit as evidence of your repentance. And do not presume to say to yourselves, 'We have Abraham as our father.' For I tell you, God can raise up children to Abraham from these stones. Even now the ax lies at the root of the trees. Therefore every tree that does not bear good fruit will be cut down and thrown into the fire. I am baptizing you with water, for repentance, but the one who is coming after me is mightier than I. I am not worthy to carry his sandals. He will baptize you with the Holy Spirit and fire. His winnowing fan is in his hand. He will clear his threshing floor and gather his wheat into his barn, but the chaff he will burn with unquenchable fire."

Understanding the Word

Israelite kings were to act as God's representatives, ensuring justice by ruling wisely and fairly; they often failed in this regard. In Isaiah's vision, God raises up an ideal Davidic king who will perfectly reflect the rule of the God he represents. Endowed with divine gifts, the king will bring down the "ruthless" and the "wicked" through right judgment ("the rod of his mouth"). Further, he will usher in an era in which all creaturely violence will end. "Natural enemies" will belong to the "peaceable kingdom" brought about by the royal icon of God. Such will be the magnificence and beneficence of the kingdom that other nations will be drawn to it.

Paul reminds his Roman readers that the story of Israel, in which the promises to the ancestors were fulfilled first in ancient times and then more completely in Christ, gives evidence of God's trustworthiness. One aspect of those promises was that all the families of the earth would find blessing through Abraham's descendants (Genesis 12:3). Thus, the fulfillment of those promises also included the extension of God's mercy not just to Israel but ultimately, in Jesus Christ, to all the nations. God wishes to gather all peoples together in Christ—a divine intention that encourages the Romans to seek unity among themselves.

John the Baptist's message of repentance (*metanoia*, change of mind and direction) draws large crowds, who are preparing for the coming of God's kingdom. This kingdom is understood eschatologically, as a time of consummation and judgment. Foreshadowing what is to come, John has harsh words for the religious leaders, who do not possess a repentant disposition. Anticipating a claim that they have no need of repentance to prepare themselves, John assures them that God is sending One who will see, not one's birth status, but one's heart, and will judge accordingly, baptizing in fire and the Holy Spirit, which is to say, with the power and wisdom of God. John's message highlights that this is a moment of decision for everyone.

Reflecting on the Word

When I was in forestry school in the Upper Peninsula of Michigan, I recall skiing one winter morning through a birch grove as the sun rose. The white birch bark glowed pink in the snow, reflecting the sunrise. Around me, trees had fallen, some had been chopped up for firewood. Yet each of the ancient trees had stump sprouts rising from its base. (That is the nature of birch trees.) In three years, young trees had grown fifteen feet. How so tall? They didn't have to start from scratch; the saplings were fed by the root systems of the older trees.

Our Christian faith is like a stump sprout that rises from our Jewish roots. We share a common vision: that peace will reign and justice will thrive. Isaiah envisions a king who will make creation flourish in solidarity: even a cobra will be so tame that a baby can handle it. Together we are rooted in God's vision, a hope for a more glowing future.

At the same time, John the Baptist bursts in wielding an axe with rough words for the Pharisees—repent! Cut down every tree that does not bear good fruit! Yet he too sees a radiant vision: One who is coming after him who will baptize with the Holy Spirit and fire!

We are rooted in God's vision of what can be. The courage of Advent is this faith in the future. We await Christmas. We await eternity. Earthly life will be cut down and pass away, yet we live on the brink of a blessed and infinite future. That mode of seeing can fill the way that we live our lives today. Like the fiery glow in the birch forest, as people of Advent we live within the sunrise of a new day.

Consider/Discuss

❖ Isaiah tells us that a shoot shall sprout from the stump of Jesse. None of us start from scratch either. Our faith is rooted in the faith of those who have gone before us. Our faith is now supported by those who travel with us. We hope that our faith will bear fruit in those who arise from our roots. What do each of those roots look like—past, present, and future?

❖ In this season of preparation for the coming of Jesus, as God sees into our hearts, what is one thing that we could chop off or prune in order to bear stronger fruit?

Living and Praying with the Word

God of the future, thank you for your vision. Open our eyes to see you as you surround and enfold us on this journey. Help us to see this sunrise in which we live. We want to walk with you more robustly. We give ourselves to you this day, for you are the source of our hope. Fill us with the fullness of your peace forever. Thank you and thank you again for your goodness to us.

DECEMBER 9, 2019

THE IMMACULATE CONCEPTION OF THE BLESSED VIRGIN MARY

Today's Focus: Planted and Tended in the Soil of Faith

All great things have tiny beginnings: the mightiest trees,
the most magnificent works of art, the longest journeys, and every one of us.
God's grace can turn that tininess into something wonderful.

FIRST READING
Genesis 3:9–15, 20

After the man, Adam, had eaten of the tree, the LORD God called to the man and asked him, "Where are you?" He answered, "I heard you in the garden; but I was afraid, because I was naked, so I hid myself." Then he asked, "Who told you that you were naked? You have eaten, then, from the tree of which I had forbidden you to eat!" The man replied, "The woman whom you put here with me—she gave me fruit from the tree, and so I ate it." The LORD God then asked the woman, "Why did you do such a thing?" The woman answered, "The serpent tricked me into it, so I ate it."

Then the LORD God said to the serpent:
"Because you have done this, you shall be banned
    from all the animals
    and from all the wild creatures;
on your belly shall you crawl,
    and dirt shall you eat
    all the days of your life.
I will put enmity between you and the woman,
    and between your offspring and hers;
he will strike at your head,
    while you strike at his heel."

The man called his wife Eve, because she became the mother of all the living.

PSALM RESPONSE
Psalm 98:1a

Sing to the Lord a new song, for he has done marvelous deeds.

SECOND READING
Ephesians 1:3–6, 11–12

Brothers and sisters: Blessed be the God and Father of our Lord Jesus Christ, who has blessed us in Christ with every spiritual blessing in the heavens, as he chose us in him, before the foundation of the world, to be holy and without blemish before him. In love he destined us for adoption to himself through Jesus Christ, in accord with the favor of his will, for the praise of the glory of his grace that he granted us in the beloved.

15

In him we were also chosen, destined in accord with the purpose of the One who accomplishes all things according to the intention of his will, so that we might exist for the praise of his glory, we who first hoped in Christ.

GOSPEL

Luke 1:26–38

The angel Gabriel was sent from God to a town of Galilee called Nazareth, to a virgin betrothed to a man named Joseph, of the house of David, and the virgin's name was Mary. And coming to her, he said, "Hail, full of grace! The Lord is with you." But she was greatly troubled at what was said and pondered what sort of greeting this might be. Then the angel said to her, "Do not be afraid, Mary, for you have found favor with God. Behold, you will conceive in your womb and bear a son, and you shall name him Jesus. He will be great and will be called Son of the Most High, and the Lord God will give him the throne of David his father, and he will rule over the house of Jacob forever, and of his kingdom there will be no end." But Mary said to the angel, "How can this be, since I have no relations with a man?" And the angel said to her in reply, "The Holy Spirit will come upon you, and the power of the Most High will overshadow you. Therefore the child to be born will be called holy, the Son of God. And behold, Elizabeth, your relative, has also conceived a son in her old age, and this is the sixth month for her who was called barren; for nothing will be impossible for God." Mary said, "Behold, I am the handmaid of the Lord. May it be done to me according to your word." Then the angel departed from her.

Understanding the Word

The story of Eden describes an idyllic past marked divine-human intimacy, which was destroyed when the snake suggested that God, jealous of divine prerogatives, did not have the humans' best interests at heart. The result, as later chapters make clear, was a breakdown of the divine-human relationship as well as relationships between humans. God's judgment on the snake, read on one level, explains why snakes are dangerous and why humans try to crush their heads rather than be bitten. But the story calls for a symbolic reading, in which the snake represents temptation, and thus the enmity between humans and the snake represents the constant and universal struggle to trust and obey God.

The reading from Ephesians focuses on divine election apart from human merit. Paul emphasizes that this election results in "blessing" from God in Christ, which takes different forms. One is holiness, perfect conformity to the will of God, "without blemish." Another is adoption into the household of God, not having earned this as a right, but receiving it as a gift, "in accord with the favor of his will." Those in God's household achieve their salvation because this is God's will, and this is therefore cause for praise and glory.

The Gospel scene is filled with references to God's earlier work, suggesting that Gabriel is announcing the culmination of a plan long in the making. References to David point toward the divine election of that king and his descendants, whose rule over Israel God promised to be "firmly established forever" (2 Samuel 7:16). The child who will fulfill this promise forever is to be born to Mary, who has found favor with God and so is prepared to be the mother of "the Son of God." Mary, of course, is perplexed by how all this can be. Gabriel's explanation itself might seem incredible, until he also announces that the aged and barren Elizabeth will also give birth, pointedly noting that "nothing will be impossible with God."

Reflecting on the Word

One afternoon, as I sliced a red onion to sauté in butter, the storyboard of my mind floated back to the previous January and the tiny onion seeds that I had planted. I kept the grow lights low. One day, up popped tiny blades that looked like grass. I was so excited! I watered. They grew. Every Saturday, I trimmed back those shoots of green to five inches tall so that they would grow stocky and strong. In March, I tilled the soil and prepared the beds. In late April, I planted small onion plants. Even when our border collie ran through the beds and trampled the tops in July, I kept weeding. I kept watering. Then, in December, one red onion slides off the cutting board to sizzle in the pan.

Mary of the Immaculate Conception was like that one tiny onion seed. Amid the brokenness of the human race, God spent centuries preparing the soil of the Chosen People. Born of the faithful remnant, the *anawim*, Mary was planted in the rich soil of faith, graced with every spiritual blessing. She was nurtured. She was cared for. She rejoiced and bore fruit. And even after the world had trampled her heart and crucified her Son, the Holy Spirit kept nourishing her with strength.

Do you remember your conception, before you were the size of an onion seed? I don't either. But if I, as a gardener, can put so much care into one red onion, with how much more care does our Creator tend to us? Even though we are trampled and wounded as part of the human condition, the reading from Ephesians tells us that we too are nourished by Christ with every spiritual blessing. God is a good gardener.

Consider/Discuss

❖ Mary probably didn't recall the moment of her conception. But imagine the elation of the angels and the saints at that moment. They were so excited—a human being immaculately conceived! In reflection and prayer, travel back to that day when you were created. See how excited they were about you also. Perhaps not immaculately conceived, but most dearly beloved! Relish their jubilation. Be washed with their love. Be healed, and rejoice.

❖ Think about what nurtured Mary's spiritual life—the psalms, the stories of Moses and the prophets, the prayers of her people. As this Advent continues to unfold, how can we purposefully enrich the soil of faith in which we grow? What do we need to trim back? What will help us to flourish?

Living and Praying with the Word

Lord God, Creator of the universe and our Creator, we remember your continuing kindness and faithfulness toward us. Give us the grace to glorify you by carefully nourishing ourselves and nurturing all those you put into our care. You have made us for yourself. Keep us trimmed. Mary of the Immaculate Conception, pray for our strong and stocky spiritual growth.

THIRD SUNDAY OF ADVENT

Today's Focus: Darkness Is Not the Final Answer

Though the world around us is filled with lights during this season,
sometimes it can still feel very dark. In this darkness,
we remember God sending us Light from light.

FIRST READING

Isaiah 35:1–6a, 10

The desert and the parched land will exult;
    the steppe will rejoice and bloom.
They will bloom with abundant flowers,
    and rejoice with joyful song.
The glory of Lebanon will be given to them,
    the splendor of Carmel and Sharon;
they will see the glory of the LORD,
    the splendor of our God.
Strengthen the hands that are feeble,
    make firm the knees that are weak,
say to those whose hearts are frightened:
    Be strong, fear not!
Here is your God,
    he comes with vindication;
with divine recompense
    he comes to save you.
Then will the eyes of the blind be opened,
    the ears of the deaf be cleared;
then will the lame leap like a stag,
    then the tongue of the mute will sing.

Those whom the LORD has ransomed will return
    and enter Zion singing,
    crowned with everlasting joy;
they will meet with joy and gladness,
    sorrow and mourning will flee.

PSALM RESPONSE

Isaiah 35:4

Lord, come and save us.

SECOND READING

James 5:7–10

Be patient, brothers and sisters, until the coming of the Lord. See how the farmer waits for the precious fruit of the earth, being patient with it until it receives the early and the late rains. You too must be patient. Make your hearts firm, because the coming of the Lord is at hand. Do not complain, brothers and sisters, about one another, that you may not be judged. Behold, the Judge is standing before the gates. Take as an example of hardship and patience, brothers and sisters, the prophets who spoke in the name of the Lord.

GOSPEL

Matthew 11:2–11

When John the Baptist heard in prison of the works of the Christ, he sent his disciples to Jesus with this question, "Are you the one who is to come, or should we look for another?" Jesus said to them in reply, "Go and tell John what you hear and see: the blind regain their sight, the lame walk, lepers are cleansed, the deaf hear, the dead are raised, and the poor have the good news proclaimed to them. And blessed is the one who takes no offense at me."

As they were going off, Jesus began to speak to the crowds about John, "What did you go out to the desert to see? A reed swayed by the wind? Then what did you go out to see? Someone dressed in fine clothing? Those who wear fine clothing are in royal palaces. Then why did you go out? To see a prophet? Yes, I tell you, and more than a prophet. This is the one about whom it is written:

Behold, I am sending my messenger ahead of you;
he will prepare your way before you.

Amen, I say to you, among those born of women there has been none greater than John the Baptist; yet the least in the kingdom of heaven is greater than he."

Understanding the Word

In the first reading God offers a vision of Israel's restoration after the Babylonian exile. This is conveyed first through the image of the flowering wilderness: what is presently "lifeless" will soon host "abundant flowers" and "joyful song." This reversal represents God's ability to bring life where there is none. Thus, this affirmation is accompanied by a general exhortation: "Be strong, fear not!" God the redeemer comes to bring the people back home. The healing of the parched land is mirrored by the healing of the weak and infirm, the sorrowful and grieving, who will—like the wilderness—sing joyfully.

James offers an exhortation to remain firm in belief and steadfast in moral uprightness while waiting for the coming of the Lord. The emphasis throughout is on "patience," mentioned four times. Just as crops cannot be rushed, neither can Christ's return, which will happen in due time. All the same, James assures his audience that "the coming of the Lord is at hand." So, do not allow Christ's apparent delay to be the occasion either for losing hope or growing slack. James particularly focuses on complaining about others, which is a form of judging. When Christ does come, he will come as Judge; it is proper for him, not for us, to judge.

In prison John the Baptist has heard rumors of Jesus, whom he had earlier baptized (3:13–17). Now he seeks to know if Jesus is, in fact, the Messiah ("the one who is to come"). Jesus lets John draw his own conclusions. He has proclaimed good news to the poor and he has healed, activities expected of the Messiah. Jesus, in turn, asks the crowds about John, affirming that he is indeed the prophet they went out to see, and he is the one sent to announce the Messiah. Thus, Jesus' identity as Messiah is confirmed both by his actions and by the fact that someone they had all recognized as a prophet had prepared the way for him.

Reflecting on the Word

John the Baptist sits in prison. He waits for the one who is to come. No angel bursts his bonds. No heavenly blast levels the stones to release him. The holy prophet expects death, for he had dared to speak out, challenging those in power. There is anticipation outside the walls, but the excitement passes him by. He waits in darkness.

The hubbub that surrounds Christmas may pass some of us by as well. We may be praying for healing. We may ache for reconciliation. We may dwell in deep grief or loneliness or heartache. Christmas can be a particularly painful time for some of us. Like John the Baptist, we may feel the darkness.

But John the Baptist was not just a reed swaying in the wind. Jesus says of him that there has been none greater. From his Jewish roots, he knew to hold fast to the Lord who loves the just, to the Most High who sets captives free, to the One who causes the desert to bloom again. And Jesus showed him an answer to fuel his faith: Look, the lame walk! Lepers are cleansed! The dead are raised! The darkness was not the final answer.

Advent is a contemplative time, a season for quiet hopefulness. Isaiah says, "Be strong! Fear not!" We too are waiting for the one who is to come. We know the conclusion to the story of Advent: Baby Jesus was born. Yet we are still waiting for the final dawning, to see the glory of God. Jesus shows us answers today as well, revealing himself sometimes in very small ways—in the sparkle of snow, in the tiny toenails of a newborn child, and in the smile of a loved one. The darkness is not our final answer either.

Consider/Discuss

❖ We have been looking at the edginess of Advent. We are looking for light. Yet sometimes the darkness of the winter and the challenges of life can make us feel as if we are sitting with John the Baptist as he waits for one to come. Where in our lives could we use more of the Lord's light? In what situations could we use courage?

❖ What "small ways" have we seen that give us hope?

Living and Praying with the Word

Lord, as the winter season grows darker, sometimes we feel as though we are trying to manufacture light. All of the Christmas hubbub does not always feel real. Give us grace to sit quietly in your blessed darkness. We appreciate that you are our only Light, our only Savior. Stir our will to surrender all of our Christmas preparations to you. Let us do only what is for your glory and let the rest go, and rest in your peace.

FOURTH SUNDAY OF ADVENT

Today's Focus: God Takes Us In; We Belong to God.

---

*Even the most secure lives have some insecurities,
and life can change in an instant. Through every possible future,
we know that our true place of safety and rest is in God alone.*

FIRST READING
Isaiah 7:10–14

The LORD spoke to Ahaz, saying: Ask for a sign from the LORD, your God; let it be deep as the netherworld, or high as the sky! But Ahaz answered, "I will not ask! I will not tempt the LORD!" Then Isaiah said: Listen, O house of David! Is it not enough for you to weary people, must you also weary my God? Therefore the LORD himself will give you this sign: the virgin shall conceive, and bear a son, and shall name him Emmanuel.

PSALM RESPONSE
Psalm 24:7c and 10b

Let the Lord enter; he is king of glory.

SECOND READING
Romans 1:1–7

Paul, a slave of Christ Jesus, called to be an apostle and set apart for the gospel of God, which he promised previously through his prophets in the holy Scriptures, the gospel about his Son, descended from David according to the flesh, but established as Son of God in power according to the Spirit of holiness through resurrection from the dead, Jesus Christ our Lord. Through him we have received the grace of apostleship, to bring about the obedience of faith, for the sake of his name, among all the Gentiles, among whom are you also, who are called to belong to Jesus Christ; to all the beloved of God in Rome, called to be holy. Grace to you and peace from God our Father and the Lord Jesus Christ.

GOSPEL
Matthew 1:18–24

This is how the birth of Jesus Christ came about. When his mother Mary was betrothed to Joseph, but before they lived together, she was found with child through the Holy Spirit. Joseph her husband, since he was a righteous man, yet unwilling to expose her to shame, decided to divorce her quietly. Such was his intention when, behold, the angel of the Lord appeared to him in a dream and said, "Joseph, son of David, do not be afraid to take Mary your wife into your home. For it is through the Holy Spirit that this child has been conceived in her. She will bear a son and you are to name him Jesus, because he will save his people from their sins." All this took place to fulfill what the Lord had said through the prophet:

Behold, the virgin shall conceive and bear a son,
and they shall name him Emmanuel,
which means "God is with us."

When Joseph awoke, he did as the angel of the Lord had commanded him and took his wife into his home.

Understanding the Word

Isaiah understood that the "house of David" was protected by God, according to God's promise to David (2 Samuel 7:11–16). King Ahaz, threatened by surrounding states seeking to depose him, contemplates turning to the Assyrian Empire for help, an act reflecting a lack of faith in God's protection. Not wishing not be dissuaded from his political course, the king "piously" declines God's offer of a sign of his continued support of the Davidic monarchy. Nevertheless, the prophet points to a sign, which is a "young woman" (in Hebrew; "virgin" in the Greek translation) who is pregnant (future tense in the Greek). The son to be born will inherit the throne of David, making him a sign of fidelity to God's promise.

Paul begins his letter to the Romans by setting out the core of his message about Christ Jesus, which is the good news, earlier announced in Israel's scriptures, that God has sent a descendant of David and confirmed him as Messiah and Lord by raising him from the dead. Paul himself is a "slave" of Christ—not degraded chattel but an apostle of the gospel to the Gentiles, a role he has been given by God that they too may belong to Christ through the "obedience of faith." This phrase refers to the summons to acknowledge Jesus' lordship and so enter into covenant relationship with God by "belonging to Christ."

The Matthean annunciation focuses on Joseph, a "son of David." The child to born will come from the house of David, as most expected the Messiah would. An adopted child was as much a child of the adoptive parents as any biological child. So, Joseph, the adoptive father, could be considered the "real" (human) father of Jesus. Jesus' descent from David is not "apparent" but, according to Jewish cultural norms, actual. Two names point toward his identity. Jesus (in Aramaic *Yeshua*) means "He will save," while "Emmanuel" indicates that he will be both the sign and the reality of God's presence to Israel.

Reflecting on the Word

We humans hunger to belong. As a result, tracing one's genealogy has become very popular. Ancestry.com has three million members. People upload family histories and search for connections. Studies of young people reveal that they are more passionate about where they belong than about what they believe.

Belonging was important for Jesus as well. The angel said to Joseph, "Do not be afraid to take Mary into your home." Joseph could have quietly thrown her out. Instead, the just man from Nazareth took her in. He offered the young pregnant Mary a roof over her head and a family lineage. He provided her a place and a people. Thus Jesus, adopted as his son under the Law of Israel, became a descendant of Joseph's "house of David."

Having a land and a people was important to the Hebrews. These things are important to us as well. Yet many people in this world are uprooted. Refugees and immigrants have no country, no place of belonging. Children who are passed from foster home to foster home do not know that security of belonging. They live on the edge of place.

We belong in this world, but at the same time, we don't belong. As an Advent people, we acknowledge that we are pilgrims on this earth. We too live on the edge of place. St. Paul says that we are called to belong to Jesus Christ. We don't abandon our family and our heritage, but we acknowledge that all that is, is God's. God is our home. God is our Source and our Goal. The Lord does not throw us out, but has taken us in and fully adopted us. God has given us a place to belong.

Consider/Discuss

❖ We wonder, "Where do I belong?" and "To whom do I belong?" As we come close to Christmas, think about the joys that God has given you in belonging, especially those you may take for granted. Think about the ache of not belonging as well. What can we do today to strengthen those bonds?

❖ On this Sunday, three days before Christmas, how we spend our money, our time, and our energy reveals much about to what we belong. Where and how are we invested?

Living and Praying with the Word

O come, Emmanuel, God-with-us; come into our hearts, hear the sound of our cry. The tensions of Christmas are intensifying. We need to rest in you. We need a place to belong. Like Joseph, take us into your home. We are searching not for a God of distance but the God of presence. When we need it most, hold us in your loving arms.

THE NATIVITY OF THE LORD, MASS DURING THE DAY

Today's Focus: The Gaze Turns to Love

Few things change the world like the arrival of a newborn. Gazing on today's newborn, in love, we are called to be changed, and to change the world.

FIRST READING
Isaiah 52:7–10

How beautiful upon the mountains
    are the feet of him who brings glad tidings,
announcing peace, bearing good news,
    announcing salvation, and saying to Zion,
    "Your God is King!"
Hark! Your sentinels raise a cry,
    together they shout for joy,
for they see directly, before their eyes,
    the LORD restoring Zion.
Break out together in song,
    O ruins of Jerusalem!
For the LORD comforts his people,
    he redeems Jerusalem.
The LORD has bared his holy arm
    in the sight of all the nations;
all the ends of the earth will behold
    the salvation of our God.

PSALM RESPONSE
Psalm 98:3c

All the ends of the earth have seen the saving power of God.

SECOND READING
Hebrews 1:1–6

Brothers and sisters: In times past, God spoke in partial and various ways to our ancestors through the prophets; in these last days, he has spoken to us through the Son, whom he made heir of all things and through whom he created the universe, who is the refulgence of his glory, the very imprint of his being, and who sustains all things by his mighty word. When he had accomplished purification from sins, he took his seat at the right hand of the Majesty on high, as far superior to the angels as the name he has inherited is more excellent than theirs.

For to which of the angels did God ever say:

You are my son; this day I have begotten you?

Or again:

I will be a father to him, and he shall be a son to me?

And again, when he leads the firstborn into the world, he says:

Let all the angels of God worship him.

GOSPEL   *John 1:1–18 or 1:1–5, 9–14*

In the shorter form of the reading, the passages in brackets are omitted.

In the beginning was the Word,
and the Word was with God,
and the Word was God.
He was in the beginning with God.
All things came to be through him,
and without him nothing came to be.

What came to be through him was life,
and this life was the light of the human race;
the light shines in the darkness,
and the darkness has not overcome it.

[A man named John was sent from God. He came for testimony, to testify to the light, so that all might believe through him. He was not the light, but came to testify to the light.] The true light, which enlightens everyone, was coming into the world.

He was in the world,
and the world came to be through him,
but the world did not know him.
He came to what was his own,
but his own people did not accept him.

But to those who did accept him he gave power to become children of God, to those who believe in his name, who were born not by natural generation nor by human choice nor by a man's decision but of God.

And the Word became flesh
and made his dwelling among us,
and we saw his glory,
the glory as of the Father's only Son,
full of grace and truth.

[John testified to him and cried out, saying, "This was he of whom I said, 'The one who is coming after me ranks ahead of me because he existed before me.' " From his fullness we have all received, grace in place of grace, because while the law was given through Moses, grace and truth came through Jesus Christ. No one has ever seen God. The only Son, God, who is at the Father's side, has revealed him.]

Understanding the Word

The Isaian passage, from near the end of the Babylonian exile, is a proclamation of salvation made by one who brings "glad tidings" (in the Greek translation of the Hebrew Scriptures: *euangelion*). An important element of the proclamation is the notion that this salvation will be visible to "all the nations" and "all the ends of the earth." This public salvation is intended to manifest to the whole world both the graciousness and the power of the God of Israel. Thus, the redemption of Israel will contribute to a larger project, seen in other parts of Isaiah, of drawing other nations to praise and worship the God of Israel, and thus share in Israel's salvation (see Isaiah 2:1–5; 56:3–8).

The Letter to the Hebrews focuses on Christ's relationship to God as son, heir, and "imprint of [God's] being." Precisely as God's Son, Jesus has accomplished what could not be done otherwise. Although God had truly, but partially, spoken through earlier prophets, now in Jesus—God's Son and imprint—God speaks fully and clearly. Whereas earlier God had provided for regular and repeated purification from sin, now God has provided a great High Priest who accomplishes purification once and for all (Hebrews 4:14—5:10; 7:1—8:6). Jesus, as heir, reigns in heaven with God and thus is worthy of the worship of all creation.

The beginning of the Gospel of John announces that Jesus Christ, as the Word (*logos*) of God, has come into the world and made his dwelling among us (literally, "tabernacled among us"; see Exodus 40:34–35). The Greek word *logos* reflects, among other things, the "mind" and wisdom of God, or God's creative plan that governs the world. Thus, the Word made flesh brings light, grace, truth, the very life of God. Those who believe in him, accepting this free gift, become children of God. Already we hear a key Johannine theme: the gracious gift of God demands a response.

Reflecting on the Word

It is Christmas Day! The long night of Mary's labor is over. The holy night when the angels sang has turned to day. The sun has risen. Jesus is here! Red and wrinkled, the baby rests in Mary's arms. Joseph gazes at the boy's little fingernails as Mary sleeps. Even the cave where the animals are stabled begins to brighten and warm. Time stands still. The everlasting Word has become flesh and dwells among us. He is here. He is now.

What happens when a newborn arrives? The hours after birth, if not interrupted by emergencies, are a time to gaze. A first-time mother can't quite believe that her enormous belly is now that tiny child; two eyes, that nose, and "look at his hair!" A father gets shaky inside at how protective he feels when he looks at this little one. Someone exclaims, "Oh, look, he's got the family chin!" Words feel trivial, unable to capture the amazement. Time stands still.

And then something happens. Time begins anew. Inside of each of these "watchers," a miracle rises up. Little by little, those who look upon the helpless creature are changed by their gazing. They begin to fall in love. Warmth spreads in the chest. Tears of joy run down the cheeks. Wonder overwhelms the mind. This child is here. This child is now. Can you feel it?

Christmas Day is a moment for gazing. Christmas Day is a time to look at Baby Jesus, the Word who became flesh and who dwells among us. In the manger, in the Eucharist, in moments of prayer, in the bond of family and friends, in service to the community: Look! Jesus is here! Let the tears of joy run down your cheeks. Jesus is here!

Consider/Discuss

❖ The experience of today's Christmas may be joyous. Or it may be difficult. How is God with you on this day? How is the Word taking flesh and dwelling with you today?

❖ Think back to your most tender, most loving Christmas. What comes to mind? What was it that warmed your heart? How can that memory transform your experience today?

Living and Praying with the Word

Emmanuel, God who is with us, sometimes there is nothing to say. Today is your Christmas. Allow me to have some quiet time just to gaze at you, the newborn in the manger, the Word become flesh. Holy Spirit, come and fill the quiet of my gaze with the strength of your love. You may warm my heart. You may overwhelm my brain. You may send tears of joy down my cheeks. Give me the grace just to sit here and gaze at you with love.

THE HOLY FAMILY OF JESUS, MARY, AND JOSEPH

Today's Focus: The Eyes Have It

---

*Even during a traumatic time like the flight into Egypt,
the Holy Family surely looked at one another in love,
to calm the anxious fear of their journey.
May their gaze comfort us today.*

FIRST READING

Sirach 3:2–6, 12–14

God sets a father in honor over his children;
 a mother's authority he confirms over her sons.
Whoever honors his father atones for sins,
 and preserves himself from them.
When he prays, he is heard;
 he stores up riches who reveres his mother.
Whoever honors his father is gladdened by children,
 and, when he prays, is heard.
Whoever reveres his father will live a long life;
 he who obeys his father brings comfort to his mother.
My son, take care of your father when he is old;
 grieve him not as long as he lives.
Even if his mind fail, be considerate of him;
 revile him not all the days of his life;
kindness to a father will not be forgotten,
 firmly planted against the debt of your sins
 —a house raised in justice to you.

PSALM RESPONSE

Psalm 128:1

Blessed are those who fear the Lord and walk in his ways.

SECOND READING

Colossians 3:12–21 or 3:12–17

In the shorter form of the reading, the passage in brackets is omitted.

Brothers and sisters: Put on, as God's chosen ones, holy and beloved, heartfelt compassion, kindness, humility, gentleness, and patience, bearing with one another and forgiving one another, if one has a grievance against another; as the Lord has forgiven you, so must you also do. And over all these put on love, that is, the bond of perfection. And let the peace of Christ control your hearts, the peace into which you were also called in one body. And be thankful. Let the word of Christ dwell in you richly, as in all wisdom you teach and admonish one another, singing psalms, hymns, and spiritual songs with gratitude in your hearts to God. And whatever you do, in word or in deed, do everything in the name of the Lord Jesus, giving thanks to God the Father through him.

[Wives, be subordinate to your husbands, as is proper in the Lord. Husbands, love your wives, and avoid any bitterness toward them. Children, obey your parents in everything, for this is pleasing to the Lord. Fathers, do not provoke your children, so they may not become discouraged.]

GOSPEL

Matthew 2:13–15, 19–23

When the magi had departed, behold, the angel of the Lord appeared to Joseph in a dream and said, "Rise, take the child and his mother, flee to Egypt, and stay there until I tell you. Herod is going to search for the child to destroy him." Joseph rose and took the child and his mother by night and departed for Egypt. He stayed there until the death of Herod, that what the Lord had said through the prophet might be fulfilled,

Out of Egypt I called my son.

When Herod had died, behold, the angel of the Lord appeared in a dream to Joseph in Egypt and said, "Rise, take the child and his mother and go to the land of Israel, for those who sought the child's life are dead." He rose, took the child and his mother, and went to the land of Israel. But when he heard that Archelaus was ruling over Judea in place of his father Herod, he was afraid to go back there. And because he had been warned in a dream, he departed for the region of Galilee. He went and dwelt in a town called Nazareth, so that what had been spoken through the prophets might be fulfilled,

He shall be called a Nazorean.

Understanding the Word

Traditional biblical wisdom holds that order and stability promote human flourishing. Here the focus is on family roles and what is due to each member of the household: Duty toward parents is a common Wisdom trope, appearing often in Proverbs. Sirach reflects in particular on the challenge of dealing with an elderly parent, and closely binds duty toward God with honoring parents. It is God who set the father and mother over the family; honoring one's parents brings favor from God. At the same time, the language of comfort, consideration, and kindness points to a sense that caring for one's parents is ultimately grounded in basic human decency as much as hope of divine reward.

The emphasis in the second reading is on decent behavior toward all, which reflects one's experience of having been transformed by Christ. Precisely as "God's chosen ones," who have put away "earthly" vices (Colossians 3:5–10) and been transformed in Christ, Christians should behave in a manner that reflects the character of God, who is compassionate, patient, forgiving, and loving. Marked by these traits, those gathered around Christ support each other, learning together from him and strengthening each other through admonishment, common worship, and especially gratitude. In the final section the writer exhorts his listeners to honor the family order as ordained by God. Christian family life also is to be marked by mutual care, without bitterness, provocation, or discouragement.

In the Gospel reading, Joseph fulfills his duty as protector of God's Son and his mother. Jesus' vulnerability is highlighted by six references to him as "child." Prompted three times, Joseph responds with quick obedience. Not only does Joseph lead mother and child away from danger, his actions also allow for the fulfillment of prophecy. The more significant of these is the first, from Hosea (11:1), which refers to the redemption of Israel, God's son (Exodus 4:22), from Egypt. It is applied now to Jesus, God's Son, as exemplar and perfect representative of Israel.

Reflecting on the Word

I never get quite enough Christmas. Liturgically, this week we are still singing Christmas songs. Poinsettias still decorate the altar. Yet we have already abandoned the infancy stories. In today's reading, Joseph uproots his family to flee to Egypt to keep the holy child safe. Does the glow of "Silent Night, Holy Night" have to dissolve into the shadows quite so quickly?

Jesus was born into a messy world. In my mind, I know that. In my heart, I don't want that.

A glimmer of insight came to me when I noticed a painting by Federico Barocci. In the *Rest on the Flight to Egypt* (c.1570), Mary sits in the center of the Holy Family. She looks to the left, as though to draw attention away from herself. St. Joseph hovers above her. He reaches out his fingers to place a twig into the fist of Jesus, a chubby toddler. The leading line in the painting is that connection between father and son. The dawning sun rises in the background. That light is reflected in the bearded man's eyes as they shimmer with tenderness for the child. The eyes of the baby gleam back with love. A placid donkey looks on. Had they just barely escaped Herod's bloodbath? Is there anxiety in Joseph's heart? This paints a picture of calm. Jesus doesn't look old enough to talk, but he shoots Joseph a playful grin as though to say, "Daddy, don't worry. We are here together."

In mutual love, there is calm amidst the messiness—holy rest, Christmas peace. It doesn't fade away. We find it in family. We find it in friendship. We find it in the solidarity of community. We find it in Jesus' gleam: "Don't worry. We are in this together."

Consider/Discuss

❖ We yearn for peace, but life can be messy. What is in Jesus' eyes when he looks at us? How can we be enveloped by Christmas peace through that loving gaze?

❖ Much of togetherness is communicated with the eyes, both in family relationships and in friendship. Storytellers suggest looking at people with two seconds of loving eye contact. Try that tender attention this week and see how family and friends respond.

Living and Praying with the Word

Jesus our Savior, you lived through all of the messiness of human life. You know more of trauma than we could ever imagine. Yet you have not abandoned us. You are here. You are with us. Help us to put on heartfelt compassion, kindness, humility, and love, especially in our families. Strengthen the bond of perfection in all of our relationships. This flight of faith is challenging. We cannot do it without you. Thank you for abiding with us and surrounding us with your gleam of love.

MARY, THE HOLY MOTHER OF GOD

Today's Focus: Mary Watches Over Jesus as the Lord Watches Over Us.

Mary, in the turmoil of her remarkable child's remarkable birth, still is able to watch over Jesus in blessing, as God watches over us, keeps us, and gives us peace.

FIRST READING   *Numbers 6:22–27*

The LORD said to Moses: "Speak to Aaron and his sons and tell them: This is how you shall bless the Israelites. Say to them:

The LORD bless you and keep you!
The LORD let his face shine upon you, and be gracious to you!
The LORD look upon you kindly and give you peace!

So shall they invoke my name upon the Israelites, and I will bless them."

PSALM RESPONSE   *Psalm 67:2a*

May God bless us in his mercy.

SECOND READING   *Galatians 4:4–7*

Brothers and sisters: When the fullness of time had come, God sent his Son, born of a woman, born under the law, to ransom those under the law, so that we might receive adoption as sons. As proof that you are sons, God sent the Spirit of his Son into our hearts, crying out, "Abba, Father!" So you are no longer a slave but a son, and if a son then also an heir, through God.

GOSPEL   *Luke 2:16–21*

The shepherds went in haste to Bethlehem and found Mary and Joseph, and the infant lying in the manger. When they saw this, they made known the message that had been told them about this child. All who heard it were amazed by what had been told them by the shepherds. And Mary kept all these things, reflecting on them in her heart. Then the shepherds returned, glorifying and praising God for all they had heard and seen, just as it had been told to them. When eight days were completed for his circumcision, he was named Jesus, the name given him by the angel before he was conceived in the womb.

Understanding the Word

The first reading features the well-known "priestly blessing," probably originally to be imparted to visitors to the Jerusalem temple or other worship sites. Blessing is a form of prayer that asks for God's gifts. This blessing asks for God's protection, good favor, and peace. To "keep" here means to watch over or guard. To "shine one's face on," or simply to show one's face, means to have a favorable disposition toward someone (see Psalm 4:7). Thus, the second line of the blessing asks for God's positive attitude and gracious favor toward the blessed. The third strophe repeats the hope for God's good favor before asking for God's "peace," in Hebrew, *shalom*, a word that sums up all that the blessing asks of God: wholeness, well-being, harmony, long life, etc.

In his letter to the Galatians, Paul argues that the coming of Christ has made both Jews and Gentiles children of God by freeing them from "elemental powers" (4:3), spiritual forces that somehow prevent humans from living in full conformity with God's will. Christ was born into this human condition of bondage in order to deliver us from that misery, and to bring all who accept the gift into familial relationship with God. As "sons and daughters" and therefore "heirs" in Christ, Christians inherit the promises made to Abraham (3:29) and passed on to his freeborn children.

Onto a quiet birth scene burst several shepherds, to whom an angel has announced the birth of the Messiah (Luke 2:8–15). Finding the child in a manger, as the angel had said, they immediately inform Mary and Joseph and probably some helpful neighbor folk that the savior's birth has been announced to them. While the neighbor folk are amazed at the notion that the child born under such unpromising circumstances could be "Messiah and Lord," Mary merely reflects on "these things." Jesus' circumcision on the eighth day, in accordance with the law (Leviticus 12:3), signals his solidarity with the covenant community that he will save.

Reflecting on the Word

I have an elderly friend who took a hard fall. Now, nurses and family hover over her continually, watching for a brain bleed and signs of confusion. What will her future hold?

I have a grandson who was recently born. His mother and father look at him continually, beholding his tiny hands and feet and admiring his shock of hair. What will this child be?

In our reading, there is a lot of clamor surrounding the shepherds. "They went with speed" and "they told everyone" and "all who heard it were astonished"—it sounds like a lot of noise, doesn't it? Like the steady stream of visitors to the hospital, they ask, "What does the future hold?"

In the middle of the shepherds' commotion are these few words about Mary: "She [treasured] all these things, reflecting on them in her heart." She is the quiet anchor in the center of the tumult. She feeds the baby. She rocks him. He is near to her. In the midst of the chaos, she gives a maternal gaze of blessing upon that infant child. Like the Virgin of Guadalupe, she wraps her mantle around him. And all of these experiences remain in her memory.

This same gaze of blessing is found in the blessing of Aaron in the book of Numbers. Watch over, keep, hover, safeguard—these are all images of protectiveness and care. We too are watched over. It is a blessed hovering, a nearness that we should not fear: The LORD bless you and keep you, watch over you; The LORD let his face to shine upon you. Life can sometimes worry us. But no matter what the future holds, a gaze of love enfolds us. We know Who holds our future.

Consider/Discuss

❖ Put yourself into the Gospel story as a townsperson or a friend of one of the shepherds. How would you respond when he tells you this remarkable story of angels and a baby in the manger?

❖ When a pregnant woman sits down with a group of older mothers, they suddenly and naturally start swapping birth stories. To whom do you think that Mary might have later told Jesus' birth stories? What stories did your mother tell about your birth?

Living and Praying with the Word

Hover over us, Spirit of God. We want to be independent. We want to believe that we can succeed in life all by ourselves. Yet when we were children, we needed a mother's care. Today, we need your care, too. We cry out from our hearts, "Abba, Father!" You are the source of our elation. Stir us to taste more deeply the sweetness of your love.

THE EPIPHANY OF THE LORD

Today's Focus: Underdogs Become Stars.

We can lose sight of how unexpected and lowly the circumstances surrounding the birth of Jesus were, how much of an underdog he was in the eyes of the world. But God grants underdogs a star in the sky.

FIRST READING
Isaiah 60:1–6

Rise up in splendor, Jerusalem! Your light has come,
    the glory of the Lord shines upon you.
See, darkness covers the earth,
    and thick clouds cover the peoples;
but upon you the LORD shines,
    and over you appears his glory.
Nations shall walk by your light,
    and kings by your shining radiance.
Raise your eyes and look about;
    they all gather and come to you:
your sons come from afar,
    and your daughters in the arms of their nurses.

Then you shall be radiant at what you see,
    your heart shall throb and overflow,
for the riches of the sea shall be emptied out before you,
    the wealth of nations shall be brought to you.
Caravans of camels shall fill you,
    dromedaries from Midian and Ephah;
all from Sheba shall come
    bearing gold and frankincense,
    and proclaiming the praises of the LORD.

PSALM RESPONSE
Psalm 72:11

Lord, every nation on earth will adore you.

SECOND READING
Ephesians 3:2–3a, 5–6

Brothers and sisters: You have heard of the stewardship of God's grace that was given to me for your benefit, namely, that the mystery was made known to me by revelation. It was not made known to people in other generations as it has now been revealed to his holy apostles and prophets by the Spirit: that the Gentiles are coheirs, members of the same body, and copartners in the promise in Christ Jesus through the gospel.

When Jesus was born in Bethlehem of Judea, in the days of King Herod, behold, magi from the east arrived in Jerusalem, saying, "Where is the newborn king of the Jews? We saw his star at its rising and have come to do him homage." When King Herod heard this, he was greatly troubled, and all Jerusalem with him. Assembling all the chief priests and the scribes of the people, he inquired of them where the Christ was to be born. They said to him, "In Bethlehem of Judea, for thus it has been written through the prophet:

And you, Bethlehem, land of Judah,
*   are by no means least among the rulers of Judah;*
since from you shall come a ruler,
*   who is to shepherd my people Israel."*

Then Herod called the magi secretly and ascertained from them the time of the star's appearance. He sent them to Bethlehem and said, "Go and search diligently for the child. When you have found him, bring me word, that I too may go and do him homage." After their audience with the king they set out. And behold, the star that they had seen at its rising preceded them, until it came and stopped over the place where the child was.

They were overjoyed at seeing the star, and on entering the house they saw the child with Mary his mother. They prostrated themselves and did him homage. Then they opened their treasures and offered him gifts of gold, frankincense, and myrrh. And having been warned in a dream not to return to Herod, they departed for their country by another way.

Understanding the Word

The beginning of the book of Isaiah presents a vision in which, one day, Zion will attract "all nations" seeking to learn from the God of Israel (Isaiah 2:1–4). Here too, toward the end of the book, we hear a similar proclamation in an oracle from the post-exilic period, during which the returnees from exile are slowly rebuilding Jerusalem and a new temple. The hopeful vision announces that because of God's presence ("the glory of the LORD") the city is filled with light shining forth over the whole earth, presently darkened (by ignorance or violence?). Once again, we hear that nations will be attracted to Jerusalem because of the God who dwells within, bringing with them tribute to God, whose sovereignty they acknowledge, whose praises they proclaim.

The reading from Ephesians explores the extension of God's relationship with Israel to include, in Christ, Gentiles also. Here the emphasis is on God's "outreach" to the nations. Paul has been entrusted with the message of God's grace. The content of that grace is precisely that Gentiles are now called to join with Jews as heirs of God's ancient promises. Like the original promises to the Jews, this inheritance has not been earned, but is founded solely on the graciousness of God, whose benevolence is now extending beyond ethnic Israel to include all those who become members of the body of Christ.

The magi, wise men and astrologers who were part of the priestly class in Persia, would have shared the cultural belief that the birth of kings was "announced" through celestial phenomena, such as the "rising of a star." Thus, they arrive, having ascertained the birth of a Jewish king. Herod, a Jewish client king of the Romans, is understandably threatened. Having determined exactly where such a newborn king might be found, he slyly sends the magi to search him out for him. The gifts of the magi are costly and appropriate for a king; they do not seem particularly dismayed to find the newborn king sleeping in a manger.

Reflecting on the Word

In the movie *Rudy*, Rudy isn't smart enough to get into Notre Dame. He's too small to play football. Could he make a touchdown for the Fighting Irish in the final game of his senior year? There's no way. Not a chance. In the story *Hidden Figures*, Katherine Johnson is a mathematical genius. She works at NASA as a "calculator." Yet she is a black woman in the early 1960s. Could she do the mathematical calculations for John Glenn's return from orbit? There's no way. Not a chance.

We love these underdog stories, don't we? The one full of grit and determination, the one who was not supposed to be there—a light shines, someone cracks open a door. The hero(ine) pushes through and comes to victory. The elation! The joy! The success!

Today's readings give us other underdog stories. St. Paul didn't walk with Jesus. He persecuted Christians. There's no way. Not a chance. The magi—astrologers from the east, they were not of the Chosen People. How could they ever see the Messiah? There's no way. Not a chance.

Yet God opens a crack in the door. Light from heaven strikes Paul to the ground. The risen Lord draws him in. In turn, Paul opens the door for those other underdogs, the Gentiles.

A star in the heavens directs the magi to the King of the Jews, and by that light they are overjoyed to see that baby. The elation! The thrill! The success! Unlikely heroes, we still sing their song, "We Three Kings."

You and I, we are unlikely heroes, too. People of faith, in love with the Lord? No way. Not a chance. Yet a light has shone into our darkness, too—a glimmer, a taste of the Holy Spirit, and a touch of glory. Wow. Sing praise!

Consider/Discuss

❖ What is your favorite underdog story? With whom do you identify most? Who is it that shines the light, opens the door for the hero(ine)? At the conclusion, what causes you to feel elation and joy at their success?

❖ Sometimes we take our faith for granted. Yet glimpses of light have enlightened our darkness. God is faithful. The heavens have opened and we are allowed to enter. How has that door opened for us?

Living and Praying with the Word

Lord Jesus, you came into this world as an underdog, born in a small backwater of a vast empire. But when the magi saw you, they knew that you truly reigned over all. Thank you for opening the door for us. We are not worthy of you, but you have let us in, too. Show us the elation—the joy—the unexpected successes that you want for us in our own lives.

THE BAPTISM OF THE LORD

Today's Focus: The Spirit Breaks In, Expanding Our Vision.

Like the Christmas story, the story of Jesus' baptism can become so familiar that we shut out its Holy Spirit. Today, take time to note the remarkable aspects of this story, and your own story.

FIRST READING

Isaiah 42:1–4, 6–7

Thus says the LORD:
Here is my servant whom I uphold,
    my chosen one with whom I am pleased,
upon whom I have put my spirit;
    he shall bring forth justice to the nations,
not crying out, not shouting,
    not making his voice heard in the street.
A bruised reed he shall not break,
    and a smoldering wick he shall not quench,
until he establishes justice on the earth;
    the coastlands will wait for his teaching.

I, the LORD, have called you for the victory of justice,
    I have grasped you by the hand;
I formed you, and set you
    as a covenant of the people,
    a light for the nations,
to open the eyes of the blind,
    to bring out prisoners from confinement,
    and from the dungeon, those who live in darkness.

PSALM RESPONSE

Psalm 29:11b

The Lord will bless his people with peace.

SECOND READING

Acts 10:34–38

Peter proceeded to speak to those gathered in the house of Cornelius, saying: "In truth, I see that God shows no partiality. Rather, in every nation whoever fears him and acts uprightly is acceptable to him. You know the word that he sent to the Israelites as he proclaimed peace through Jesus Christ, who is Lord of all, what has happened all over Judea, beginning in Galilee after the baptism that John preached, how God anointed Jesus of Nazareth with the Holy Spirit and power. He went about doing good and healing all those oppressed by the devil, for God was with him."

Jesus came from Galilee to John at the Jordan to be baptized by him. John tried to prevent him, saying, "I need to be baptized by you, and yet you are coming to me?" Jesus said to him in reply, "Allow it now, for thus it is fitting for us to fulfill all righteousness." Then he allowed him. After Jesus was baptized, he came up from the water and behold, the heavens were opened for him, and he saw the Spirit of God descending like a dove and coming upon him. And a voice came from the heavens, saying, "This is my beloved Son, with whom I am well pleased."

Understanding the Word

In the Isaian passage God presents an unnamed servant: chosen, upheld, and pleasing to God, who has endowed the servant with the divine spirit. This enables him to serve God faithfully. The nature of his service is to bring forth justice, not just to Israel, as one might expect, but also to the nations, establishing justice "on the earth." The Hebrew word for justice, *mishpat*, here refers to the restoration of God's order. This "victory for justice" will not be accomplished through physical or military force. Instead the servant will bring the nations into covenantal relationship with God, opening up the path for God's light and healing.

Cornelius is a Roman centurion who, as a "devout and God-fearing" man (Acts 10:2), has always treated the Jews with respect. Just before the present scene, Peter has received a vision in which he is commanded to eat "profane and unclean" food (10:9–16), which he interprets to mean that the mission of Christ is to be extended to the Gentiles. Thus, we hear him say today that God shows no partiality regarding nationality. While it is true that Jesus himself was sent to the Israelites, he is Lord of all, and thus the healing ministry begun in him is now extended beyond the bounds of ethnic Israel to encompass all those who believe in him and accept the offer of forgiveness of sins (10:43).

Matthew notes that Jesus went to John in the wilderness specifically to be baptized. In response to John's question, Jesus does not suggest that he needs to receive John's baptism for repentance (3:11), but "to fulfill all righteousness." Righteousness here means doing God's will, and it has been suggested that by being baptized, Jesus is placing himself in solidarity with the sinners he will save. In any case, the baptism is the occasion for a confirmation of his identity as God's Son and the empowerment for his mission by the Holy Spirit, who will immediately lead him into the wilderness.

Reflecting on the Word

Imagine that you are a seagull casually flying in from the Mediterranean, hovering for a spell above the Jordan River. It is a beautifully hot day and the wind floats you aloft. All is good. All is peaceful.

Suddenly the heavens open. Power fills the sky. You can feel the air vibrate. The Spirit breaks in. A dove descends. The God of glory thunders, the voice of the Lord over the waters: "This is my beloved Son, with whom I am well pleased."

You're knocked off guard, for you haven't seen pictures of a furry man pouring water over a guy with his head bowed, a little bird fluttering overhead; you haven't heard this baptism of Jesus story before. This Spirit of God is not like any other dove that you have ever seen. This is not like any other day. What is going on?

Below you, people walk with their heads bowed, trudging in the dirt, tired by their humdrum existence. You want to caw out, "Looooook, loooook, looook, looook! Come and soar with me! The Spirit of God is here!" The voice of the Lord is power. The voice of the Lord is splendor. You are roused with courage, feeling that you could keep flying even through the worst of thunderstorms.

Who are these two men? One stays by the water. The other turns toward the desert, where he will remain for forty days. The dove disappears to lead the man to the desert, that power remains with the man who walks away. Who could this be? Wherever he goes, you want to go. Wherever he stops, you want to stop. Life is richer in his presence. The air still vibrates. The splendor has not gone away. Something just feels fitting and right and abundant. What was crooked is now straight. All is good. All is warm. God is here!

Consider/Discuss

❖ How often do we take the story of the inbreaking of the Spirit at the baptism of the Lord for granted, as though we have seen it before? How often do we take the inbreaking of the Spirit in our own lives for granted—a nice story, but not very real?

❖ The next time you hear a seagull crying or a bird calling, look up. Look around. The Spirit of God is here. The God of glory thunders. The God of splendor whispers. Do we have ears to hear?

Living and Praying with the Word

O Jesus, give us a heart for you. Spirit of God, fill us to the max! Help us to soar and to dance above the humdrum of life, to be empowered anew. You have done something fresh. Break into our lives as well. Thank you for your glory!

Notes

Ordinary Time I

In Week Seven of Ordinary Time we hear God say to Israel: "Be holy, for I, the LORD, your God, am holy" (Leviticus 19:102, 17–18). This command reflects a certain reciprocity in the divine–human relationship, a notion that is inherent in the Old Testament readings in these first weeks of Ordinary Time. On the one hand, we have the holiness of God, which is made manifest in God's saving power on behalf of the whole world. God will send a Servant to bring healing to Israel and light to the nations (Isaiah 49:3, 5–6), and those who now walk in darkness will rejoice in this light (Isaiah 8:23–9:3). On the other hand, we have the human response to this divine initiative, which is to reflect the light of God's holiness by being a saving presence in the world also: "Share your bread with the hungry, shelter the oppressed and the homeless . . . Then your light shall break forth like the dawn" (Isaiah 58:7–10).

Most of the second readings in these weeks are from the beginning of Paul's First Letter to the Corinthians, and he too will focus on holiness. Paul begins by reminding the faction–riven community that they have been called to be holy (1:1–3), a call that must be grounded in recognition that they follow the *crucified* Messiah (1:10–13, 17; 2:1–5). The Corinthians are struggling in their call to holiness because they have not yet grasped the implications for them of the cross. Instead, they are still viewing the world according to "the wisdom of the age," which understands nothing of God (2:6–10), and is not even wisdom, but "foolishness in the eyes of God." Worldly wisdom has blinded the Corinthians to the fact that they are now, in the Spirit, God's temple, which is holy (3:16–23). They have yet to start acting like it.

In the Gospel readings from Matthew Jesus begins to lay out his program for discipleship. He begins by preaching "Repent, for the kingdom of heaven is at hand" and calling his first disciples (4:12–23). Repentance means conforming one's life to God's values. Jesus' disciples must be instructed in these values not only for themselves, but for the whole world (5:13–16). While God's kingdom is beautiful, it also requires of those who would live in it surpassing righteousness (i.e., holiness). This means, in the first place, not just observing the letter of the divine law, but comprehending and living by its logic. Peacefulness, fidelity, truth, and generosity are all values of the kingdom of God because they are all marks of the divine perfection, and Jesus' disciples are called to set their sights on nothing less than this perfection for themselves (5:17–37; 5:38–48).

SECOND SUNDAY IN ORDINARY TIME

Today's Focus: Ordinary Time, Holy Life

*Much of life is ordinary, but God has graced us with
the ability to recall the extraordinary moments of blessing,
and to act on them to fill all of life with holiness.*

FIRST READING
Isaiah 49:3, 5–6

The LORD said to me: You are my servant,
    Israel, through whom I show my glory.
Now the LORD has spoken
    who formed me as his servant from the womb,
that Jacob may be brought back to him
    and Israel gathered to him;
and I am made glorious in the sight of the LORD,
    and my God is now my strength!
It is too little, the LORD says, for you to be my servant,
    to raise up the tribes of Jacob,
    and restore the survivors of Israel;
I will make you a light to the nations,
    that my salvation may reach to the ends of the earth.

PSALM RESPONSE
Psalm 40:8a, 9a

Here am I, Lord; I come to do your will.

SECOND READING
1 Corinthians 1:1–3

Paul, called to be an apostle of Christ Jesus by the will of God, and Sosthenes our brother, to the church of God that is in Corinth, to you who have been sanctified in Christ Jesus, called to be holy, with all those everywhere who call upon the name of our Lord Jesus Christ, their Lord and ours. Grace to you and peace from God our Father and the Lord Jesus Christ.

GOSPEL
John 1:29–34

John the Baptist saw Jesus coming toward him and said, "Behold, the Lamb of God, who takes away the sin of the world. He is the one of whom I said, 'A man is coming after me who ranks ahead of me because he existed before me.' I did not know him, but the reason why I came baptizing with water was that he might be made known to Israel." John testified further, saying, "I saw the Spirit come down like a dove from heaven and remain upon him. I did not know him, but the one who sent me to baptize with water told me, 'On whomever you see the Spirit come down and remain, he is the one who will baptize with the Holy Spirit.' Now I have seen and testified that he is the Son of God."

Understanding the Word

In Exodus 19:6, God announces that Israel is being formed to be "a holy nation," a people that shows to the rest of the earth the holiness of God by its way of life. Just so, the servant in the first reading is intended to take up Israel's role and show forth God's glory. The servant is first charged with a mission to bring back Israel ("Jacob") to God, that is, to gather Israel back into faithful relationship with God. The servant will then take up the role of Israel and act as a light to the nations, drawing them to God so that they, like Israel, may receive salvation.

Paul's greeting to the Corinthians signals a theme of the letter, namely the Corinthians' holiness. He first alludes to his authority as an apostle of Christ. He will rely on this authority to address problems in the church at Corinth, all of which relate in some way to a failure on the Corinthians' part to appreciate the implications of their life in Christ, which is to be sanctified and sanctifying. Those who call on the name of Christ are of the church of God—and Paul will remind them of what this means for their conduct, especially with each other.

John the Baptist identifies Jesus as both "Lamb of God" and "Son of God." The former points toward Jesus' death on the cross, which the Evangelist will associate with the sacrifice of the Passover lamb (Jesus dies on the "preparation day" when the lambs are slaughtered and his legs are not broken, just as the bones of the Passover lamb are not to be broken [John 19:33, 36; Exodus 12:46]). This image is combined with that of the Suffering Servant of Isaiah 53:5–7, who, "like a lamb led to slaughter" will take on the sins of the people. The death of Jesus as the Lamb of God will be effective because Jesus is the Son of God, on whom now, as at his baptism, the Spirit rests.

Reflecting on the Word

Blah! We have moved into Ordinary Time. Christmas is over. The January doldrums have set in. We are surrounded by the same plain old life and the same plain old people.

The Super Bowl might break the post-Christmas blahs for football fans. Snow banks can become snow forts for those who like to dig. Otherwise, blah. Where's the adventure? Where's the excitement? Those big moments like Christmas and weddings and vacations *mark* our lives; it's the six-tiered cake pictures that go into our memory books!

The baptism of Jesus was a big moment. In today's Gospel, John the Baptist is still talking about it. He is remembering: "I have seen!" He is telling others about how the dove descended and how the Lord spoke: "and I have testified!" He is about to send his followers into action.

Ordinary Time is the time for remembering. Then we put memory into action. Isaiah remembers how God formed him in the womb and called him to a life of prophetic service; therefore, he calls the Israelites back, to be a holy nation. The psalmist remembers how God drew him out of a pit of destruction and put a new song in his mouth. Therefore, he wants to follow: "To do your will is my delight."

So how do we work our way through Ordinary Time? We remember. Then we act. Every day is a remembering, followed by the noble adventure of following Jesus. Thus it is the everyday moments that *make* our lives. We may not have a picture of mom's oatmeal in our memory books, but it nourished us daily. We may not have a picture of the hug that quieted our tears, but it shaped our soul. Day-to-day personal holiness—the faithfulness, kindness, and honesty of everyday life—that is what history is made of.

Consider/Discuss

❖ We don't have to achieve holiness all by ourselves; the Holy Spirit is called the Sanctifier for a reason. If we grow attuned to listening to the Spirit, we will be brought to holiness. What do you remember of what God has done for you? How does that spur you to act?

❖ Step by step, we are to be transformed into the person of Christ—to be a gift of love to this world. Tell a story of what everyday holiness has looked like in your life.

Living and Praying with the Word

God Almighty, you are grand and glorious! We see your grandeur when we look at the vastness of the stars and the radiance of the sun. Yet our lives are lived in littleness. Getting out of bed each day, taking one step after another, we mark the days of our lives. Send us your grace in abundance so that we will do each little task for love of you. Let your Spirit rest on us as well and make holy our actions, even when they lead through the desert.

THIRD SUNDAY IN ORDINARY TIME

Today's Focus: Called to Follow, No Matter the Cost

The command (or invitation) from Jesus, "Follow me," seems simple enough at first. But to follow Jesus means that we leave other things behind, and our following could change our lives.

FIRST READING
Isaiah 8:23—9:3

First the LORD degraded the land of Zebulun and the land of Naphtali; but in the end he has glorified the seaward road, the land west of the Jordan, the District of the Gentiles.

Anguish has taken wing, dispelled is darkness:
  for there is no gloom where but now there was distress.
The people who walked in darkness
  have seen a great light;
upon those who dwelt in the land of gloom
  a light has shone.
You have brought them abundant joy
  and great rejoicing,
as they rejoice before you as at the harvest,
  as people make merry when dividing spoils.
For the yoke that burdened them,
  the pole on their shoulder,
and the rod of their taskmaster
  you have smashed, as on the day of Midian.

PSALM RESPONSE
Psalm 27:1a

The Lord is my light and my salvation.

SECOND READING
1 Corinthians 1:10–13, 17

I urge you, brothers and sisters, in the name of our Lord Jesus Christ, that all of you agree in what you say, and that there be no divisions among you, but that you be united in the same mind and in the same purpose. For it has been reported to me about you, my brothers and sisters, by Chloe's people, that there are rivalries among you. I mean that each of you is saying, "I belong to Paul," or "I belong to Apollos," or "I belong to Cephas," or "I belong to Christ." Is Christ divided? Was Paul crucified for you? Or were you baptized in the name of Paul? For Christ did not send me to baptize but to preach the gospel, and not with the wisdom of human eloquence, so that the cross of Christ might not be emptied of its meaning.

Matthew 4:12–23 or 4:12–17

In the shorter form of the reading, the passage in brackets is omitted.

When Jesus heard that John had been arrested, he withdrew to Galilee. He left Nazareth and went to live in Capernaum by the sea, in the region of Zebulun and Naphtali, that what had been said through Isaiah the prophet might be fulfilled:
Land of Zebulun and land of Naphtali,
  the way to the sea, beyond the Jordan,
  Galilee of the Gentiles,
the people who sit in darkness have seen a great light,
on those dwelling in a land overshadowed by death
  light has arisen.

From that time on, Jesus began to preach and say, "Repent, for the kingdom of heaven is at hand."

[As he was walking by the Sea of Galilee, he saw two brothers, Simon who is called Peter, and his brother Andrew, casting a net into the sea; they were fishermen. He said to them, "Come after me, and I will make you fishers of men." At once they left their nets and followed him. He walked along from there and saw two other brothers, James, the son of Zebedee, and his brother John. They were in a boat, with their father Zebedee, mending their nets. He called them, and immediately they left their boat and their father and followed him.

He went around all of Galilee, teaching in their synagogues, proclaiming the gospel of the kingdom, and curing every disease and illness among the people.]

Understanding the Word

The Isaian passage refers to the devastation wrought by the Assyrians around the year 732 B.C., when the northernmost tribal areas of Zebulun and Naphtali were annexed by the empire (2 Kings 15:29). This area, which included a number of non-Israelites, was referred to as the Galilee (District) of the Gentiles. The full oracle, which continues beyond the Lectionary reading, announces that the degradation of that event has come to an end with the birth of a new Davidic king (8:5–6). This king will surely take back for Israel the northern lands, just as Gideon rescued these northern tribes from the hands of the Midianites back in the days of the Judges (Judges 6–7).

Paul this week attends to divisions that have arisen within the church at Corinth. These reflect a fundamental misunderstanding about the nature of the church as a whole. Whereas in the larger society it was customary to "belong" to a particular teacher or political or social group, distinct from others who belonged to other groups, the church of Christ is formed around Christ alone, and it is he who unites all Christians in "the same mind and in the same purpose." To divide the church along factional lines is, for Paul, to deny its special nature, which is not meant to mirror the larger society.

Jesus' hometown of Nazareth lies to the southwest of the Sea of Galilee, whereas Capernaum is situated to the north, in the middle of the former area of Naphtali. The Evangelist's citation of the Isaiah passage points to Jesus' identity as the long-expected Davidic king who has brought salvation not only to Israel but also to the Gentiles. Jesus begins his public ministry by preaching repentance and the reign of God—the former part of the acceptance of the latter. Jesus' first act is to call together his coworkers who, having learned from him, will help him cast as wide a net as possible for the proclamation of the kingdom of heaven.

Reflecting on the Word

Imagine you are Simon Peter's mother-in-law. How do you confront him when he tells you about this call of Jesus. "What? You're leaving fishing? You love fishing! You love being on the water! You're going to follow who? A carpenter's son from Nazareth? Nazareth! Really?" But you've never seen Peter's bearded face so radiant, at least not since the day he married your daughter. Since her death, inescapable gloom has engulfed him. Despondency has surrounded him like a dark cloud on the Sea of Galilee. He is such a passionate man. He's been really difficult to live with.

Now? Something has changed. Joy floods his eyes. Love fills his words. Something new overflows from his heart. This Jesus hasn't asked him to leave fishing, he exclaims, but tells him that he'll be fishing for "men"! What in the world does "fishing for men" mean? How can he ask that much from Simon? Does he know how broken he is inside or does he only see those strong muscles? Does this Jesus understand that the big fisherman really doesn't handle loss very well?

You try to get Andrew to change his brother's mind. Andrew is the more level-headed one. But he says that he's going ,too. He says that we can trust this Jesus. Then he sings, "The Lord is my light and my salvation." As he turns to go, he shouts, "He might be the one! He could be the Messiah that we have been waiting for!" Then he skips down the path. Andrew, sensible Andrew, skips! You've heard of mountains skipping like rams, but—Andrew?

And yet worry seizes you—Simon is leaving all? How will we eat? Who will run the business? You've got so much fear. So much anxiety. It just might make you sick.

Consider/Discuss

❖ The call of Jesus is an unrelenting call to leave everything behind. What worries do we have about that? In what ways is it hard to trust, for our own life or for that of others? How can that anxiety make us sick?

❖ In the middle of Isaiah's oracle of gloom and doom, the prophet suddenly describes a new radiance that will dawn. When you have been in a deep darkness, what does it feel like to see a great light? Do you ever feel so much joy that you feel like skipping?

Living and Praying with the Word

Lord, you have come to the shore of our lives. You have called us by name. Thank you for the honor of following you. On our own, we've got nothing. With you, all is possible. Help us to trust that where you lead will be abundant and rich. Hold our worries in your hands and deliver us from all anxiety, for your call is our call, your path is our path. Let us never be separated from you.

THE PRESENTATION OF THE LORD

Today's Focus: Faith—Assurance That God Is at Work

We sometimes think that holiness is for other people, and it's likely that we all know people who we'd consider holier than ourselves. Our life of faith tells us otherwise, and must lead us to holiness.

FIRST READING   *Malachi 3:1–4*

Thus says the Lord God:
   Lo, I am sending my messenger
     to prepare the way before me;
   And suddenly there will come to the temple
     the Lord whom you seek,
   And the messenger of the covenant whom you desire.
     Yes, he is coming, says the Lord of hosts.
   But who will endure the day of his coming?
     And who can stand when he appears?
   For he is like the refiner's fire,
     or like the fuller's lye.
   He will sit refining and purifying silver,
     and he will purify the sons of Levi,
   Refining them like gold or like silver
     that they may offer due sacrifice to the Lord.
   Then the sacrifice of Judah and Jerusalem
     will please the Lord,
     as in the days of old, as in years gone by.

PSALM RESPONSE   *Psalm 24:8*

Who is this king of glory? It is the Lord!

SECOND READING   *Hebrews 2:14–18*

Since the children share in blood and flesh, Jesus likewise shared in them, that through death he might destroy the one who has the power of death, that is, the devil, and free those who through fear of death had been subject to slavery all their life. Surely he did not help angels but rather the descendants of Abraham; therefore, he had to become like his brothers and sisters in every way, that he might be a merciful and faithful high priest before God to expiate the sins of the people. Because he himself was tested through what he suffered, he is able to help those who are being tested.

53

In the shorter form of the reading, the passages in brackets are omitted.

When the days were completed for their purification according to the law of Moses, Mary and Joseph took Jesus up to Jerusalem to present him to the Lord, just as it is written in the law of the Lord,

Every male that opens the womb shall be consecrated to the Lord,
and to offer the sacrifice of
a pair of turtledoves or two young pigeons,
in accordance with the dictate in the law of the Lord.

Now there was a man in Jerusalem whose name was Simeon. This man was righteous and devout, awaiting the consolation of Israel, and the Holy Spirit was upon him. It had been revealed to him by the Holy Spirit that he should not see death before he had seen the Christ of the Lord. He came in the Spirit into the temple; and when the parents brought in the child Jesus to perform the custom of the law in regard to him, he took him into his arms and blessed God, saying:

"Now, Master, you may let your servant go
in peace, according to your word,
for my eyes have seen your salvation,
which you prepared in the sight of all the peoples:
a light for revelation to the Gentiles,
and glory for your people Israel."

[The child's father and mother were amazed at what was said about him; and Simeon blessed them and said to Mary his mother, "Behold, this child is destined for the fall and rise of many in Israel, and to be a sign that will be contradicted— and you yourself a sword will pierce—so that the thoughts of many hearts may be revealed." There was also a prophetess, Anna, the daughter of Phanuel, of the tribe of Asher. She was advanced in years, having lived seven years with her husband after her marriage, and then as a widow until she was eighty-four. She never left the temple, but worshiped night and day with fasting and prayer. And coming forward at that very time, she gave thanks to God and spoke about the child to all who were awaiting the redemption of Jerusalem.

When they had fulfilled all the prescriptions of the law of the Lord, they returned to Galilee, to their own town of Nazareth. The child grew and became strong, filled with wisdom; and the favor of God was upon him.]

Understanding the Word

A major theme in Malachi is God's apparent inattention to injustice. Immediately before the reading, God notes that the people have demanded, "Where is the just God?" (2:17). God responds that soon the messenger of the covenant will appear in advance of the one whom they seek. It is not clear from the biblical text who this messenger is or how the messenger relates to God. Understood eschatologically, it refers to the figure who will come to be known as the Messiah. In any case, the advent of this figure will bring about the justice the people seek, beginning with cleaning up corrupt priests (Levites) and their worship.

The focus of the reading from Hebrews is on the fact that Jesus shared our human nature (flesh and blood) precisely so he could deliver us from the fear of death. It is this fear, and not death itself, that holds us in bondage to the devil. In a time of persecution, it is fear of suffering and death that the author sees as potentially leading his audience into infidelity (3:1—4:14). Thus, the message: they have nothing to fear from death, because Jesus has endured it and come out the other side. Because he acts now as high priest, merciful and faithful, those who die have nothing to fear.

The Torah prescribes that a newborn son be circumcised, marking his acceptance into the covenant community, and that the mother should be ritually purified (Leviticus 12:1–5). This gesture of obeying the Torah indicates the larger Gospel theme that Jesus himself will perfectly fulfill the Law. More than that, with Jesus' advent God is fulfilling covenant promises to Israel, and ultimately to all nations. Thus, inspired by the Holy Spirit, Simeon announces that in Jesus God has brought consolation and salvation—a gift that some will oppose ("contradict"). The widow Anna also recognizes Jesus, and likewise announces the good news of the redemption of God's people.

Reflecting on the Word

Have you ever met someone who is really old and really wise? I have met several such men and women, mostly at daily Mass. Their eyes are gentle. Smile lines are etched into the wrinkles of their faces. In some, a lifetime of generosity is written into their bodies, as though their hands reach out to hug you, even when they have not moved. Others are quieter, but their faces radiate peace. Kindliness and holiness have become a way of life for them.

Simeon and Anna are the first-century equivalent of those saints whom you and I have met. These two pray. They pray a lot. Simeon is described as "upright and devout." When he sees the child, he believes. He believes! An eight-day-old baby is being presented to the Lord. And Simeon sees in that child the Savior of the world. How does that work? Something must have moved within him.

Faith is an inner assurance that rises within us to convince us that God is at work. That belief, at that moment, is a gift.

Anna has prayed night and day in the temple for years and years and years. Many of us have tasted the seasoning of the Spirit. But there are saints who have tasted of the pure Spirit, as though it were something they drank straight. Anna seems to be one of those people, those who live on the borderline between God and the world.

You might just be one of those people. If you are, thank you for your life of holiness. If you are not, then like me, let's keep working to drink deeply of God's Spirit, day after day. God is real, at work at all times. Faith is a gift, an inner assurance that this is so.

Consider/Discuss

❖ Think about those moments when you have been gifted with an inner certainty about God's movement or action in your life. It could be a delicate touch or an overwhelming conversion experience. Share that story with someone this week.

❖ Sometimes we start to think and act as though the living God were just an idea. If God is real, at work at all times, what does that mean for how we listen, how we are attentive? What does that divine presence mean for how we live our lives day after day?

Living and Praying with the Word

On this day of presentation, God of glory, we present ourselves to you. Purify us to become more holy. We see in others what beauty a lifetime of grace can create. We want to be like that. Lead us in your everlasting way.

FIFTH SUNDAY IN ORDINARY TIME

Today's Focus: Team "Light for the World!"

The individualism of our surrounding culture can invade our spiritual lives, and we despair of being able to counter all the sin in the world. But we are part of a team, powered by the light of Christ!

FIRST READING
Isaiah 58:7–10

Thus says the LORD:
　Share your bread with the hungry,
　　shelter the oppressed and the homeless;
　clothe the naked when you see them,
　　and do not turn your back on your own.
　Then your light shall break forth like the dawn,
　　and your wound shall quickly be healed;
　your vindication shall go before you,
　　and the glory of the LORD shall be your rear guard.
　Then you shall call, and the LORD will answer,
　　you shall cry for help, and he will say: Here I am!
　If you remove from your midst
　　oppression, false accusation and malicious speech;
　if you bestow your bread on the hungry
　　and satisfy the afflicted;
　then light shall rise for you in the darkness,
　　and the gloom shall become for you like midday.

PSALM RESPONSE
Psalm 112:4a

The just man is a light in darkness to the upright.

SECOND READING
1 Corinthians 2:1–5

When I came to you, brothers and sisters, proclaiming the mystery of God, I did not come with sublimity of words or of wisdom. For I resolved to know nothing while I was with you except Jesus Christ, and him crucified. I came to you in weakness and fear and much trembling, and my message and my proclamation were not with persuasive words of wisdom, but with a demonstration of Spirit and power, so that your faith might rest not on human wisdom but on the power of God.

Jesus said to his disciples: "You are the salt of the earth. But if salt loses its taste, with what can it be seasoned? It is no longer good for anything but to be thrown out and trampled underfoot. You are the light of the world. A city set on a mountain cannot be hidden. Nor do they light a lamp and then put it under a bushel basket; it is set on a lampstand, where it gives light to all in the house. Just so, your light must shine before others, that they may see your good deeds and glorify your heavenly Father."

Understanding the Word

This post-exilic Isaiah passage reflects a time when the full restoration of God's people in the land had yet to materialize. Agricultural and economic conditions led to a general failure to thrive. The people have complained that, although they have fasted and prayed, God has not responded (58:3). Thus, God's retort: This is the fast I want—to take care of one another, to remove oppression and injustice from among you. Only when God's people have attended to these traditional, well-known covenantal expectations will they experience full restoration, when God answers and quickly heals their "wound." This is God's desire and final intention.

Paul has been arguing that God's wisdom, God's way of acting in the world, makes no sense from the perspective of "human wisdom" (1:18–31). Thus it was that when Paul came proclaiming God's plan of salvation through the cross of Christ ("the mystery of God"), he did not rely on persuasive arguments or "sublimity of words." Rather, he simply proclaimed what God had done, relying on God—through the Spirit and power—to persuade that Paul spoke the truth. Ultimately for Paul, the Christian message cannot be demonstrated using human logic; its truth can only be shown and believed through the power of God.

Jesus exhorts his disciples that they are charged not just to follow and learn from him, but to manifest the glory of God through their lives. Salt is only useful when it seasons food. Likewise, discipleship is not just for the good of the individual but for others as well; disciples must therefore make sure that they are faithful followers of Christ. Light provides illumination, and is thus a prominent biblical metaphor for the attractive power of God's teaching and actions for others (for example, Isaiah 2:2–5; 42:6). Just as salt must be salty or it stops being salt, and light that does not illuminate cannot really be light, so Christians in whom others cannot see the glory of God are not really (good) disciples.

Reflecting on the Word

My husband and I are season ticket holders for Notre Dame women's basketball. What we really like to watch is how the players work together as a team. Because women are generally shorter than men, they cannot just run down the court solo and slam the ball into the hoop. They have to work together. Women's basketball is a team sport.

In today's reading, Jesus is talking to a team. In the passages "You are the salt of the earth" and "You are the light of the world," the "you" is plural. It might be more accurately translated with a southern accent as "y'all are the light of the world." We are to be a team. We are not tall enough to knock the lights out of "darkness" by ourselves. We have to work together. The Christian life is a team endeavor.

In the readings for the last several weeks, St. Paul has been berating the Corinthians for their lack of solidarity: You fight over privilege and power! You fight over food! You look first to your own interests! Is this Christian team behavior? He can't change them through persuasive arguments. He points them to the cross of Christ who models for "y'all" a new way to live.

We are called to be a team. How do we conquer the darkness together? Isaiah says, share food with the hungry. Clothe the naked. Satisfy the needs of the wretched. Then, when we (plural) call for help, "the Lord will answer, 'Here I am'." Then our light will rise like dawn out of darkness. Our fans in the stands, the saints of heaven who have played this game before us, will cheer as the lights come up; they will "give praise to our Father" and shout out to us, "Go team!"

Consider/Discuss

❖ Sometimes the darkness feels too great. We cannot overcome it by ourselves. Do you ever get discouraged? Where might the Lord be leading you to become a part of a team that makes a difference in this world?

❖ We are to be a team that is light for the world. On any team, some sit on the sidelines and others actively contribute. Are you willing to train hard enough to get into the game? What spiritual exercises do you need to take up to be stronger?

Living and Praying with the Word

Angels and saints in heaven, pray for our solidarity. Even in the Church, we struggle to play and pray together. But in the battle against the darkness, we need each other, all players on the field. Father, Son, and Spirit, you are one. Strengthen us so that we look past our differences and learn to work together to be one as you are one. Help us be light for the world and salt of the earth, to your glory and praise. St. Paul, pray for us as you prayed for the Corinthian community.

SIXTH SUNDAY IN ORDINARY TIME

Today's Focus: Not a Law-destroyer But a Law-fulfiller.

Israel thought their observance of the Law of Moses was the way to the unseen God. In Jesus Christ, that way to God was made incarnate, visible, and is a way that we still can take.

FIRST READING

Sirach 15:15–20

If you choose you can keep the commandments,
    they will save you;
  if you trust in God, you too shall live;
he has set before you fire and water;
  to whichever you choose, stretch forth your hand.
Before man are life and death, good and evil,
  whichever he chooses shall be given him.
Immense is the wisdom of the Lord;
  he is mighty in power, and all-seeing.
The eyes of God are on those who fear him;
  he understands man's every deed.
No one does he command to act unjustly,
  to none does he give license to sin.

PSALM RESPONSE

Psalm 119:1b

Blessed are they who follow the law of the Lord!

SECOND READING

1 Corinthians 2:6–10

Brothers and sisters: We speak a wisdom to those who are mature, not a wisdom of this age, nor of the rulers of this age who are passing away. Rather, we speak God's wisdom, mysterious, hidden, which God predetermined before the ages for our glory, and which none of the rulers of this age knew; for, if they had known it, they would not have crucified the Lord of glory. But as it is written:

What eye has not seen, and ear has not heard,
  and what has not entered the human heart,
    what God has prepared for those who love him,
this God has revealed to us through the Spirit.

For the Spirit scrutinizes everything, even the depths of God.

In the shorter form of the reading, the passages in brackets are omitted.

Jesus said to his disciples: ["Do not think that I have come to abolish the law or the prophets. I have come not to abolish but to fulfill. Amen, I say to you, until heaven and earth pass away, not the smallest letter or the smallest part of a letter will pass from the law, until all things have taken place. Therefore, whoever breaks one of the least of these commandments and teaches others to do so will be called least in the kingdom of heaven. But whoever obeys and teaches these command- ments will be called greatest in the kingdom of heaven.] I tell you, unless your righteousness surpasses that of the scribes and Pharisees, you will not enter the kingdom of heaven.

"You have heard that it was said to your ancestors,
You shall not kill; and whoever kills will be liable to judgment.

But I say to you, whoever is angry with his brother will be liable to judgment; [and whoever says to brother, 'Raqa,' will be answerable to the Sanhedrin; and whoever says, 'You fool,' will be liable to fiery Gehenna. Therefore, if you bring your gift to the altar, and there recall that your brother has anything against you, leave your gift there at the altar, go first and be reconciled with your brother, and then come and offer your gift. Settle with your opponent quickly while on the way to court. Otherwise your opponent will hand you over to the judge, and the judge will hand you over to the guard, and you will be thrown into prison. Amen, I say to you, you will not be released until you have paid the last penny.]

"You have heard that it was said,
You shall not commit adultery.

But I say to you, everyone who looks at a woman with lust has already commit- ted adultery with her in his heart. [If your right eye causes you to sin, tear it out and throw it away. It is better for you to lose one of your members than to have your whole body thrown into Gehenna. And if your right hand causes you to sin, cut it off and throw it away. It is better for you to lose one of your members than to have your whole body go into Gehenna.

"It was also said,
Whoever divorces his wife must give her a bill of divorce.

But I say to you, whoever divorces his wife—unless the marriage is unlawful— causes her to commit adultery, and whoever marries a divorced woman commits adultery.]

"Again you have heard that it was said to your ancestors,
Do not take a false oath,
but make good to the Lord all that you vow.

But I say to you, do not swear at all; [not by heaven, for it is God's throne; nor by the earth, for it is his footstool; nor by Jerusalem, for it is the city of the great King. Do not swear by your head, for you cannot make a single hair white or black.] Let your 'Yes' mean 'Yes,'and your 'No' mean 'No.' Anything more is from the evil one."

Understanding the Word

Biblical wisdom literature, as here in Sirach, often talks about the choice between two paths: wisdom or foolishness, life or death. The point of traditional wisdom literature is to make this choice clear and to argue for the way of wisdom and of life. The commands of God are intended also to point toward the way of life. God's commands are not impossible to fulfill, otherwise they would be unjust. Humans must learn to trust that what God commands is, in fact, the truly good. Sin, in this reading, is failure to trust God and so choose the wrong path.

Although Paul declared that he did not come to the Corinthians speaking wisdom (2:1–5), he now concedes that, in fact, he did come speaking wisdom. But it was not the "wisdom of this age." Instead, he spoke God's wisdom, which only those who are "mature" can understand. God's wisdom is not likely to be persuasive to those who think with the mind of the age rather than with the mind of God (see Romans 12:2). This wisdom is only accessible through the power and gift of the Spirit, who alone comprehends the "mysterious, hidden" plan of God. Paul will go on to insist that it is this same Spirit that the Corinthians have received, so that they may "judge spiritually," and not according to the wisdom of the world (2:11–15).

Jesus insists to his disciples that he has not come to abrogate a single divine command or prophetic exhortation. Instead, he insists that the law exists not merely to be "observed," but to be lived. It is intended to point toward and inculcate those dispositions and virtues that together comprise "righteousness." The way to the kingdom of heaven is not merely to follow the rules, as if they in themselves were the point. Rather it is to become formed into people whose wills reflect the values embodied by the law (which of course does not excuse one from keeping the commandments).

Reflecting on the Word

In a world of kings and emperors and governors and rulers, how can someone get access to the "big man at the top?" He has many guards. He lives in a mighty palace. You have to know the right people even to get a glimpse of him. Ordinary folks just cannot get access to the "Boss."

In the same way, the Israelites revered God, the Holy One, as unapproachable, mighty, pure, and majestic, the "biggest (boss) at the top." They believed that you would die if you saw God. Their reverence was rich and deep. Even Moses, who was the greatest of prophets, only saw where God had passed by. Thus they wondered, how do we get access to the Divine?

How did they solve that "access" question? If you wanted to get to Jerusalem, you followed the road to Jerusalem. If you wanted to get to the God of purity, you followed the road that led you to become pure, for the Most Holy could not look upon sin. How do you become pure? By following the laws of purity. What we may not understand from our vantage point is that observing the law meant everything to the religious people of Jesus' day—not for the sake of "the law" itself, but because they wanted to be able to approach God. They wanted to come to God with a clean heart. The law was their way to get access to the Most High God.

Jesus understood that theology. When Jesus said that he didn't come to destroy the law but to fulfill it, he understood their longing: they wanted access to God. That was admirable. Jesus honored that. Moving forward from the written law, he offered *himself* as the road to the Father: "*I* am the way."

Consider/Discuss

❖ St. Paul got into many arguments about the law. He also understood the theology that following the law granted access to the Father. After his conversion, he understood that Jesus was now the way to the Father. The law may not have passed away, but how often do we try to gain access to God's favor through adherence to law? What does it mean to you for Jesus to be "the Way"?

❖ Reverence for God seems to be on the wane in our culture. Purity is not reverenced much either. How does that cultural attitude affect your own spiritual and moral life? Where do you hold yourself accountable? Where do you feel that you can let yourself slack off?

Living and Praying with the Word

Jesus, you have promised us that you are the way of access to the Father. We live in that hope. Help us not to be presumptuous about purity, thinking that we can live any way we choose and you will blithely forgive us. Help us to be perfect as you are perfect, pure as you are pure. We cannot do this on our own. We come through you who are the Way, the Truth, and the Life. Lead us to the One who is Unapproachable Radiance!

SEVENTH SUNDAY IN ORDINARY TIME

Today's Focus: Be Holy as the Lord Is Holy

The command to be holy, as God is holy, can seem like a return to the sin of Eden—thinking that we are gods. Rather, we are to let God's grace guide us and draw us near, so we are filled with divine holiness.

FIRST READING
Leviticus 19:1–2, 17–18

The Lord said to Moses, "Speak to the whole Israelite community and tell them: Be holy, for I, the Lord, your God, am holy.

"You shall not bear hatred for your brother or sister in your heart. Though you may have to reprove your fellow citizen, do not incur sin because of him. Take no revenge and cherish no grudge against any of your people. You shall love your neighbor as yourself. I am the Lord."

PSALM RESPONSE
Psalm 103:8a

The Lord is kind and merciful.

SECOND READING
1 Corinthians 3:16–23

Brothers and sisters: Do you not know that you are the temple of God, and that the Spirit of God dwells in you? If anyone destroys God's temple, God will destroy that person; for the temple of God, which you are, is holy.

Let no one deceive himself. If any one among you considers himself wise in this age, let him become a fool, so as to become wise. For the wisdom of this world is foolishness in the eyes of God, for it is written:
God catches the wise in their own ruses,
and again:
The Lord knows the thoughts of the wise,
that they are vain.

So let no one boast about human beings, for everything belongs to you, Paul or Apollos or Cephas, or the world or life or death, or the present or the future: all belong to you, and you to Christ, and Christ to God.

Jesus said to his disciples: "You have heard that it was said,
An eye for an eye and a tooth for a tooth.

But I say to you, offer no resistance to one who is evil. When someone strikes you on your right cheek, turn the other one as well. If anyone wants to go to law with you over your tunic, hand over your cloak as well. Should anyone press you into service for one mile, go for two miles. Give to the one who asks of you, and do not turn your back on one who wants to borrow.

"You have heard that it was said,
You shall love your neighbor and hate your enemy.

But I say to you, love your enemies and pray for those who persecute you, that you may be children of your heavenly Father, for he makes his sun rise on the bad and the good, and causes rain to fall on the just and the unjust. For if you love those who love you, what recompense will you have? Do not the tax collectors do the same? And if you greet your brothers only, what is unusual about that? Do not the pagans do the same? So be perfect, just as your heavenly Father is perfect."

Understanding the Word

Much of Leviticus focuses on God's formative intentions for Israel by repeating often the phrase, "Be holy, for I, the LORD, your God, am holy." These words punctuate a section of ethical and cultic laws scholars call the Holiness Code (chapters 17–26). The command put forward in the reading this week is exemplary of the ethical commands, and it highlights that these commands are meant form one's "heart." One is not to hate even secretly, or to "cherish" a grudge. Instead, Israelites are called to love one another as much as they love themselves. Thus, they will become as holy as their God.

Paul comes back to an earlier concern, which is the divisions among the Corinthians (1:10–17), the fruit of "the wisdom of this world." Paul, Apollos, and Cephas (Peter) are not leaders of factions, but coworkers and instruments of God's construction of a temple, the Corinthians as a whole (the "you" here is plural). Divisions form when one considers oneself part of an "in group" and derives self-worth from that membership ("boasting about human beings"). Paul reminds the Corinthians that their worth comes not from "belonging" to human beings, but to Christ, who himself belongs to God. By virtue of this fact, everything belongs to them. So they can stop trying to gain their worth through posturing and division.

Jesus has been instructing his disciples how the Law is intended to form a certain kind of person. Now he turns to the theme of retaliation. The ancient *lex talionis* is meant to limit vengeance (Exodus 21:23–24; Leviticus 24:19–20). Jesus deepens this point by commanding his followers to reject vengeance altogether, and further, to respond to demands with generosity. Jesus' command to love enemies is founded on the observable fact that God also shows kindness to the unjust and the bad (who might be considered God's "enemies"). Just as Israel was commanded to be holy as God is holy, so Jesus' followers are commanded to be "perfect" as God is perfect.

Reflecting on the Word

When I taught high school theology, on the first day of the semester, I had a student proudly walk into my sophomore morality class with a colorfully decorated binder. She showed off to me her cover picture of Moses holding two stone tablets. On the tablets was written, "The Ten Suggestions." She grinned at me as only a teenager can, whimsically testing, as if to ask, "What do you, teacher, think about my cleverness in re-casting the Ten Commandments?" with a shrug of the shoulder of "Who do you think *you* are to tell *me* what I should do?" Having lived with teenagers at my house for the previous twenty years, I just nodded and smiled. It was going to be an interesting semester.

In the world in which we live, what are we to do with ethical laws and commandments? Are they just "suggestions"? Are there any absolutes? Is anything always wrong? Is anything always right? Is there anyone to Whom we are accountable? Is there really a test at the end of life, or is God such a "nice guy" that no one goes to hell? Who is in charge anyway?

My fifteen-year-old student presumed a world that was kind and benevolent. She may never have experienced killing and war and infidelity and betrayal. Her parents were probably good people. Her friends may have been, too. If that were the case, then why did we need the ten "ethical suggestions"? Our access to God comes through Jesus and does not rely on our perfection, right?

Right, but the flourishing of life certainly does. Forming the heart to love and be generous and prayerful and forgiving—this bears fruit, fruit that lasts, in relationships that are solid and enduring. A holy life is a life worth living.

Consider/Discuss

❖ In the Sermon on the Mount, Jesus lays out clear principles for holy living, commanding us to be perfect as our heavenly Father is perfect. Similarly, the Levitical holiness code reveals how to be holy as God is holy. What does holiness look like in your life? Why does it matter to you?

❖ Does someone you love dismiss ethical laws as though they were just "suggestions"? What life stories could you tell to respond to that person?

Living and Praying with the Word

Lord, sometimes, we throw up our hands at what is happening in our world. There are so many things that we cannot control. Help us to make an impact in the small world in which we live, by living lives of holiness and goodness and prayer. With your grace, please help us. And bless all those who do not believe in you or follow you, for you send blessings on the just and the unjust. We entrust all of that to you—it is not ours, but yours. Thank you for taking this world and carrying it for us.

Notes

LENT

The first readings for Lent tell the story of humanity's troubled relationship with God and the various efforts God makes to draw us back. The tragic disobedience in the Garden introduces into the relationship a human tendency to distrust God, resulting in spiritual and physical death (Genesis 2:7–9; 3:1–7). Not content to leave things thus, God seeks to repair the damage, first by creating a people, beginning with a little old couple, in whom eventually all the families of the earth will find blessing (Genesis 12:1–4a). In its history, Israel—in whom we are invited to see ourselves—struggles to trust in a God who continually provides (Exodus 17:3–7). But the human tendency to distrust eventually leads to the death of exile, a death from which God promises to deliver, prefiguring the promise of physical resurrection (Ezekiel 37:12–14). Finally, Isaiah speaks of a servant sent by God to bring a message of comfort, which nevertheless arouses hostility (Isaiah 50:4–7). Throughout Lent we see God continually seeking to repair the damage caused so long ago and the persistent human resistance to God's efforts, even as they long for salvation. In a word, the first readings present us with a diagnosis of our situation.

The epistles take up this question of the human condition by affirming that God has done something definitive about it in Christ and outlining the appropriate human response. Paul presents us with the indisputable fact that through the ages humans have been captive to sin and thus condemned to both spiritual and physical death (Romans 5:12–19). But Christ has brought an end to the judgment all humans incur through the guilt of Adam, and through grace (and the Spirit) brings us out of the realm of sin and death into the realm of righteousness and life (Ephesians 5:8–14; Romans 8:8–11). At the same time, Christ reconciles us to God and makes it possible to love God, which we call holiness, a calling all Christians have received by virtue of having received new life in Christ (2 Timothy 1:8b–10; Romans 5:1–2, 5–8).

The Gospels present us with various answers to the question, Who is Jesus? He is the New Israel—or the new humanity—who overcomes the sins and failings of the past by resisting the satanic temptations to turn away from God in selfishness and fear (Matthew 4:1–11). He is God's Son, beloved and endowed with divine authority (Matthew 17:1–9). To a humanity thirsty for it-knows-not-what, he is the Living Water (John 4:5–42). To the blind who are barely able to glimpse him, he is the Light (John 9:1–41). To those who have died, he is the Resurrection (John 11:1–45). And to all of us who desperately need him, he is God's humble servant who has come to serve us and bring us back from death to life, darkness to light, alienation to reconciliation with God (Matthew 26:14 — 27:66).

FIRST SUNDAY OF LENT

Today's Focus: Called to Be True

A new Lent is a new opportunity to examine our relationship with God and to follow the example of Jesus, who remained true to the end.

FIRST READING *Genesis 2:7–9; 3:1–7*

The LORD God formed man out of the clay of the ground and blew into his nostrils the breath of life, and so man became a living being.

Then the LORD God planted a garden in Eden, in the east, and placed there the man whom he had formed. Out of the ground the LORD God made various trees grow that were delightful to look at and good for food, with the tree of life in the middle of the garden and the tree of the knowledge of good and evil.

Now the serpent was the most cunning of all the animals that the LORD God had made. The serpent asked the woman, "Did God really tell you not to eat from any of the trees in the garden?" The woman answered the serpent: "We may eat of the fruit of the trees in the garden; it is only about the fruit of the tree in the middle of the garden that God said, 'You shall not eat it or even touch it, lest you die.' " But the serpent said to the woman: "You certainly will not die! No, God knows well that the moment you eat of it your eyes will be opened and you will be like gods who know what is good and what is evil." The woman saw that the tree was good for food, pleasing to the eyes, and desirable for gaining wisdom. So she took some of its fruit and ate it; and she also gave some to her husband, who was with her, and he ate it. Then the eyes of both of them were opened, and they realized that they were naked; so they sewed fig leaves together and made loincloths for themselves.

PSALM RESPONSE *Psalm 51:3a*

Be merciful, O Lord, for we have sinned.

SECOND READING *Romans 5:12–19 or 5:12, 17–19*

In the shorter form of the reading, the passage in brackets is omitted.

Brothers and sisters: Through one man sin entered the world, and through sin, death, and thus death came to all men, inasmuch as all sinned—[for up to the time of the law, sin was in the world, though sin is not accounted when there is no law. But death reigned from Adam to Moses, even over those who did not sin after the pattern of the trespass of Adam, who is the type of the one who was to come.

But the gift is not like the transgression. For if by the transgression of the one, the many died, how much more did the grace of God and the gracious gift of the one man Jesus Christ overflow for the many. And the gift is not like the result of the one who sinned. For after one sin there was the judgment that brought condemnation; but the gift, after many transgressions, brought acquittal.] For if, by the transgression of the one, death came to reign through that one, how much more will those who receive the abundance of grace and of the gift of justification come to reign in life through the one Jesus Christ. In conclusion, just as through one transgression condemnation came upon all, so, through one righteous act, acquittal and life came to all. For just as through the disobedience of the one man the many were made sinners, so, through the obedience of the one, the many will be made righteous.

GOSPEL *Matthew 4:1–11*

At that time Jesus was led by the Spirit into the desert to be tempted by the devil. He fasted for forty days and forty nights, and afterwards he was hungry. The tempter approached and said to him, "If you are the Son of God, command that these stones become loaves of bread." He said in reply, "It is written:

One does not live on bread alone,
but on every word that comes forth
from the mouth of God."

Then the devil took him to the holy city, and made him stand on the parapet of the temple, and said to him, "If you are the Son of God, throw yourself down. For it is written:

He will command his angels concerning you
and with their hands they will support you,
lest you dash your foot against a stone."

Jesus answered him, "Again it is written,

You shall not put the Lord, your God, to the test."

Then the devil took him up to a very high mountain, and showed him all the kingdoms of the world in their magnificence, and he said to him, "All these I shall give to you, if you will prostrate yourself and worship me." At this, Jesus said to him, "Get away, Satan! It is written:

The Lord, your God, shall you worship
and him alone shall you serve."

Then the devil left him and, behold, angels came and ministered to him.

Understanding the Word

The Genesis reading relates how an original intimacy between humans and God was damaged by distrust. The serpent's question to the woman implies that God has placed an unreasonable limitation on the couple. Although Eve does not take the bait, she does note that God said they would die if they ate from the tree. Knowing that they will not physically die, the serpent tells a half-truth, suggesting that God does not have their best interest at heart. But once the couple has eaten of the tree, they do experience death in the form of estrangement from God, the source of life. Exile from the Garden, where God and the tree of life reside, symbolizes this rupture of the divine-human relationship, the devastating consequences of sin.

In his letter to the Romans, Paul articulates the problem to which Christ is the solution—human captivity to sin. He develops this theme by drawing a contrast between the actions of Adam and their consequences and those of Christ. Adam's disobedience brought judgment and death, not only for himself but for all his descendants, such that "death reigned" in the world. Christ's obedience reversed all of this: sinners are made righteous, the condemned are "acquitted," and the reign of death comes to an end. Through the "abundance of grace," a sheer gift of God, the acquitted now "reign in life" through Christ.

In Matthew's Gospel Jesus, who represents all of Israel (2:15), recapitulates and perfects Israel's history with God. Now Jesus is led into the wilderness and tested, as Israel was after the Exodus. Whereas in the desert Israel lacked trust and was unfaithful to God, Jesus resists the temptation to use his powers for his own needs, to put God to the test, or to worship anyone other than God. The rest of the Gospel will show Jesus, as Son of God, serving others rather than himself and, even to the Cross, trusting and remaining faithful to the Father.

Reflecting on the Word

In the fourth century A.D., Christianity became legal and then mandatory. To "follow Jesus" grew to be a soft way of life. Anybody and everybody could (and then should) be a Christian. Within one lifetime, the faith that had required its followers to be willing to be torn apart by lions now became "good for business." What happened as a result? Men and women, turned off to a tamed Christianity, flocked to the Egyptian desert. In the desert, they shed the "fat" of mainstream acceptance. They strove to be pure and obedient and true in their faith. Desert monasticism flourished.

Jesus also was led into the desert. The Judean desert is stark. No trees offer shade. The sun beats down mercilessly. Ninety-five degrees is a cool day in May. For forty days, Jesus' hunger intensified. If he had any fat on his body, it shriveled up. Three times he was tempted to take the easier path. Three times he stayed true to his mission and to his God: I will love the Lord alone!

Adam and Eve didn't think that they needed to do what God told them. When found out, they tried to evade the One who sought them in love, like a guilty toddler hiding behind the couch crying out, "Don't look at me!" They squirmed away from right and wrong.

As you and I move into this season of Lent, what does it mean for us to be true to God? The world around us may tempt us to be soft: lies and posturing and deceit proliferate in our culture and even in our Church. Lent is the season to grow more holy, our time to go to the desert. This is our ascetic season. This is our opportunity to strip away the fat that weighs down our spiritual and moral life.

Consider/Discuss

❖ King David is called to truth by the prophet Nathan (2 Samuel 11—13). He cries out, "O God, create a pure heart in me. Give me a new and steadfast spirit!" What does it mean to you to be true? What tempts you to take a "softer" path?

❖ As we come before God in prayer, is there some part within us that wants to hide behind the couch and not be seen?

Living and Praying with the Word

Lord, sometimes we squirm away from obedience. You call us to look you straight in the eye and remain steadfast in following you, no matter the cost. But sometimes it is more comfortable to go the softer way. When we are tempted to disregard what our conscience tells us is right, fill us with the strength to stand fast. As we enter into this Lenten season, strip away the fat that encases our spiritual and moral life. Give us the grace to follow you more purely.

SECOND SUNDAY OF LENT

Today's Focus: The Divine Brilliance

God is more brilliant than we can ever imagine, and we will see flickers of that brilliance if we open our eyes of faith.

FIRST READING
Genesis 12:1–4a

The LORD said to Abram: "Go forth from the land of your kinsfolk and from your father's house to a land that I will show you.

"I will make of you a great nation,
and I will bless you;
I will make your name great,
so that you will be a blessing.
I will bless those who bless you
and curse those who curse you.
All the communities of the earth
shall find blessing in you."

Abram went as the LORD directed him.

PSALM RESPONSE
Psalm 33:22

Lord, let your mercy be on us, as we place our trust in you.

SECOND READING
2 Timothy 1:8b–10

Beloved: Bear your share of hardship for the gospel with the strength that comes from God.

He saved us and called us to a holy life, not according to our works but according to his own design and the grace bestowed on us in Christ Jesus before time began, but now made manifest through the appearance of our savior Christ Jesus, who destroyed death and brought life and immortality to light through the gospel.

Jesus took Peter, James, and John his brother, and led them up a high mountain by themselves. And he was transfigured before them; his face shone like the sun and his clothes became white as light. And behold, Moses and Elijah appeared to them, conversing with him. Then Peter said to Jesus in reply, "Lord, it is good that we are here. If you wish, I will make three tents here, one for you, one for Moses, and one for Elijah." While he was still speaking, behold, a bright cloud cast a shadow over them, then from the cloud came a voice that said, "This is my beloved Son, with whom I am well pleased; listen to him." When the disciples heard this, they fell prostrate and were very much afraid. But Jesus came and touched them, saying, "Rise, and do not be afraid." And when the disciples raised their eyes, they saw no one else but Jesus alone.

As they were coming down from the mountain, Jesus charged them, "Do not tell the vision to anyone until the Son of Man has been raised from the dead."

Understanding the Word

The early chapters of Genesis display the repercussions of the disobedience of Adam and Eve, passed on as an inclination to sin. In the call of Abram we see the beginning of a long-term divine plan to deal with the problem of the human heart. In the promise that initiates the relationship that will eventually lead to the creation of God's covenant partner, Israel, God assures Abram not only of descendants and land, but also that "all the communities of the earth shall find blessing in you." It is through Israel that God will bring all humanity back into that harmonious relationship with God they originally enjoyed in the Garden.

In his letter to Timothy, Paul reminds the young man that he has received a gift from God that must be "stirred into flame" (2 Timothy 1:6). Timothy has received a commission to teach the Christian message in its integrity. This task will bring hardship, yet Timothy is to take heart and be strong; like all Christians, he has been saved and called by Christ to a holy life. This is not the result of anything Timothy has done, but is purely through the design and call of God. The "life and immortality" that Christ brings is pure gift, but it calls for a response: a holy life that manifests the "light" of the gospel that Timothy is called to proclaim.

On a mountain called Sinai (or Horeb), God appeared to Moses, the people of Israel met their Deliverer, and Elijah encountered God in silence. It is fitting, then, that the divine sonship of Christ, just confessed by Peter (16:16), should now be confirmed on a mountain. The Transfiguration of Jesus reveals not only his identity and authority as God's beloved Son, and as the fulfillment of the law (Moses) and the prophets (Elijah), but also a hint of his post-resurrection glory. Since the truth revealed on the mountain can only be understood and accepted in light of that future event, the disciples are ordered not to speak of it for the time being.

Reflecting on the Word

I have been to the Holy Land once. I recall sitting on the bus with the sunshine of the morning sky flickering through the windows. As we bounced along, I realized how my early sandbox experiences of the warmth of the sun have deeply impacted my image of God.

As we drove north from Nazareth, I wondered how the radiance of the sunshine also impacted Jesus' youngest images of his God as Father. Jesus rested by the Sea of Galilee that shimmers in the midday sun. Jesus climbed Mount Tabor that radiates with light. Jesus prayed on the Mount of Olives, where the clouds and the sky gleam with vibrant color. What stands out in my memory is the Holy Land's brilliance. The Word became flesh in a place of luminous beauty.

In today's readings, Abram and Paul and the apostles have glimpsed that radiance. Later in Genesis, Abram senses glory in the splendor of the stars in a deeply black sky, and believes. Paul himself has obviously experienced that magnificence, for he calls Timothy to grab hold of it. The apostles see it in the person of Jesus, transfigured in front of them. He is dazzling! He is radiant! He is bright! This is the deeper reality of the glory of the Son of God. Peter and James and John get a preview of that glory and they don't really know what to do with it.

We may have also seen flickers of God's glory. Yet more radiance surrounds us than meets the eye. What we may have glimpsed is as faint as the light of a candle compared to the brilliance of the sun. The dazzling One surrounds us and enfolds us at all times. The holy Light will transform us if we let it.

Consider/Discuss

❖ In prayer, have you seen it? Have you ever felt your rib cage so swell up with holy warmth that you almost could burst? Have you seen that Radiance? Have you felt just on the edge of that "more?" Share your story with another believer whom you trust.

❖ We see the grandeur of a sunset, dazzling sparkles in the snow, or the shimmer of light on the water. In our sacramental understanding of the created world, flashes of earthly beauty lead us to the grandeur of God. This week, take a few extra moments to absorb and delight in the radiant beauty that surrounds you.

Living and Praying with the Word

Shower your steadfast light upon us, O Lord. You have flashed, you have revealed, and you have bathed us with your glory. Yet we cannot begin to contain your luminous beauty. Cleanse us this Lent so that we are more fitting vessels for your grandeur. Stir the spark of our faith until it has been stirred into a living flame of love. Then help us to overflow with your joy so that others may behold you as well.

THIRD SUNDAY OF LENT

Today's Focus: The Tender Voice of Jesus

In today's encounter with the Samaritan woman at the well, Jesus speaks to her directly about her life, but also offers her refreshment for days to come.

FIRST READING

Exodus 17:3–7

In those days, in their thirst for water, the people grumbled against Moses, saying, "Why did you ever make us leave Egypt? Was it just to have us die here of thirst with our children and our livestock?" So Moses cried out to the LORD, "What shall I do with this people? A little more and they will stone me!" The LORD answered Moses, "Go over there in front of the people, along with some of the elders of Israel, holding in your hand, as you go, the staff with which you struck the river. I will be standing there in front of you on the rock in Horeb. Strike the rock, and the water will flow from it for the people to drink." This Moses did, in the presence of the elders of Israel. The place was called Massah and Meribah, because the Israelites quarreled there and tested the LORD, saying, "Is the LORD in our midst or not?"

PSALM RESPONSE

Psalm 95:8

If today you hear his voice, harden not your hearts.

SECOND READING

Romans 5:1–2, 5–8

Brothers and sisters: Since we have been justified by faith, we have peace with God through our Lord Jesus Christ, through whom we have gained access by faith to this grace in which we stand, and we boast in hope of the glory of God.

And hope does not disappoint, because the love of God has been poured out into our hearts through the Holy Spirit who has been given to us. For Christ, while we were still helpless, died at the appointed time for the ungodly. Indeed, only with difficulty does one die for a just person, though perhaps for a good person one might even find courage to die. But God proves his love for us in that while we were still sinners Christ died for us.

In the shorter form of the reading, the passages in brackets are omitted.

Jesus came to a town of Samaria called Sychar, near the plot of land that Jacob had given to his son Joseph. Jacob's well was there. Jesus, tired from his journey, sat down there at the well. It was about noon.

A woman of Samaria came to draw water. Jesus said to her, "Give me a drink." His disciples had gone into the town to buy food. The Samaritan woman said to him, "How can you, a Jew, ask me, a Samaritan woman, for a drink?"—For Jews use nothing in common with Samaritans.—Jesus answered and said to her, "If you knew the gift of God and who is saying to you, 'Give me a drink,' you would have asked him and he would have given you living water." The woman said to him, "Sir, you do not even have a bucket and the cistern is deep; where then can you get this living water? Are you greater than our father Jacob, who gave us this cistern and drank from it himself with his children and his flocks?" Jesus answered and said to her, "Everyone who drinks this water will be thirsty again; but whoever drinks the water I shall give will never thirst; the water I shall give will become in him a spring of water welling up to eternal life." The woman said to him, "Sir, give me this water, so that I may not be thirsty or have to keep coming here to draw water."

[Jesus said to her, "Go call your husband and come back." The woman answered and said to him, "I do not have a husband." Jesus answered her, "You are right in saying, 'I do not have a husband.' For you have had five husbands, and the one you have now is not your husband. What you have said is true." The woman said to him, "Sir, [I can see that you are a prophet. Our ancestors worshiped on this mountain; but you people say that the place to worship is in Jerusalem." Jesus said to her, "Believe me, woman, the hour is coming when you will worship the Father neither on this mountain nor in Jerusalem. You people worship what you do not understand; we worship what we understand, because salvation is from the Jews. But the hour is coming, and is now here, when true worshipers will worship the Father in Spirit and truth; and indeed the Father seeks such people to worship him. God is Spirit, and those who worship him must worship in Spirit and truth." The woman said to him, "I know that the Messiah is coming, the one called the Christ; when he comes, he will tell us everything." Jesus said to her, "I am he, the one speaking with you."

[At that moment his disciples returned, and were amazed that he was talking with a woman, but still no one said, "What are you looking for?" or "Why are you talking with her?" The woman left her water jar and went into the town and said to the people, "Come see a man who told me everything I have done. Could he possibly be the Christ?" They went out of the town and came to him. Meanwhile, the disciples urged him, "Rabbi, eat." But he said to them, "I have food to eat of which you do not know." So the disciples said to one another, "Could someone have brought him something to eat?" Jesus said to them, "My food is to do the will of the one who sent me and to finish his work. Do you not say, 'In four months the harvest will be here'? I tell you, look up and see the fields ripe for the harvest. The reaper is already receiving payment and gathering crops for eternal life, so that the sower and reaper can rejoice together. For here the saying is verified that 'One sows and another reaps.' I sent you to reap what you have not worked for; others have done the work, and you are sharing the fruits of their work."]

Many of the Samaritans of that town began to believe in him because of the word of the woman who testified, "He told me everything I have done." When the Samaritans came to him, they invited him to stay with them; and he stayed there two days. Many more began to believe in him because of his word, and they said to the woman, "We no longer believe because of your word; for we have heard for ourselves, and we know that this is truly the savior of the world."

Understanding the Word

After their deliverance from Egypt, the work of forming Israel into God's people continues. Although they have seen God's power to save, they have not experienced God's ability to provide. Until they come to trust that their God is capable of meeting all of their needs, they will not be able to be faithful to the covenant relationship. The cry for water, revealing doubts that God is "in their midst," is thus a "test" of God's trustworthiness. God's quick provision is intended not only to provide life-giving water, but also to inspire trust in the God with whom they will shortly enter into covenant relationship.

In his letter to the Romans, Paul explains that, whereas sin alienates us from God, faith in Christ brings about peace with God. More than this, Christ makes it possible to share in the divine life, which gives hope of future glory. This hope is firm because the believer already experiences the "love of God," which can mean God's love for the believer, the believer's love of God, or both. In the first case, the Spirit and the life of grace are from God, a gift of love and a firm promise for the future. In the second case, the believer is able to love God through the transforming power of grace.

Today's Johannine reading dramatizes a central theme found in the Prologue. Just as the Word was in the world but the world did not know or accept him (1:10–11), so at first the woman resists Jesus, "knowing" only that he is a Jew, estranged from Samaritans. But Jesus persists, declaring that if she really knew who he was she would have asked for "living water" from him, a metaphor for divine life and grace ("to those who did accept him, he gave power to become children of God" [1:12]). Eventually the woman comes to believe that he might "possibly be the Christ." As a result of her testimony, others encounter Jesus and come to "know that he is truly the savior of the world."

Reflecting on the Word

Around the corner from my office is a statue by sculptor Ivan Mestrovic of the encounter between Christ and the Samaritan woman at the well. The Lord is looking straight at the woman. The woman is clinging to a large jar and looking down. It is midday. What did this woman expect when she woke up that day? Another dry and empty day as the pariah of the town? In Mosaic law, it is the husband who divorces the wife, so she has already been cast off five times. And her current live-in has not married her. Yet here is a bone-weary male Jewish stranger, asking her for a drink. Asking *her* for a drink. Apparently from *her* bucket. No wonder she is looking down.

This statue on the Notre Dame campus freezes time right there. But in the Gospel, we hear Jesus tenderly poke and prod and speak to her until she opens up and lifts her head. He holds out to her an abundance of the water of life, greater than she has ever imagined. And she takes it.

She drops her bucket (to which she clings so tightly in the statue) and runs to tell the news about the stranger. When she comes back, she doesn't bring a bucket; she brings a whole village!

In art, we look at spaces, not just objects. What most impresses me about Mestrovic's statue is the tenderness in the space between the two characters. Some of us are preachers, some are teachers. Whatever our ministry in life, when we seek to help people come to God, it is that tone of tenderness that crosses divides. More important than words, come into the space with gentleness. Living water will flow.

Consider/Discuss

❖ Jesus also entrusts his thirst to us. We encounter him in order to be filled. Yet he has no bucket but ours. What is our role in fulfilling Jesus' mission to the thirsty world in which we live?

❖ Read through the Gospel again, this time imagining great tenderness in the voice of Jesus. How do you hear the passage differently?

Living and Praying with the Word

Like the woman at the well and the Israelites in the desert, Lord, sometimes we wonder if you—or anyone—cares. Yet you continue to tenderly poke and prod and speak to us. Help us to raise our eyes and see you looking at us with love. As we continue on through this Lent, bring us to repentance and to glory, but also deepen our tenderness in our mission to bring living water to those who thirst for you.

MARCH 22, 2020

FOURTH SUNDAY OF LENT

Today's Focus: Led by the Light

Jesus, the Light of the world, leads us out of darkness,
a beacon of God's merciful care and love for us.

FIRST READING   *1 Samuel 16:1b, 6–7, 10–13a*

The LORD said to Samuel: "Fill your horn with oil, and be on your way. I am sending you to Jesse of Bethlehem, for I have chosen my king from among his sons."

As Jesse and his sons came to the sacrifice, Samuel looked at Eliab and thought, "Surely the Lord's anointed is here before him." But the LORD said to Samuel: "Do not judge from his appearance or from his lofty stature, because I have rejected him. Not as man sees does God see, because man sees the appearance but the LORD looks into the heart." In the same way Jesse presented seven sons before Samuel, but Samuel said to Jesse, "The LORD has not chosen any one of these." Then Samuel asked Jesse, "Are these all the sons you have?" Jesse replied, "There is still the youngest, who is tending the sheep." Samuel said to Jesse, "Send for him; we will not begin the sacrificial banquet until he arrives here." Jesse sent and had the young man brought to them. He was ruddy, a youth handsome to behold and making a splendid appearance. The LORD said, "There—anoint him, for this is the one!" Then Samuel, with the horn of oil in hand, anointed David in the presence of his brothers; and from that day on, the spirit of the LORD rushed upon David.

PSALM RESPONSE   *Psalm 23:1*

The Lord is my shepherd; there is nothing I shall want.

SECOND READING   *Ephesians 5:8–14*

Brothers and sisters: You were once darkness, but now you are light in the Lord. Live as children of light, for light produces every kind of goodness and righteousness and truth. Try to learn what is pleasing to the Lord. Take no part in the fruitless works of darkness; rather expose them, for it is shameful even to mention the things done by them in secret; but everything exposed by the light becomes visible, for everything that becomes visible is light. Therefore, it says:

"Awake, O sleeper,
and arise from the dead,
and Christ will give you light."

In the shorter form of the reading, the passages in brackets are omitted.

As Jesus passed by he saw a man blind from birth. [His disciples asked him, "Rabbi, who sinned, this man or his parents, that he was born blind?" Jesus answered, "Neither he nor his parents sinned; it is so that the works of God might be made visible through him. We have to do the works of the one who sent me while it is day. Night is coming when no one can work. While I am in the world, I am the light of the world." When he had said this,] he spat on the ground and made clay with the saliva, and smeared the clay on his eyes, and said to him, "Go wash in the Pool of Siloam"—which means Sent—. So he went and washed, and came back able to see.

His neighbors and those who had seen him earlier as a beggar said, "Isn't this the one who used to sit and beg?" Some said, "It is," but others said, "No, he just looks like him." He said, "I am." [So they said to him, "How were your eyes opened?" He replied, "The man called Jesus made clay and anointed my eyes and told me, 'Go to Siloam and wash.' So I went there and washed and was able to see." And they said to him, "Where is he?" He said, "I don't know."]

They brought the one who was once blind to the Pharisees. Now Jesus had made clay and opened his eyes on a sabbath. So then the Pharisees also asked him how he was able to see. He said to them, "He put clay on my eyes, and I washed, and now I can see." So some of the Pharisees said, "This man is not from God, because he does not keep the sabbath." But others said, "How can a sinful man do such signs?" And there was a division among them. So they said to the blind man again, "What do you have to say about him, since he opened your eyes?" He said, "He is a prophet."

[Now the Jews did not believe that he had been blind and gained his sight until they summoned the parents of the one who had gained his sight. They asked them, "Is this your son, who you say was born blind? How does he now see?" His parents answered and said, "We know that this is our son and that he was born blind. We do not know how he sees now, nor do we know who opened his eyes. Ask him, he is of age; he can speak for himself." His parents said this because they were afraid of the Jews, for the Jews had already agreed that if anyone acknowledged him as the Christ, he would be expelled from the synagogue. For this reason his parents said, "He is of age; question him."

So a second time they called the man who had been blind and said to him, "Give God the praise! We know that this man is a sinner." He replied, "If he is a sinner, I do not know. One thing I do know is that I was blind and now I see." So they said to him, "What did he do to you? How did he open your eyes?" He answered them, "I told you already and you did not listen. Why do you want to hear it again? Do you want to become his disciples, too?" They ridiculed him and said, "You are that man's disciple; we are disciples of Moses! We know that God spoke to Moses, but we do not know where this one is from." The man answered and said to them, "This is what is so amazing, that you do not know where he is from, yet he opened my eyes. We know that God does not listen to sinners, but if one is devout and does his will, he listens to him. It is unheard of that anyone ever opened the eyes of a person born blind. If this man were not from God, he would not be able to do anything."] They answered and said to him, "You were born totally in sin, and are you trying to teach us?" Then they threw him out.

When Jesus heard that they had thrown him out, he found him and said, "Do you believe in the Son of Man?" He answered and said, "Who is he, sir, that I may believe in him?" Jesus said to him, "You have seen him, the one speaking with you is he." He said, "I do believe, Lord," and he worshiped him. [Then Jesus said, "I came into this world for judgment, so that those who do not see might see, and those who do see might become blind."

Some of the Pharisees who were with him heard this and said to him, "Surely we are not also blind, are we?" Jesus said to them, "If you were blind, you would have no sin; but now you are saying, 'We see,' so your sin remains."]

Understanding the Word

In the Bible, God typically chooses leaders who, while always flawed and sometimes sinful, nevertheless are fundamentally obedient and loyal to God. An exception to this rule was the first king chosen to lead Israel, Saul, who proved to be unwilling to listen to God's spokesman, the prophet Samuel. Now God chooses another king, the youngest son of Jesse, who will turn out to be a man after God's own heart (Acts 13:22). God looks past David's youth and sees a child who, with divine help, will be capable of following God "wholeheartedly." And so immediately the newly chosen king receives God's Spirit, equipping him to rule God's people.

The New Testament letters make it clear that receiving new life in Christ entails personal transformation right now, not just forgiveness of past sins and future beatitude. To be reborn in Christ is to be rescued from the darkness of the world and to live in the light of the Lord. This light allows Christians to assess reality from the divine perspective, exposing "the fruitless works of darkness." It also allows for transformation, producing in the individual "every kind of goodness and righteousness and truth." It is in this sense that Christians have already woken up from the death of darkness and now walk in the life of Christ's light.

At the end of today's Gospel, Jesus says he came so that those who do not see might see, and those who do see might become blind. The blind man received healing because he knew he could not see (i.e., was a sinner), and knowing it left him open to spiritual healing. The physically sighted leaders, who do see, paradoxically do not see their sinfulness. Their "sight" is illusory; they are just as "spiritually blind" as the blind man, but they don't know it. Jesus forces a choice on them: will they recognize that they do not see, or will their hardheartedness lead them to reject the light of the world (John 1:9) and thus become truly blind.

Reflecting on the Word

In some places in the U.S., flowers are blooming and the sun is shining: spring has come. Here at my house in the Midwest, it is still late winter. This particular week in March is when I plant my tomatoes and my peppers in my seed room. I suspend bright lights two inches above the flats to keep them warm. Where light glows, the plants spring upward when they germinate. Did you know that seeds with no light will grow in any direction—sidewise, upwards, or upside down?

Similarly, people in nursing homes or hospitals, having only artificial lightbulbs, can lose track of the natural rhythms of night and day. Third-shift workers may experience that same disorientation. The body does not know when it is dark and when it is light.

I recall a disoriented time in my life at seventeen. The world felt directionless. Was there was a purpose to anything that I did? I remember thinking, as we sped down the interstate, "If I opened the door and fell out of this car and died, nobody would really care." I had a vague sense of God's care, but that love was like a weak light bulb far away.

The letter to the Ephesians calls us from darkness to light: "Live like those who are at home in the daylight." Jesus touches the blind man's eyes and he sees. The "Light of the world" changes things. He did for me. I hope that he has done so for you.

Yet some may prefer the darkness, Jesus says. Nobody enjoys being directionless, so other directions are marketed to "save us," to lift us from darkness to light —from football to coffee, yoga, and massage therapy. But can any "thing" truly replace Jesus as Savior, the true Light of the world?

Consider/Discuss

❖ Depression and despair are growing in our culture. Suicides and drug use rates have lowered life expectancy. How do we help those we love to transform from a perception of God as "a weak light bulb far away" to the radiant Love who is near? What can we personally do to be Jesus' light to a world that feels hopeless and directionless?

❖ When have you ever felt like the man born blind? When have you experienced Jesus as the light who brings you out of that darkness? Personal stories are most effective in bringing about transformation. Could you share that story with someone who is feeling as though he or she lives in the shadows?

Living and Praying the Word

Jesus, Light of the world, thank you for leading us through dark valleys and out of despair. Like young David, anoint us to follow you wholeheartedly wherever you direct. We want to sprout. We want to grow. We want to bear fruit that will nourish others. Help us to grow always toward your light.

FIFTH SUNDAY OF LENT

Today's Focus: Sweet Mystery of Life—and Death

Facing death—of those we love or our own—is a profoundly human moment in every life, a moment into which we know Jesus will step.

FIRST READING   *Ezekiel 37:12–14*

Thus says the LORD GOD: O my people, I will open your graves and have you rise from them, and bring you back to the land of Israel. Then you shall know that I am the LORD, when I open your graves and have you rise from them, O my people! I will put my spirit in you that you may live, and I will settle you upon your land; thus you shall know that I am the LORD. I have promised, and I will do it, says the LORD.

PSALM RESPONSE   *Psalm 130:7*

With the Lord there is mercy and fullness of redemption.

SECOND READING   *Romans 8:8–11*

Brothers and sisters: Those who are in the flesh cannot please God. But you are not in the flesh; on the contrary, you are in the spirit, if only the Spirit of God dwells in you. Whoever does not have the Spirit of Christ does not belong to him. But if Christ is in you, although the body is dead because of sin, the spirit is alive because of righteousness. If the Spirit of the one who raised Jesus from the dead dwells in you, the one who raised Christ from the dead will give life to your mortal bodies also, through his Spirit dwelling in you.

GOSPEL   *John 11:1–45 or 11:3–7, 17, 20–27, 33b–45*

In the shorter form of the reading, the passages in brackets are omitted.

[Now a man was ill, Lazarus from Bethany, the village of Mary and her sister Martha. Mary was the one who had anointed the Lord with perfumed oil and dried his feet with her hair; it was her brother Lazarus who was ill.] So the sisters sent word to Jesus saying, "Master, the one you love is ill." When Jesus heard this he said, "This illness is not to end in death, but is for the glory of God, that the Son of God may be glorified through it." Now Jesus loved Martha and her sister and Lazarus. So when he heard that he was ill, he remained for two days in the place where he was. Then after this he said to his disciples, "Let us go back to Judea." [The disciples said to him, "Rabbi, the Jews were just trying to stone you, and you want to go back there?" Jesus answered, "Are there not twelve hours in a day? If one walks during the day, he does not stumble, because he sees the light of this world. But if one walks at night, he stumbles, because the light is not in him."

He said this, and then told them, "Our friend Lazarus is asleep, but I am going to awaken him." So the disciples said to him, "Master, if he is asleep, he will be saved." But Jesus was talking about his death, while they thought that he meant ordinary sleep. So then Jesus said to them clearly, "Lazarus has died. And I am glad for you that I was not there, that you may believe. Let us go to him." So Thomas, called Didymus, said to his fellow disciples, "Let us also go to die with him."]

When Jesus arrived, he found that Lazarus had already been in the tomb for four days. [Now Bethany was near Jerusalem, only about two miles away. And many of the Jews had come to Martha and Mary to comfort them about their brother.] When Martha heard that Jesus was coming, she went to meet him; but Mary sat at home. Martha said to Jesus, "Lord, if you had been here, my brother would not have died. But even now I know that whatever you ask of God, God will give you." Jesus said to her, "Your brother will rise." Martha said to him, "I know he will rise, in the resurrection on the last day." Jesus told her, "I am the resurrection and the life; whoever believes in me, even if he dies, will live, and everyone who lives and believes in me will never die. Do you believe this?" She said to him, "Yes, Lord. I have come to believe that you are the Christ, the Son of God, the one who is coming into the world."

[When she had said this, she went and called her sister Mary secretly, saying, "The teacher is here and is asking for you." As soon as she heard this, she rose quickly and went to him. For Jesus had not yet come into the village, but was still where Martha had met him. So when the Jews who were with her in the house comforting her saw Mary get up quickly and go out, they followed her, presuming that she was going to the tomb to weep there. When Mary came to where Jesus was and saw him, she fell at his feet and said to him, "Lord, if you had been here, my brother would not have died." When Jesus saw her weeping and the Jews who had come with her weeping,] he became perturbed and deeply troubled, and said, "Where have you laid him?" They said to him, "Sir, come and see." And Jesus wept. So the Jews said, "See how he loved him." But some of them said, "Could not the one who opened the eyes of the blind man have done something so that this man would not have died?"

So Jesus, perturbed again, came to the tomb. It was a cave, and a stone lay across it. Jesus said, "Take away the stone." Martha, the dead man's sister, said to him, "Lord, by now there will be a stench; he has been dead for four days." Jesus said to her, "Did I not tell you that if you believe you will see the glory of God?" So they took away the stone. And Jesus raised his eyes and said, "Father, I thank you for hearing me. I know that you always hear me; but because of the crowd here I have said this, that they may believe that you sent me." And when he had said this, he cried out in a loud voice, "Lazarus, come out!" The dead man came out, tied hand and foot with burial bands, and his face was wrapped in a cloth. So Jesus said to them, "Untie him and let him go."

Now many of the Jews who had come to Mary and seen what he had done began to believe in him.

Understanding the Word

In Ezekiel's time, Israel was in exile, estranged from God. Thus in his vision of the "dry bones" (37:1–14), he sees Israel as truly dead. This "death" easily led to despair of eventual reconciliation with God and a return to life. In response to doubts of God's continued love of them, Israel receives divine assurance that although they are dead now, the time of alienation will come to an end. Israel will be restored to God and to the land. This spiritual rebirth is characterized as resurrection from the grave. God confirms that Israel remains "my people," and will certainly bring them back to life: "I have promised, and I will do it."

For Saint Paul, physical and spiritual death are inherently related. Bodily death is ultimately the result of sin—the body is dead because of sin. In Christ, the Spirit of God brings life first by attending to the condition of sin, conquering it and "replacing" it with righteousness, spiritual life. This same Spirit is also able to raise the physical body from the dead, as the Spirit did for Jesus. The Spirit of Christ, belonging to those who have turned away from "the flesh" (a metaphor for all that is in us opposed to the will of God), resurrects us from both spiritual and physical death.

When Jesus hears that his friend Lazarus is ill, he first says that the illness will not end in death. One gets the impression from this that he is not worried that Lazarus will actually die, which would explain his delay of two days before returning to Bethany. Yet Jesus knows in fact that Lazarus has died in that time, and we realize that he has allowed this to happen so that he can "awaken him." In this final and most dramatic sign, Jesus allows the death of Lazarus so that he can publicly raise him from the dead. Such a feat is intended to provoke belief that he is who he has been claiming to be all along, the One sent by God, who alone has the power to give life.

Reflecting on the Word

Martha cried out, "Lord if you had been here, my brother would not have died!" What had she been thinking and discussing with Mary during the days of her brother's illness and now after his death? Surrounded by friends, she did not find the one friend that she was looking for—he who had the ability to help. She may have whispered, "Jesus, where are you? Where are you right now when Mary and Lazarus and I so need you?"

Have you ever been in a situation in which someone who could have chosen to help you would not? Someone who is in a position of authority—who you thought had your back and did not? The betrayal cuts deeply, causing anguish, high blood pressure, anger, grief, hurt, and sleepless nights—in short, a crisis of trust in the one who could have helped, but did not. Where was he/she when I needed him/her?

We don't always know why things work out as they do. Human beings let us down. Sometimes it feels as though God lets us down—our prayers are not answered as we expect. These are our personal crucifixion moments. We may later see clearly why things happened and God is glorified: these are resurrection moments. Sometimes we never know why and life and death remain a mystery.

In today's story, the Lord did finally show up. Then he quaked with grief. Jesus wept. For the sake of his friends, he called Lazarus out of the tomb. It was personally perilous for him to do so. But out of love, he revealed his power. At the same time, he was about to take the pains of the world upon himself. When he saw his friends' grief, did that reveal how much they would suffer from *his* upcoming death? No wonder he trembled.

Consider/Discuss

❖ Every person has foretastes of death and resurrection in this life. In difficult moments, how have you (or have you not) identified with Martha's whisper, "Where are you, Lord?"

❖ In bleak moments, we may be tempted to give ourselves (and others) glib answers that do not satisfy or are suspect or hollow, shallow answers like "God wanted another angel in heaven" or "Well, it was God's will" or . . . How does that artificial certainty belittle the mystery dimension of God and life? How else could we respond more truly to the puzzlement of betrayal and/or grief?

Living and Praying with the Word

Lord, I hope you don't mind the honesty, but sometimes it feels as though you aren't showing up. We need you. We believe that you are the resurrection and the life; help our unbelief. Give us the strength to cling tightly to your steadfast love when life bears down hard. Most of all, thank you for taking our pains upon yourself. Ezekiel's dry bones give us hope in this parched valley. We look forward to the day when you bring us to a new and fresh life, good and gracious God.

PALM SUNDAY OF THE PASSION OF THE LORD

Today's Focus: Hearing the Story Again—for the First Time

The Passion reveals the depths to which the Lord will go to show us his love. It is our calling to listen and hear this love story again, in a new and fresh way.

FIRST READING   *Isaiah 50:4–7*

The Lord GOD has given me
  a well-trained tongue,
that I might know how to speak to the weary
  a word that will rouse them.
Morning after morning
  he opens my ear that I may hear;
and I have not rebelled,
  have not turned back.
I gave my back to those who beat me,
  my cheeks to those who plucked my beard;
my face I did not shield
  from buffets and spitting.

The Lord GOD is my help,
  therefore I am not disgraced;
I have set my face like flint,
  knowing that I shall not be put to shame.

PSALM RESPONSE   *Psalm 22:2a*

My God, my God, why have you abandoned me?

SECOND READING   *Philippians 2:6–11*

Christ Jesus, though he was in the form of God,
    did not regard equality with God
    something to be grasped.
Rather, he emptied himself,
    taking the form of a slave,
    coming in human likeness;
    and found human in appearance,
    he humbled himself,
    becoming obedient to the point of death,
    even death on a cross.

Because of this, God greatly exalted him
> and bestowed on him the name
> which is above every name,
> that at the name of Jesus
> every knee should bend,
> of those in heaven and on earth and under the earth,
> and every tongue confess that
> Jesus Christ is Lord,
> to the glory of God the Father.

GOSPEL   *Matthew 26:14 — 27:66 or 27:11-54*

In the shorter form of the Passion, the passages in brackets are omitted.

[One of the Twelve, who was called Judas Iscariot, went to the chief priests and said, "What are you willing to give me if I hand him over to you?" They paid him thirty pieces of silver, and from that time on he looked for an opportunity to hand him over.

On the first day of the Feast of Unleavened Bread, the disciples approached Jesus and said, "Where do you want us to prepare for you to eat the Passover?" He said, "Go into the city to a certain man and tell him, 'The teacher says, "My appointed time draws near; in your house I shall celebrate the Passover with my disciples." ' " The disciples then did as Jesus had ordered, and prepared the Passover.

When it was evening, he reclined at table with the Twelve. And while they were eating, he said, "Amen, I say to you, one of you will betray me." Deeply distressed at this, they began to say to him one after another, "Surely it is not I, Lord?" He said in reply, "He who has dipped his hand into the dish with me is the one who will betray me. The Son of Man indeed goes, as it is written of him, but woe to that man by whom the Son of Man is betrayed. It would be better for that man if he had never been born." Then Judas, his betrayer, said in reply, "Surely it is not I, Rabbi?" He answered, "You have said so."

While they were eating, Jesus took bread, said the blessing, broke it, and giving it to his disciples said, "Take and eat; this is my body." Then he took a cup, gave thanks, and gave it to them, saying, "Drink from it, all of you, for this is my blood of the covenant, which will be shed on behalf of many for the forgiveness of sins. I tell you, from now on I shall not drink this fruit of the vine until the day when I drink it with you new in the kingdom of my Father." Then, after singing a hymn, they went out to the Mount of Olives.

Then Jesus said to them, "This night all of you will have your faith in me shaken, for it is written:
I will strike the shepherd,
> *and the sheep of the flock will be dispersed;*

but after I have been raised up, I shall go before you to Galilee." Peter said to him in reply, "Though all may have their faith in you shaken, mine will never be." Jesus said to him, "Amen, I say to you, this very night before the cock crows, you will deny me three times." Peter said to him, "Even though I should have to die with you, I will not deny you." And all the disciples spoke likewise.

Then Jesus came with them to a place called Gethsemane, and he said to his disciples, "Sit here while I go over there and pray." He took along Peter and the two sons of Zebedee, and began to feel sorrow and distress. Then he said to them, "My soul is sorrowful even to death. Remain here and keep watch with me." He advanced a little and fell prostrate in prayer, saying, "My Father, if it is possible, let this cup pass from me; yet, not as I will, but as you will." When he returned to his disciples he found them asleep. He said to Peter, "So you could not keep watch with me for one hour? Watch and pray that you may not undergo the test. The spirit is willing, but the flesh is weak." Withdrawing a second time, he prayed again, "My Father, if it is not possible that this cup pass without my drinking it, your will be done!" Then he returned once more and found them asleep, for they could not keep their eyes open. He left them and withdrew again and prayed a third time, saying the same thing again. Then he returned to his disciples and said to them, "Are you still sleeping and taking your rest? Behold, the hour is at hand when the Son of Man is to be handed over to sinners. Get up, let us go. Look, my betrayer is at hand."

While he was still speaking, Judas, one of the Twelve, arrived, accompanied by a large crowd, with swords and clubs, who had come from the chief priests and the elders of the people. His betrayer had arranged a sign with them, saying, "The man I shall kiss is the one; arrest him." Immediately he went over to Jesus and said, "Hail, Rabbi!" and he kissed him. Jesus answered him, "Friend, do what you have come for." Then stepping forward they laid hands on Jesus and arrested him. And behold, one of those who accompanied Jesus put his hand to his sword, drew it, and struck the high priest's servant, cutting off his ear. Then Jesus said to him, "Put your sword back into its sheath, for all who take the sword will perish by the sword. Do you think that I cannot call upon my Father and he will not provide me at this moment with more than twelve legions of angels? But then how would the Scriptures be fulfilled which say that it must come to pass in this way?" At that hour Jesus said to the crowds, "Have you come out as against a robber, with swords and clubs to seize me? Day after day I sat teaching in the temple area, yet you did not arrest me. But all this has come to pass that the writings of the prophets may be fulfilled." Then all the disciples left him and fled.

Those who had arrested Jesus led him away to Caiaphas the high priest, where the scribes and the elders were assembled. Peter was following him at a distance as far as the high priest's courtyard, and going inside he sat down with the servants to see the outcome. The chief priests and the entire Sanhedrin kept trying to obtain false testimony against Jesus in order to put him to death, but they found none, though many false witnesses came forward. Finally two came forward who stated, "This man said, 'I can destroy the temple of God and within three days rebuild it.' " The high priest rose and addressed him, "Have you no answer? What are these men testifying against you?" But Jesus was silent. Then the high priest said to him,

The high priest rose and addressed him, "Have you no answer? What are these men testifying against you?" But Jesus was silent. Then the high priest said to him, "I order you to tell us under oath before the living God whether you are the Christ, the Son of God." Jesus said to him in reply, "You have said so. But I tell you:

From now on you will see 'the Son of Man
seated at the right hand of the Power'
and 'coming on the clouds of heaven.' "

Then the high priest tore his robes and said, "He has blasphemed! What further need have we of witnesses? You have now heard the blasphemy; what is your opinion?" They said in reply, "He deserves to die!" Then they spat in his face and struck him, while some slapped him, saying, "Prophesy for us, Christ: who is it that struck you?"

Now Peter was sitting outside in the courtyard. One of the maids came over to him and said, "You too were with Jesus the Galilean." But he denied it in front of everyone, saying, "I do not know what you are talking about!" As he went out to the gate, another girl saw him and said to those who were there, "This man was with Jesus the Nazarene." Again he denied it with an oath, "I do not know the man!" A little later the bystanders came over and said to Peter, "Surely you too are one of them; even your speech gives you away." At that he began to curse and to swear, "I do not know the man." And immediately a cock crowed. Then Peter remembered the word that Jesus had spoken: "Before the cock crows you will deny me three times." He went out and began to weep bitterly.

When it was morning, all the chief priests and the elders of the people took counsel against Jesus to put him to death. They bound him, led him away, and handed him over to Pilate, the governor.

Then Judas, his betrayer, seeing that Jesus had been condemned, deeply regretted what he had done. He returned the thirty pieces of silver to the chief priests and elders, saying, "I have sinned in betraying innocent blood." They said, "What is that to us? Look to it yourself." Flinging the money into the temple, he departed and went off and hanged himself. The chief priests gathered up the money, but said, "It is not lawful to deposit this in the temple treasury, for it is the price of blood." After consultation, they used it to buy the potter's field as a burial place for foreigners. That is why that field even today is called the Field of Blood. Then was fulfilled what had been said through Jeremiah the prophet,

And they took the thirty pieces of silver,
the value of a man with a price on his head,
a price set by some of the Israelites,
and they paid it out for the potter's field
just as the Lord had commanded me.

Now] Jesus stood before the governor, who questioned him, "Are you the king of the Jews?" Jesus said, "You say so." And when he was accused by the chief priests and elders, he made no answer. Then Pilate said to him, "Do you not hear how many things they are testifying against you?" But he did not answer him one word, so that the governor was greatly amazed.

Now on the occasion of the feast the governor was accustomed to release to the crowd one prisoner whom they wished. And at that time they had a notorious prisoner called Barabbas. So when they had assembled, Pilate said to them, "Which one do you want me to release to you, Barabbas, or Jesus called Christ?" For he knew that it was out of envy that they had handed him over. While he was still seated on the bench, his wife sent him a message, "Have nothing to do with that righteous man. I suffered much in a dream today because of him." The chief priests and the elders persuaded the crowds to ask for Barabbas but to destroy Jesus. The governor said to them in reply, "Which of the two do you want me to release to you?" They answered, "Barabbas!" Pilate said to them, "Then what shall I do with Jesus called Christ?" They all said, "Let him be crucified!" But he said, "Why? What evil has he done?" They only shouted the louder, "Let him be crucified!" When Pilate saw that he was not succeeding at all, but that a riot was breaking out instead, he took water and washed his hands in the sight of the crowd, saying, "I am innocent of this man's blood. Look to it yourselves." And the whole people said in reply, "His blood be upon us and upon our children." Then he released Barabbas to them, but after he had Jesus scourged, he handed him over to be crucified.

Then the soldiers of the governor took Jesus inside the praetorium and gathered the whole cohort around him. They stripped off his clothes and threw a scarlet military cloak about him. Weaving a crown out of thorns, they placed it on his head, and a reed in his right hand. And kneeling before him, they mocked him, saying, "Hail, King of the Jews!" They spat upon him and took the reed and kept striking him on the head. And when they had mocked him, they stripped him of the cloak, dressed him in his own clothes, and led him off to crucify him.

As they were going out, they met a Cyrenian named Simon; this man they pressed into service to carry his cross.

And when they came to a place called Golgotha—which means Place of the Skull—, they gave Jesus wine to drink mixed with gall. But when he had tasted it, he refused to drink. After they had crucified him, they divided his garments by casting lots; then they sat down and kept watch over him there. And they placed over his head the written charge against him: This is Jesus, the King of the Jews. Two revolutionaries were crucified with him, one on his right and the other on his left. Those passing by reviled him, shaking their heads and saying, "You who would destroy the temple and rebuild it in three days, save yourself, if you are the Son of God, and come down from the cross!" Likewise the chief priests with the scribes and elders mocked him and said, "He saved others; he cannot save himself. So he is the king of Israel! Let him come down from the cross now, and we will believe in him. He trusted in God; let him deliver him now if he wants him. For he said, 'I am the Son of God.' " The revolutionaries who were crucified with him also kept abusing him in the same way.

From noon onward, darkness came over the whole land until three in the afternoon. And about three o'clock Jesus cried out in a loud voice, *"Eli, Eli, lema sabachthani?"* which means, "My God, my God, why have you forsaken me?" Some of the bystanders who heard it said, "This one is calling for Elijah." Immediately one of them ran to get a sponge; he soaked it in wine, and putting it on a reed, gave it to him to drink. But the rest said, "Wait, let us see if Elijah comes to save him." But Jesus cried out again in a loud voice, and gave up his spirit.

And behold, the veil of the sanctuary was torn in two from top to bottom. The earth quaked, rocks were split, tombs were opened, and the bodies of many saints who had fallen asleep were raised. And coming forth from their tombs after his resurrection, they entered the holy city and appeared to many. The centurion and the men with him who were keeping watch over Jesus feared greatly when they saw the earthquake and all that was happening, and they said, "Truly, this was the Son of God!" [There were many women there, looking on from a distance, who had followed Jesus from Galilee, ministering to him. Among them were Mary Magdalene and Mary the mother of James and Joseph, and the mother of the sons of Zebedee.

When it was evening, there came a rich man from Arimathea named Joseph, who was himself a disciple of Jesus. He went to Pilate and asked for the body of Jesus; then Pilate ordered it to be handed over. Taking the body, Joseph wrapped it in clean linen and laid it in his new tomb that he had hewn in the rock. Then he rolled a huge stone across the entrance to the tomb and departed. But Mary Magdalene and the other Mary remained sitting there, facing the tomb. The next day, the one following the day of preparation, the chief priests and the Pharisees gathered before Pilate and said, "Sir, we remember that this impostor while still alive said, 'After three days I will be raised up.' Give orders, then, that the grave be secured until the third day, lest his disciples come and steal him and say to the people, 'He has been raised from the dead.' This last imposture would be worse than the first." Pilate said to them, "The guard is yours; go, secure it as best you can." So they went and secured the tomb by fixing a seal to the stone and setting the guard.]

Understanding the Word

The servant in Isaiah is God's emissary, equipped with eloquence to console and encourage the weary. This true and obedient ambassador listens carefully to God before speaking. Yet almost inevitably a message of comfort for some rouses suspicion and hostility in others, whom it implicitly critiques; there is a reason some of God's people are weary and despondent. In the face of such hostility, the temptation is to abandon the mission, yet this servant is faithful, not rebelling or turning back, but daily returning to receive from God a new message. Not only a message, but also strength to endure animosity and humiliation for the sake of the consolation he brings to the weary.

The hymn from Philippians focuses on the profound humility of Christ, who "empties himself" to accept the role of a "slave." This slavery or servitude is twofold. One the one hand, Jesus serves God, doing God's will obediently even to the point of death. On the other hand, the reason for the death is to save humanity, and so Jesus also serves his brothers and sisters, again, to the point of death. This self-emptying, this *kenosis*, reflects the supremely ego-free goodness of God. It is this "form" of God that Jesus embodies, and which Paul would have the Philippians emulate, setting aside their own agendas and prerogatives to serve Christ and one another.

Matthew's Passion narrative shows what the Son of God pays to save God's people. Humility, service, strength, and especially trust in God—all are on display throughout. This trust appears even where it seems particularly absent, in the cry from the cross: "My God, why have you abandoned me?" The words are from Psalm 22, a lament that cries to God from the midst of mockery and physical danger. Like most biblical laments, though, the psalm ends with an affirmation of trust in God's deliverance: "I will live for the LORD" (22:31). The Passion narrative thus ends with Christ proclaiming not despair but hope that the God who has delivered in the past will now prove faithful again.

Reflecting on the Word

One thing that I love about working with the Rite of Christian Initiation of Adults (RCIA) is how new the Gospel is for those who have never heard it before. A few years ago on Palm Sunday, we headed downstairs from the sanctuary to break open the Word. We were not even to the basement door, when Roy, a man in his fifties, touched my arm and said, with tears in his eyes, "I never heard that story before!" The day before I wrote this, because it was a snow day from RCIA, one of our catechumens and her eleven-year-old son read Luke's account of the death and resurrection by candlelight at home for their homework. The mom texted me afterward. "What an amazing story!" she said.

For a heart of innocence, what could be so breathtaking about the death of Jesus? When I read it afresh, what flabbergasts me is what also impressed St. Paul—the degree of self-emptying, self-giving, self-sacrifice that Jesus was willing to undergo in obedience and for our sakes. Where did he get the strength to do that? "I gave my back to those who beat me, my cheeks to those who plucked my beard." Isaiah says, "The Lord GOD is my help . . . He who declares my innocence is near." Our God is Deliverer. God lifts us up. God is faithful. God is for us.

For someone who has never heard this story, to have the Lord of the universe care, to take our side, to be willing to die to lift us up from the muck of life—that is not something to be taken lightly. For those who are used to feeling adrift and alone, this is fresh and life-giving! After being baptized at the Easter Vigil, Roy broke into a smile and his whole body radiated happiness. New life! Not just a theological idea, but a gift from the One who cares.

Consider/Discuss

❖ How often might we listen to scriptures and think, "Yeah, yeah, I've heard that time and time again"? How could we get back to a heart of innocence about the story of Jesus? In this time before Easter, read through one whole Gospel narrative about the Passion and Resurrection. Try to read it as though you had never heard it before. What resonates within you?

❖ Many of us already live self-sacrificing and self-emptying lives, and those around us are grateful. Where do we get the strength to see each day through? When we are weary, even beaten, Who and what sustains us? If you know someone who lives a self-sacrificing and self-emptying life, thank him/her this week.

Living and Praying with the Word

Lord, as we enter into this most sacred of weeks, give us new eyes to see the beauty of what you have done for us. Bless those who minister—the preachers and lectors, the musicians and artists, and all who serve liturgically. Help us to create liturgies that move and inspire our people and show forth your presence. Please bring back those who are far from faith and enlighten those who do not yet know you. Thank you, most of all, for giving yourself to us so completely.

Notes

EASTER

The first readings of Easter present vignettes from the Acts of the Apostles that show the early church carrying out its evangelical mission. The community struggles to organize itself and figure out how to overcome social divisions that have followed the new believers into the church (Acts 2:42–47; 6:1–7). More difficulties are met in the world, which must be persuaded that a crucified Jew was not only the Messiah of Israel, but the savior of the entire world, sent by the One God (Acts 10:34a, 37–43; 2:14, 22–33; 2:14a, 36–41). Yet the gospel spreads, spurred on by the very persecution that seeks to stifle it (Acts 8:5–8, 14–17). Throughout this season we see a small group of determined apostles and disciples bring an incredible story to the whole world, and—a sure sign of its truth—the acceptance of that story by Jews and Gentiles alike.

The second reading most of the season is from the First Letter of Peter, written to Christians experiencing persecution. In the face of social and civil hostility, they are tempted to waver. Peter assures them that they have the power—in Christ—to resist the temptation and to remain strong, if only they will have faith and hope in Christ, from whom they have received an imperishable inheritance the world cannot take away (1:3–9; 1:17–21). Indeed, "the world" and "worldly desires" continue to have a hold on these Christians still young in the faith (2:20b–25). Peter reminds them that their home is not in this world, yet they must remain in the world because God is building them into a temple, where as a holy nation they offer spiritual sacrifices to God (2:4–9; 2:20b–25). They are not of the world, then, but they have a role in God's plan for the world.

In the first weeks of Easter, the Gospels focus on belief in Jesus as the resurrected Messiah. When they hide from the world in fear, Jesus appears to his disciples and sends them back out with their message. The challenge of proclaiming the resurrection of Jesus is presented vividly in the story of Thomas, who must "see to believe." Others who do not see will be challenged to believe (John 20:19–31). The story of the road to Emmaus highlights the difficulty of persuading others that a crucified Jew was the Messiah. Only those who take the risk of meeting Christ in "the breaking of the bread" will be able to recognize him and believe (Luke 24:13–35). As Easter proceeds, we hear Jesus in the Gospel of John teaching his disciples that he alone is the way to the Father, the Sheepgate (John 10:1–10), the One who has seen and knows the Father and reveals the Father to those with eyes of faith (John 14:1–12). As we move toward Pentecost, Jesus prepares his disciples for the gift of the Spirit, who will bestow on them the eternal life promised to them in Christ (John 14:15–21).

APRIL 12, 2020

EASTER SUNDAY OF THE RESURRECTION OF THE LORD

Today's Focus: Christ is Risen! Let's Dance!

Our joy at the Resurrection must move our hearts, our voices, and our bodies, until our inner bliss is fully expressed in singing and dancing!

FIRST READING   *Acts 10:34a, 37–43*

Peter proceeded to speak and said: "You know what has happened all over Judea, beginning in Galilee after the baptism that John preached, how God anointed Jesus of Nazareth with the Holy Spirit and power. He went about doing good and healing all those oppressed by the devil, for God was with him. We are witnesses of all that he did both in the country of the Jews and in Jerusalem. They put him to death by hanging him on a tree. This man God raised on the third day and granted that he be visible, not to all the people, but to us, the witnesses chosen by God in advance, who ate and drank with him after he rose from the dead. He commissioned us to preach to the people and testify that he is the one appointed by God as judge of the living and the dead. To him all the prophets bear witness, that everyone who believes in him will receive forgiveness of sins through his name.

PSALM RESPONSE   *Psalm 118:24*

This is the day the Lord has made; let us rejoice and be glad.

SECOND READING   *Colossians 3:1–4*

Brothers and sisters: If then you were raised with Christ, seek what is above, where Christ is seated at the right hand of God. Think of what is above, not of what is on earth. For you have died, and your life is hidden with Christ in God. When Christ your life appears, then you too will appear with him in glory.

– or –

1 Corinthians 5:6b–8

Brothers and sisters: Do you not know that a little yeast leavens all the dough? Clear out the old yeast, so that you may become a fresh batch of dough, inasmuch as you are unleavened. For our paschal lamb, Christ, has been sacrificed.

Therefore, let us celebrate the feast, not with the old yeast, the yeast of malice and wickedness, but with the unleavened bread of sincerity and truth.

GOSPEL *John 20:1–9*

On the first day of the week, Mary of Magdala came to the tomb early in the morning, while it was still dark, and saw the stone removed from the tomb. So she ran and went to Simon Peter and to the other disciple whom Jesus loved, and told them, "They have taken the Lord from the tomb, and we don't know where they put him." So Peter and the other disciple went out and came to the tomb. They both ran, but the other disciple ran faster than Peter and arrived at the tomb first; he bent down and saw the burial cloths there, but did not go in. When Simon Peter arrived after him, he went into the tomb and saw the burial cloths there, and the cloth that had covered his head, not with the burial cloths but rolled up in a separate place. Then the other disciple also went in, the one who had arrived at the tomb first, and he saw and believed. For they did not yet understand the Scripture that he had to rise from the dead.

Understanding the Word

Peter's speech occurs within the story of Cornelius (Acts 10). Summoned by the Roman, Peter gives all those gathered in his house the gospel "in a nutshell": Jesus was anointed by God to preach and to heal, especially those "oppressed by the devil" (including those bound by the power of sin). Despite his good deeds, Jesus was crucified, but then was raised from the dead. Now he has sent others to carry on his mission of preaching and forgiving sin, freeing those in bondage to its power. As if to give divine confirmation to the mission to the Gentiles, the Holy Spirit comes upon Peter's audience, who are baptized, the first Gentile converts to the Way.

Colossians reminds us that the resurrection of Christ, while a unique event, is not isolated, but in fact has brought about a new order in the cosmos, in which the baptized are called to participate in Christ. Like Christ, they have died to earthly things, those aspects of the world that are opposed to Christ. Now "raised," believers actually live "above" with Christ, and must act accordingly. When

Christ appears again, this new life, now "hidden" (accessible only by faith), will be revealed in all its glory. In the meantime, though hidden it offers the baptized a new perspective and new way of living that must be manifest in earthly conduct.

When Mary Magdalene sees the empty tomb, she thinks at first that perhaps Jesus' body has been stolen. The Evangelist spends some time, however, describing the empty linens, something thieves would not take the time to leave behind. We remember that when Lazarus (who would die again) was raised, he came forward in his linens. Jesus, who will not die again, has left the linens, like death itself, behind. When the Beloved Disciple sees the empty tomb and the linens, he "believes" that Jesus has been raised from the dead and not stolen, but he does not yet fully comprehend the meaning of the Resurrection. Understanding only comes when one encounters the resurrected Lord.

Reflecting on the Word

In her grief and uncertainty, Mary of Magdala is heavy of heart and slow of foot: she "comes" to the tomb, looking. She does not understand. Jesus is dead. Gone. Dead. Truly dead.

On this early Easter morning, what are you and I looking for? Like Mary, we too can be heavy of heart and slow of foot. A twelve-year-old girl asked me recently, "If Jesus is really God, why doesn't he just fix all the bad things?" In the pre-dawn uncertainties of our day, we too do not understand.

But then the Gospel begins to pick up speed as the sun rises: watch the feet. Mary of Magdala sees the stone rolled away from the tomb; she takes off running. Peter and the other disciple come running. The younger man runs faster. When his sandals come back out of the tomb, they are dancing and boogying, hopping and frolicking—you can see it in his feet—the young man sees and believes! He knows! Peter dashes in, too. He is amazed. Where could Jesus be?

Watch the feet of a toddler. At the wonder of the first crocus, her whole body gets involved—her arms flap, her back sways, and her eyes radiate delight. Even before she is able to talk, she experiences joy; full of life, full of wonder—look at her face, her smile, her feet.

Look at the natural world. A month ago, my yard looked dead—deep snow, bare twigs. Now the raspberry canes are popping with tiny green leaves. The soil is warming. Even the chickadees flit at the bird feeder—just watch their feet!

The beauty of the visible world leads us to the invisible One. Candles, music, lights, movement—even the liturgy itself is like a dance. We sing "Alleluia!" Easter is real. Jesus is alive!

Consider/Discuss

❖ The tomb is empty. The Lord is alive. Lent is over. Death and darkness and despair and uncertainty are not the final answer. What are our feet going to do today? This is the day the Lord has made; let us rejoice and be glad. Are you ready to dance?

❖ On this Easter morning, you and I are also looking for the certainty of faith. The darkness cannot and must not be our final answer. We are looking for the Son. Even though we cannot totally comprehend resurrection, where do you find tastes of new life?

Living and Praying with the Word

Jesus our risen Lord, you have been set free! Open the tombs of our hearts so that we swell with your Easter joy. We thank you for transforming us from the plodding of pre-dawn heaviness to this moment when the sun comes up, when you are risen! Lighten our feet so that we too start to dance and boogie, hop and frolic, with the gift of certainty that you live. Glory to you forever and ever! Alleluia!

SECOND SUNDAY OF EASTER (DIVINE MERCY SUNDAY)

Today's Focus: Show Me!

---

*As Christ showed Thomas the signs of resurrection,
so God continues to show—to reveal—to us the risen Christ among us.
Let us, in turn, reveal the Resurrection by the way we live.*

FIRST READING   *Acts 2:42–47*

They devoted themselves to the teaching of the apostles and to the communal life, to the breaking of bread and to the prayers. Awe came upon everyone, and many wonders and signs were done through the apostles. All who believed were together and had all things in common; they would sell their property and possessions and divide them among all according to each one's need. Every day they devoted themselves to meeting together in the temple area and to breaking bread in their homes. They ate their meals with exultation and sincerity of heart, praising God and enjoying favor with all the people. And every day the Lord added to their number those who were being saved.

PSALM RESPONSE   *Psalm 118:1*

Give thanks to the Lord for he is good, his love is everlasting.

SECOND READING   *1 Peter 1:3–9*

Blessed be the God and Father of our Lord Jesus Christ, who in his great mercy gave us a new birth to a living hope through the resurrection of Jesus Christ from the dead, to an inheritance that is imperishable, undefiled, and unfading, kept in heaven for you who by the power of God are safeguarded through faith, to a salvation that is ready to be revealed in the final time. In this you rejoice, although now for a little while you may have to suffer through various trials, so that the genuineness of your faith, more precious than gold that is perishable even though tested by fire, may prove to be for praise, glory, and honor at the revelation of Jesus Christ. Although you have not seen him you love him; even though you do not see him now yet believe in him, you rejoice with an indescribable and glorious joy, as you attain the goal of your faith, the salvation of your souls.

On the evening of that first day of the week, when the doors were locked, where the disciples were, for fear of the Jews, Jesus came and stood in their midst and said to them, "Peace be with you." When he had said this, he showed them his hands and his side. The disciples rejoiced when they saw the Lord. Jesus said to them again, "Peace be with you. As the Father has sent me, so I send you." And when he had said this, he breathed on them and said to them, "Receive the Holy Spirit. Whose sins you forgive are forgiven them, and whose sins you retain are retained."

Thomas, called Didymus, one of the Twelve, was not with them when Jesus came. So the other disciples said to him, "We have seen the Lord." But he said to them, "Unless I see the mark of the nails in his hands and put my finger into the nailmarks and put my hand into his side, I will not believe."

Now a week later his disciples were again inside and Thomas was with them. Jesus came, although the doors were locked, and stood in their midst and said, "Peace be with you." Then he said to Thomas, "Put your finger here and see my hands, and bring your hand and put it into my side, and do not be unbelieving, but believe." Thomas answered and said to him, "My Lord and my God!" Jesus said to him, "Have you come to believe because you have seen me? Blessed are those who have not seen and have believed."

Now, Jesus did many other signs in the presence of his disciples that are not written in this book. But these are written that you may come to believe that Jesus is the Christ, the Son of God, and that through this belief you may have life in his name.

Understanding the Word

The new life in Christ manifested itself in the lives of the disciples through learning the Christian proclamation, caring for each other, and prayer. The apostles themselves not only teach but heal and, as with Jesus, the crowds are amazed at what God accomplishes through them. Communal life is marked by simplicity and sharing, countering cultural tendencies toward selfishness. The prayer of the disciples involves traditional forms of Jewish liturgy but also specifically Christian prayer of "breaking bread." In all they do followers of Christ present a powerful, positive witness to what it means to live the Way, and this evangelization in word, deed, and prayer draws many others to Christ.

Peter is writing to Christians who are struggling to remain faithful to their baptismal calling, which has alienated them from their society and perhaps their families. Thus his letter begins with encouragement: They have received an inheritance from God that can never be taken away from them against their will. This inheritance is an imperishable treasure that others cannot touch, steal, or destroy because it is not here on earth, but with God. Peter focuses on the necessity to have faith (mentioned three times) that Christ will see their souls through any persecution. Suffering is cause for joy because it strengthens faith. Suffering for Christ brings them closer to their goal, the inheritance waiting for them safely with Christ.

The fearful disciples have hidden from the world. Into their fear comes Christ, who twice proclaims peace and sends them back out into the world. Their mission is not only to forgive (or retain) sins, but to proclaim Jesus as God's Messiah, proof of which claim is his resurrection. While the disciples have the advantage of actually seeing the resurrected Christ, those to whom they are sent will not. Thus the story of Thomas emphasizes the necessity for those who are not able to "see the mark of the nails in his hands" to believe on the strength of the witness of others that Jesus of Nazareth, crucified as a criminal, is in fact "Lord and God."

Reflecting on the Word

We don't know the day-to-day occupation of Thomas the apostle. He asked a lot of questions. His may have been the first-century equivalent of a scientific mind: He's looking for evidence. He wants to be shown. He is not content to take the word of the others. He wants to see. He wants to understand.

The beautiful thing about this story is Jesus' divine mercy. He doesn't condemn Thomas's request. He offers to show him his hands and his side. He respects the intellectual grasping of the "scientist." Yet commentary after commentary deprecates Thomas' questions, even though Jesus did not. "Just believe on the apostles' word," they interpret as today's message. They must not live in the same world that I live in.

You can tell your scientifically-minded sixteen-year-old, "Just believe that God loves you" until you are blue in the face. She is not going to believe it on your word. She wants to see. Yet we have not seen God. With our limited minds, we cannot comprehend the Trinity; both St. Augustine and history's agnostics agree on that. The difference between a Christians and an agnostic, then, is revelation— we believe that by the mercy of God, we have been shown. The Lord has breathed on us and because of that, we have seen his glory.

When I teach my undergraduate prayer class at Notre Dame, I get a mix of believers and non-believers. Early in the course, I offer them what I call The Atheist's Prayer: "God, if you're real, show me." I cannot harangue them into belief. If God is real and they keep praying, they will be shown. I have seen it happen. God comes, not because we pray, but out of a deep desire to be with us. In every generation, age and after age, God shows up.

Consider/Discuss

❖ Faith is a gift that we have been given. We have been shown. We have responded, but it was first a gift given. On this Divine Mercy Sunday, how can we have greater mercy for those who may not believe based on our word? What is one concrete thing that we can do to strengthen or mend a relationship with a family member who is far from faith?

❖ In today's story from the Acts of the Apostles, the early community "showed" the risen Lord by the way that they lived their lives. How can we build a faith community that is so loving that others are attracted? Together, how can we reveal that following Jesus is worth living for?

Living and Praying with the Word

Lord Jesus, thank you for offering to show your hands and your side to the apostle Thomas. As a result of your mercy, he came to faith and declared you "Lord and God." Bless all those we know with scientific minds, especially those who do not now believe in you. Reveal yourself to them and show them that following you is the greatest adventure that they could ever undertake. For you are alive! You are here, now. Alleluia! Alleluia!

THIRD SUNDAY OF EASTER

Today's Focus: Aha!

Though the risen Lord is revealed in the grand Easter "Aha!"
we also can come to know his glorified presence in gentler, merciful moments.

FIRST READING   Acts 2:14, 22–33

Then Peter stood up with the Eleven, raised his voice, and proclaimed: "You who are Jews, indeed all of you staying in Jerusalem. Let this be known to you, and listen to my words. You who are Israelites, hear these words. Jesus the Nazarene was a man commended to you by God with mighty deeds, wonders, and signs, which God worked through him in your midst, as you yourselves know. This man, delivered up by the set plan and foreknowledge of God, you killed, using lawless men to crucify him. But God raised him up, releasing him from the throes of death, because it was impossible for him to be held by it. For David says of him:

I saw the Lord ever before me,
    with him at my right hand I shall not be disturbed.
Therefore my heart has been glad and my tongue has exulted;
    my flesh, too, will dwell in hope,
because you will not abandon my soul to the netherworld,
    nor will you suffer your holy one to see corruption.
You have made known to me the paths of life;
    you will fill me with joy in your presence.

"My brothers, one can confidently say to you about the patriarch David that he died and was buried, and his tomb is in our midst to this day. But since he was a prophet and knew that God had sworn an oath to him that he would set one of his descendants upon his throne, he foresaw and spoke of the resurrection of the Christ, that neither was he abandoned to the netherworld nor did his flesh see corruption. God raised this Jesus; of this we are all witnesses. Exalted at the right hand of God, he received the promise of the Holy Spirit from the Father and poured him forth, as you see and hear."

PSALM RESPONSE   Psalm 16:11a

Lord, you will show us the path of life.

SECOND READING   1 Peter 1:17–21

Beloved: If you invoke as Father him who judges impartially according to each one's works, conduct yourselves with reverence during the time of your sojourning, realizing that you were ransomed from your futile conduct, handed on by your ancestors, not with perishable things like silver or gold but with the precious blood of Christ as of a spotless unblemished lamb.

He was known before the foundation of the world but revealed in the final time for you, who through him believe in God who raised him from the dead and gave him glory, so that your faith and hope are in God.

GOSPEL

Luke 24:13–35

That very day, the first day of the week, two of Jesus' disciples were going to a village seven miles from Jerusalem called Emmaus, and they were conversing about all the things that had occurred. And it happened that while they were conversing and debating, Jesus himself drew near and walked with them, but their eyes were prevented from recognizing him. He asked them, "What are you discussing as you walk along?" They stopped, looking downcast. One of them, named Cleopas, said to him in reply, "Are you the only visitor to Jerusalem who does not know of the things that have taken place there in these days?" And he replied to them, "What sort of things?" They said to him, "The things that happened to Jesus the Nazarene, who was a prophet mighty in deed and word before God and all the people, how our chief priests and rulers both handed him over to a sentence of death and crucified him. But we were hoping that he would be the one to redeem Israel; and besides all this, it is now the third day since this took place. Some women from our group, however, have astounded us: they were at the tomb early in the morning and did not find his body; they came back and reported that they had indeed seen a vision of angels who announced that he was alive. Then some of those with us went to the tomb and found things just as the women had described, but him they did not see." And he said to them, "Oh, how foolish you are! How slow of heart to believe all that the prophets spoke! Was it not necessary that the Christ should suffer these things and enter into his glory?" Then beginning with Moses and all the prophets, he interpreted to them what referred to him in all the Scriptures. As they approached the village to which they were going, he gave the impression that he was going on farther. But they urged him, "Stay with us, for it is nearly evening and the day is almost over." So he went in to stay with them. And it happened that, while he was with them at table, he took bread, said the blessing, broke it, and gave it to them. With that their eyes were opened and they recognized him, but he vanished from their sight. Then they said to each other, "Were not our hearts burning within us while he spoke to us on the way and opened the Scriptures to us?" So they set out at once and returned to Jerusalem where they found gathered together the eleven and those with them who were saying, "The Lord has truly been raised and has appeared to Simon!" Then the two recounted what had taken place on the way and how he was made known to them in the breaking of bread.

Understanding the Word

Peter's speech at the beginning of Acts explains the meaning of the coming of the Spirit, the effects of which his audience has just witnessed. Despite doing good deeds, Jesus was put to death, yet resurrected, a sure sign that he was not under God's judgment but was, on the contrary, God's Messiah. The citation from Psalm 16 demonstrates that this resurrection was part of a divine plan foretold long ago. This same resurrected Christ is the source of the Holy Spirit, whose coming they have witnessed. Jesus himself, his works, his death, his resurrection and exaltation, and the coming of the Spirit are all the fulfillment of God's "set plan."

Peter reminds his audience of persecuted Christians that their permanent home is with God in Christ. They are sojourners who must not put their hope or faith in this world, but in Christ alone. Only in this way can they receive their eternal inheritance, which has been "bought" for them by Christ's blood. Christ came so that those who believe in him might draw closer to God. By believing in the gospel, these new Christians (many of whom, as Gentiles, had not known the God of Israel) have come to believe in the God who brought it about. It is this God, and not the world or its many gods, in whom Christians are called to hope and have faith.

One of the chief obstacles to accepting that Jesus was the Christ was his crucifixion. Jews especially would find such an apparently failed Messiah incredible. As Jesus reveals through his opening of the Scriptures that the Messiah was indeed "supposed" to "suffer these things," his listeners shed their despondency, realize that Jesus could have been the Messiah, and now find his resurrection credible. This lesson comes home to the disciples when they see Jesus "breaking the bread," recalling to them the night he told his apostles that his body and blood were being given up for them. In light of the scriptures and his own words, the death of Jesus is seen not as an "accident" but ordained as a gift.

Reflecting on the Word

Loss. Heaviness. Heartache. Jesus is dead. Two despondent disciples are going home. All their expectations and joys are gone. The mission is over. Their eyes are downcast. There is an ache in the pit of their stomach. Can you feel how disheartened they are? To understand the Resurrection as the first disciples did, we must first get inside their agony. And not just any death: Jesus' death. Have you ever felt that low?

Jesus doesn't pop in and say, "Hey, look, I'm here! There's a happy ending!" They're too dispirited for that. No, Jesus has mercy. He engages them in quiet conversation. Jesus is gentle. Each time he appears in the resurrection stories, he looks different somehow. They had known him before. They do not recognize him now.

They walked a long way together. Jesus gradually brought them out of their funk by recasting the story that they had been telling themselves. He gave them a fresh understanding of who the Redeemer was to be. Their hearts started to burn within them.

Then in the breaking of the bread, suddenly their eyes are opened. Aha! They see! Awakened to joy, they turn and dash back to Jerusalem to tell the apostles! (Remember, if you want to see jubilation, watch the feet.) The resurrection of Jesus is an earthquake-causing "Aha!" Death has no more power. Life is the final answer!

We may sometimes think that we are headed home. But our true homeland does not look like this one. The Word who became flesh transforms our despair into hope, our weariness into refreshment, our wanting to quit into perseverance, and our heartache into splendor. This is the meaning of the Paschal Mystery. This is the core of the Resurrection. This is the heart of the Christian story. This is the "Aha!" of Easter!

Consider/Discuss

❖ The psalmist says, "You will show me the path to life, abounding joy in your presence, the delights at your right hand forever." How have I been shown? When have my eyes been opened and my heart set on fire?

❖ The "Aha!" of understanding enlivens the mind. The "Aha!" of feeling burns in the heart. The "Aha!" of seeing invigorates the imagination. Though it may not compare to the immensity of the Resurrection, have you encountered an "Aha!" moment of clarity like that?

Living and Praying with the Word

Lord, sometimes we just want to go home. Life can weigh us down. The world can be discouraging. Our struggles are nothing compared to the grief from your crucifixion, but you can see that our eyes also can grow downcast. In this moment, walk with us on this road. We could use an "Aha!" moment. Reveal yourself to us! Make our hearts burn within us at your Presence. Let me delight at your right hand forever, risen Lord, for you are the joy of my life.

FOURTH SUNDAY OF EASTER

Today's Focus: From Ruin to Restoration

---

*Our Good Shepherd, weather-worn and ready to die for his flock,
leads us always through dark valleys, to places of life, safety, and light.*

FIRST READING
Acts 2:14a, 36–41

Then Peter stood up with the Eleven, raised his voice, and proclaimed: "Let the whole house of Israel know for certain that God has made both Lord and Christ, this Jesus whom you crucified."

Now when they heard this, they were cut to the heart, and they asked Peter and the other apostles, "What are we to do, my brothers?" Peter said to them, "Repent and be baptized, every one of you, in the name of Jesus Christ for the forgiveness of your sins; and you will receive the gift of the Holy Spirit. For the promise is made to you and to your children and to all those far off, whomever the Lord our God will call." He testified with many other arguments, and was exhorting them, "Save yourselves from this corrupt generation." Those who accepted his message were baptized, and about three thousand persons were added that day.

PSALM RESPONSE
Psalm 23:1

The Lord is my shepherd; there is nothing I shall want.

SECOND READING
1 Peter 2:20b–25

Beloved: If you are patient when you suffer for doing what is good, this is a grace before God. For to this you have been called, because Christ also suffered for you, leaving you an example that you should follow in his footsteps.
He committed no sin, and no deceit was found in his mouth.

When he was insulted, he returned no insult; when he suffered, he did not threaten; instead, he handed himself over to the one who judges justly. He himself bore our sins in his body upon the cross, so that, free from sin, we might live for righteousness. By his wounds you have been healed. For you had gone astray like sheep, but you have now returned to the shepherd and guardian of your souls.

Jesus said: "Amen, amen, I say to you, whoever does not enter a sheepfold through the gate but climbs over elsewhere is a thief and a robber. But whoever enters through the gate is the shepherd of the sheep. The gatekeeper opens it for him, and the sheep hear his voice, as the shepherd calls his own sheep by name and leads them out. When he has driven out all his own, he walks ahead of them, and the sheep follow him, because they recognize his voice. But they will not follow a stranger; they will run away from him, because they do not recognize the voice of strangers." Although Jesus used this figure of speech, the Pharisees did not realize what he was trying to tell them.

So Jesus said again, "Amen, amen, I say to you, I am the gate for the sheep. All who came before me are thieves and robbers, but the sheep did not listen to them. I am the gate. Whoever enters through me will be saved, and will come in and go out and find pasture. A thief comes only to steal and slaughter and destroy; I came so that they might have life and have it more abundantly."

Understanding the Word

In concluding his Pentecost speech, Peter points out to the Jerusalem crowd that Jesus, whom he has just shown to be Lord and Messiah, was the same Jesus they had crucified. Realizing that they have committed such a grievous crime, the crowd wonder what is next for them. Peter's response comes as a relief: God has not condemned for crucifying Jesus. Rather, they are offered the gift of repentance, forgiveness, and the Holy Spirit. The promises God made to them as Abraham's children are now fulfilled in Christ. Rather than chastisement, Peter holds out the promise of life, if they will allow themselves to be saved by the same Christ they condemned to death.

In his letter Peter continues to develop the implications of being Christian. He reminds his persecuted audience that in his own suffering Christ showed them how to remain faithful as "aliens and sojourners" (2:11) in a hostile world. Jesus did not respond to insults with insults, or to threats with threats of his own. The death of Christ was part of God's mysterious plan to free Christ's followers from their sins and equip them to "live for righteousness." Jesus' followers have been healed not only of the wounds of past sins, but also from sinful inclinations to hurt those who hurt them, "worldly desires that wage war against the soul" (2:11). Jesus shows them a better way and guards those very souls against which the world (and worldly desires) wage war.

The image of the people of God as God's flock is a venerable biblical metaphor. In Jesus' figure of speech, the "thieves and robbers" who have illicitly entered the sheepfold are the Pharisees and other opponents, who do not have the people's best interests at heart. Although he will soon call himself the good shepherd, here Jesus refers to himself as the gate for the sheep, an image that focuses on his role as the one who gives access to God, the source of life. Whereas others who claim to shepherd the people in fact only lead them to destruction, Jesus alone guides God's flock to abundant life and salvation.

Reflecting on the Word

When I was little, my grandpa gave me a packet of World War I postcards for my postcard collection. He had been stationed in Paris in 1918. I remember staring for long minutes at his sepia pictures of bombed-out buildings. The streets were empty and full of rubble. My ten-year-old imagination said that France was in ruins.

I went to France in 2011 to visit my brother. Streets bustled with cars. Apartment buildings were bright with petunias in window boxes. The sidewalks were full of people walking. Mothers were pushing strollers. My grown-up impression of France was of a community that had been materially restored.

Ruin comes in many forms. Thieves who break in and steal the sheep can devastate the owner of the sheep. Deceit, corruption, and insult can tear a person down. A leader who goes astray from a moral path can bomb holes in family and community. The rubble from the abuse crisis litters the streets of the Church and tests our ability to trek onward.

It is the Good Shepherd who wants to lead us from ruin to restoration and then to flourishing. Despite the impression that sentimental Jesus pictures might give us, a shepherd is not a soft character. He is weather-hardened and battle-ready. He is willing to fight to the death for his sheep so that they can safely walk through dark valleys. He restores and watches over all, for his protection is communal; sheep move in flocks.

Jesus says that he came so that we might have life and have it more abundantly. We pray for this renewal. From a personal Spirit-filled abundance, we are to work toward the reinvigoration of the Church and the whole world. We go together. The Good Shepherd will lead us to a vibrant new life.

Consider/Discuss

❖ This week we begin a subtle scriptural shift. In the first half of the Easter season, we've focused on the revelation of who Jesus is. In this second half as we build toward Pentecost, we shift our focus toward the empowerment to be the people Jesus calls us to be. Look back at today's readings. Which passages, verbs, and images speak about what we are to do and who we are to be?

❖ The hunger for restoration is a recurring theme in the Old Testament. As we form impressions of the world in which we live, do we think more about ruin than restoration, or more of restoration than ruin? Where does our information come from? How do those sources affect the way that we approach life? How does that impact our hope?

Living and Praying with the Word

Shepherd of the flock, if we are headed off of a cliff, use your staff to snatch us back. If we are scattering in all directions, herd us together and steer us where you want us to go. As we walk through today's dark valleys, help us trust that your rod and your staff will help us to travel securely together. Bring us to abundance and help us to flourish. For yours is the kingdom and the power and the glory, forever and ever.

MAY 10, 2020

FIFTH SUNDAY OF EASTER

Today's Focus: The Holy Spirit—The Tie That Binds

Because the Church is made up of human beings,
arguments and divisions have always been part of our story.
But so has turning to the Spirit in prayer, so we can return to unity.

FIRST READING

Acts 6:1–7

As the number of disciples continued to grow, the Hellenists complained against the Hebrews because their widows were being neglected in the daily distribution. So the Twelve called together the community of the disciples and said, "It is not right for us to neglect the word of God to serve at table. Brothers, select from among you seven reputable men, filled with the Spirit and wisdom, whom we shall appoint to this task, whereas we shall devote ourselves to prayer and to the ministry of the word." The proposal was acceptable to the whole community, so they chose Stephen, a man filled with faith and the Holy Spirit, also Philip, Prochorus, Nicanor, Timon, Parmenas, and Nicholas of Antioch, a convert to Judaism. They presented these men to the apostles who prayed and laid hands on them. The word of God continued to spread, and the number of the disciples in Jerusalem increased greatly; even a large group of priests were becoming obedient to the faith.

PSALM RESPONSE

Psalm 33:22

Lord, let your mercy be on us, as we place our trust in you.

SECOND READING

1 Peter 2:4–9

Beloved: Come to him, a living stone, rejected by human beings but chosen and precious in the sight of God, and, like living stones, let yourselves be built into a spiritual house to be a holy priesthood to offer spiritual sacrifices acceptable to God through Jesus Christ. For it says in Scripture:
Behold, I am laying a stone in Zion,
a cornerstone, chosen and precious,
and whoever believes in it shall not be put to shame.
Therefore, its value is for you who have faith, but for those without faith:
The stone that the builders rejected
has become the cornerstone,
and
A stone that will make people stumble,
and a rock that will make them fall.
They stumble by disobeying the word, as is their destiny.

You are "a chosen race, a royal priesthood, a holy nation, a people of his own, so that you may announce the praises" of him who called you out of darkness into his wonderful light.

GOSPEL   *John 14:1–12*

Jesus said to his disciples: "Do not let your hearts be troubled. You have faith in God; have faith also in me. In my Father's house there are many dwelling places. If there were not, would I have told you that I am going to prepare a place for you? And if I go and prepare a place for you, I will come back again and take you to myself, so that where I am you also may be. Where I am going you know the way." Thomas said to him, "Master, we do not know where you are going; how can we know the way?" Jesus said to him, "I am the way and the truth and the life. No one comes to the Father except through me. If you know me, then you will also know my Father. From now on you do know him and have seen him." Philip said to him, "Master, show us the Father, and that will be enough for us." Jesus said to him, "Have I been with you for so long a time and you still do not know me, Philip? Whoever has seen me has seen the Father. How can you say, 'Show us the Father'? Do you not believe that I am in the Father and the Father is in me? The words that I speak to you I do not speak on my own. The Father who dwells in me is doing his works. Believe me that I am in the Father and the Father is in me, or else, believe because of the works themselves. Amen, amen, I say to you, whoever believes in me will do the works that I do, and will do greater ones than these, because I am going to the Father."

Understanding the Word

The early Christian community comprised both Jews (Hebrews) and Gentiles (Graeco-Roman). Social divisions between them were not easily overcome, even in the care of the needy. The apparent neglect of the Gentile widows, whether intended or not, presents itself to the apostles as a practical problem that needs to be addressed structurally. They cannot take time from their particular ministry to make sure that everyone's needs are met. Yet they recognize the importance of solicitude for needy widows and others, as shown not only by their desire to choose men with good reputations, known to be filled with the Spirit and wisdom, but also by their prayer and imposition of hands.

Peter's audience has been born anew through the word of God (1:23). This word draws them to the Lord, who is building them into a temple where they will offer spiritual sacrifices to God. Like Israel, Christians are to be for God a chosen race, a holy and royal priesthood, and a holy nation, whose purpose is to proclaim the praises of God, and thus draw others to God as well. Like Peter's audience, Christ too was rejected by those without faith and thus became a stumbling block for them. Yet he remains alive to nurture and support them, the living cornerstone on which the church is founded.

In his farewell discourse at the Last Supper, Jesus assures his followers that they are not to be perturbed by his imminent departure, because he goes to the Father, where he will prepare a place for them. When he returns, he will take them there. Yet they will not be going someplace completely unknown to them. Indeed, the way to the Father they already know because they know Jesus, in whom they have met the Father. Not quite getting it, Philip asks that they actually see the Father, "that will be enough for us"(!). Jesus reminds his followers once again that in him they have actually seen the Father because the Father is in him.

Reflecting on the Word

I was the chaplain on call for the day shift that day. A nurse called, "Please come!"

When I got to the seventh floor, by the nursing desk two men and a woman were shouting at each other. The room opposite was bursting with large people, arguing. I bent my head to the nurse, "What's going on?" "Nine children. They're fighting over their mother's last wishes." We got them calmed enough to pray together and be silent so they could focus on their dying mother. A few minutes later, with her last words, she pleaded quietly, "Children, please don't fight."

The deepest desire of a mother's heart is for her children to flourish. Integral to that flourishing is her desire for them to get along and to care for each other. My grandma said to my dad and his six siblings, "Stay together."

If this is how a mother feels, how much greater, then, are the desires of God's heart? As we build in the next few weeks toward the empowerment of Pentecost, what are the Lord's designs for our flourishing?

The Holy Spirit is the tie who binds a community together. When the early Christians bickered over who was getting enough food, the apostles were inspired to anoint the first deacons to serve. That way the church could be at peace and prosper.

Jesus prays that we all be one. The tension in today's Gospel is that Jesus knows that he is about to go away. How are his followers to stay together? He wants them to flourish. They flourish best together. He is the Way. If they remain focused on him, they will stay together. They are about to be handed an important mission: to be Christ to the world. They need that focus. So do we.

Consider/Discuss

❖ One of the most rewarding elements in the Christian life is to find out God's vision and take it for our own. What is God's dream for the world? What is your part in that grand vision?

❖ Jesus says that he is "the Way." He doesn't say, "I am a nice idea." In a world sometimes unconvinced, is the Christian message good for human flourishing? How does faithfully following Jesus matter?

Living and Praying with the Word

Lord, we put our hope in you. There is much that pulls us apart from each other. Your vision is for us to be together. We pray earnestly for you to heal our divisions, for you are our unfailing help. We commit ourselves to you again this day. Be our Way, our Truth, and our Life.

MAY 17, 2020

SIXTH SUNDAY OF EASTER

Today's Focus: The Spirit's Joy

---

*The Holy Spirit promised by Jesus gives us our purpose:
to go out on the joyful mission of spreading the good news of salvation.*

FIRST READING

Acts 8:5–8, 14–17

Philip went down to the city of Samaria and proclaimed the Christ to them. With one accord, the crowds paid attention to what was said by Philip when they heard it and saw the signs he was doing. For unclean spirits, crying out in a loud voice, came out of many possessed people, and many paralyzed or crippled people were cured. There was great joy in that city.

Now when the apostles in Jerusalem heard that Samaria had accepted the word of God, they sent them Peter and John, who went down and prayed for them, that they might receive the Holy Spirit, for it had not yet fallen upon any of them; they had only been baptized in the name of the Lord Jesus. Then they laid hands on them and they received the Holy Spirit.

PSALM RESPONSE

Psalm 66:1

Let all the earth cry out to God with joy.

SECOND READING

1 Peter 3:15–18

Beloved: Sanctify Christ as Lord in your hearts. Always be ready to give an explanation to anyone who asks you for a reason for your hope, but do it with gentleness and reverence, keeping your conscience clear, so that, when you are maligned, those who defame your good conduct in Christ may themselves be put to shame. For it is better to suffer for doing good, if that be the will of God, than for doing evil. For Christ also suffered for sins once, the righteous for the sake of the unrighteous, that he might lead you to God. Put to death in the flesh, he was brought to life in the Spirit.

John 14:15–21

Jesus said to his disciples: "If you love me, you will keep my commandments. And I will ask the Father, and he will give you another Advocate to be with you always, the Spirit of truth, whom the world cannot accept, because it neither sees nor knows him. But you know him, because he remains with you, and will be in you. I will not leave you orphans; I will come to you. In a little while the world will no longer see me, but you will see me, because I live and you will live. On that day you will realize that I am in my Father and you are in me and I in you. Whoever has my commandments and observes them is the one who loves me. And whoever loves me will be loved by my Father, and I will love him and reveal myself to him."

Understanding the Word

In Acts, the gospel proclamation radiates from Jerusalem, eventually reaching Rome. Just previous to this passage, we read that persecution in Jerusalem has scattered the disciples "throughout the countryside of Judea and Samaria" (8:1). Philip, one of the seven "deacons" chosen in last week's reading, finds himself among the Samaritans, a people long estranged from Jews. His preaching of the Jewish Messiah, accompanied by healings and exorcisms, leads nevertheless to many being baptized. This might be considered something of a reconciliation between Jew and Samaritan, and therefore a sign of the kingdom of God. The effect of the baptisms is completed with the bestowal of the Holy Spirit through the ministry of the apostles.

The letter of Peter supports persecuted Christians in their struggle to remain faithful to Christ. Echoing one of the Beatitudes, the apostle reminds his audience that they are blessed who suffer because of righteousness (3:14). Righteousness means, among other things, responding to hostility as did Christ, the Lord of their hearts: with peace and gentleness. The animosity they face for being Christians constitutes a temptation to respond in kind, a temptation that should be resisted, lest they act with a bad conscience and do evil. Those who suffer for Christ can be strengthened by the reminder that he too suffered and although he died "in the flesh," he now lives "in the Spirit." His followers can expect the same.

The Last Supper discourse continues with Jesus' promise of the Spirit. He has just assured the apostles that he will not abandon them but will return to take them to the Father (see last week's Gospel). Now he promises them that in the meantime, he will send "another" Advocate, suggesting that the Spirit will do for them what Jesus did. And indeed the Spirit is a Spirit of truth, as Jesus himself is the truth (14:6). He then reverts to his promise to return, using language that emphasizes the mutual indwelling of Christ and his followers. It is on the basis of this indwelling that the followers are commanded to love Jesus, and thus be loved by the Father and by Jesus. To those who love, God the Father and the Son will be revealed.

Reflecting on the Word

I was having a conversation with a well-educated Catholic layman, who asked me what I was writing about. I said, "Mission." His eyes lit up. "You should go talk to Father M.; he spent a lot of time in Africa!" I grinned. Mission: the word evokes exotic places and visiting priests or nuns telling hair-raising stories. Many people of faith still interpret "mission" as something someone else does somewhere else. What is expected is to give money to the "missions."

Yet mission also means "purpose." Researchers tell us that a personal sense of purpose leads to greater well-being. A famous saying is, "The two most important days in your life are the day that you were born and the day that you find out why." Where does Christian purpose come from? Why are we here?

Jesus promises that the Advocate, the Holy Spirit, will be with us always. As we are washed with that indwelling tender Spirit, we in turn fall in love. Daily life is no longer the same. We may be fishermen or computer programmers, students or professionals, preachers or lay ministers, parents or grandparents—when we encounter the friendship of the living God, we are changed. We are filled with radiant joy. Mission is not just something someone else does somewhere else. Mission is what we do, right here, right now. It doesn't matter so much what we do in daily life, but how we do it. The Holy Spirit's joy gives us purpose.

As Pentecost approaches, we can prepare to be empowered and sent out into our ordinary twenty-first–century lives to be extraordinary people. This is our calling, our obligation. This is also our delight. We are to be an enthusiastic people of purpose, with determination, resolution, drive, tenacity, and commitment to living Jesus' joy-filled way of life.

Consider/Discuss

❖ One of the tensions in the last five weeks of the Easter season is the contrast between the first readings from Acts, which tell stories of what happens after Pentecost, and the Gospels which are rich with Jesus' admonitions to help the disciples get ready for Pentecost. How do our lives dwell within that paradox—living in the Spirit now while also waiting for the Spirit's fullness to come?

❖ We are given a mission to be light for the world. We are filled with the Spirit to accomplish that mission. To live for Jesus—is that our joy or our obligation—or both? What do we see as our purpose in everyday life?

Living and Praying with the Word

Come, Holy Spirit! We need a new Pentecost, a revival of faith. Our world needs renewal. We cannot do this by ourselves. We need you. Come with your rushing wind. Come with your mighty power. Come, hidden joy of the world. We pray together in deep need: come, Holy Spirit and renew the hearts of your faithful.

THE ASCENSION OF THE LORD

Today's Focus: Going, Going . . . Not Gone

Even though Jesus has "gone away," he is closer to us now than he could have been if he had physically remained on earth.

FIRST READING
Acts 1:1–11

In the first book, Theophilus, I dealt with all that Jesus did and taught until the day he was taken up, after giving instructions through the Holy Spirit to the apostles whom he had chosen. He presented himself alive to them by many proofs after he had suffered, appearing to them during forty days and speaking about the kingdom of God. While meeting with them, he enjoined them not to depart from Jerusalem, but to wait for "the promise of the Father about which you have heard me speak; for John baptized with water, but in a few days you will be baptized with the Holy Spirit."

When they had gathered together they asked him, "Lord, are you at this time going to restore the kingdom to Israel?" He answered them, "It is not for you to know the times or seasons that the Father has established by his own authority. But you will receive power when the Holy Spirit comes upon you, and you will be my witnesses in Jerusalem, throughout Judea and Samaria, and to the ends of the earth." When he had said this, as they were looking on, he was lifted up, and a cloud took him from their sight. While they were looking intently at the sky as he was going, suddenly two men dressed in white garments stood beside them. They said, "Men of Galilee, why are you standing there looking at the sky? This Jesus who has been taken up from you into heaven will return in the same way as you have seen him going into heaven."

PSALM RESPONSE
Psalm 47:6

God mounts his throne to shouts of joy: a blare of trumpets for the Lord.

SECOND READING
Ephesians 1:17–23

Brothers and sisters: May the God of our Lord Jesus Christ, the Father of glory, give you a Spirit of wisdom and revelation resulting in knowledge of him. May the eyes of your hearts be enlightened, that you may know what is the hope that belongs to his call, what are the riches of glory in his inheritance among the holy ones, and what is the surpassing greatness of his power for us who believe, in accord with the exercise of his great might, which he worked in Christ, raising him from the dead and seating him at his right hand in the heavens, far above every principality, authority, power, and dominion, and every name that is named not only in this age but also in the one to come. And he put all things beneath his feet and gave him as head over all things to the church, which is his body, the fullness of the one who fills all things in every way.

The eleven disciples went to Galilee, to the mountain to which Jesus had ordered them. When they saw him, they worshiped, but they doubted. Then Jesus approached and said to them, "All power in heaven and on earth has been given to me. Go, therefore, and make disciples of all nations, baptizing them in the name of the Father, and of the Son, and of the Holy Spirit, teaching them to observe all that I have commanded you. And behold, I am with you always, until the end of the age."

Understanding the Word

Luke begins his story of the gospel's spread with the conclusion of the earthly ministry of Christ. In this account of the Ascension one notices the centrality of the Holy Spirit, whose bestowal will allow the apostles to continue Jesus' work. This Spirit-informed proclamation will be the way that Jesus brings about Israel's hoped-for restoration, yet go beyond Israel to restore all peoples. Although the apostles did not witness the Resurrection itself, they do witness Jesus' ascension, confirming in their sight that Jesus is the Messiah of God, never to die. With this witness, and the power and guidance of the Holy Spirit, they will be equipped to be Jesus' witnesses "to the ends of the earth."

Paul begins his letter to the Ephesians with a lengthy thanksgiving for what the Father has done in Jesus Christ, culminating with the gift of the Spirit (1:3–14). He now prays that the same Spirit will allow them to know God. This knowledge encompasses three things: enlightening the "eyes of the heart," which probably has to do with moral conduct, the heart being the seat of the will; the glorious inheritance that awaits them; and the power of God, who raised Christ from the dead and exalted him above all created powers of the cosmos (see Colossians 1:16). In and because of Christ the church experiences the life and power of God.

Told by the women who have encountered the risen Christ to go to Galilee to meet him (Matthew 28:10), the apostles see Jesus for the first time since his passion. They respond with both worship and doubt. The latter is not skepticism, but that wavering elsewhere called being of "little faith" (6:30; 14:31). The struggle to trust will remain in the church even after the Resurrection. Despite this imperfect faith, Jesus sends the Eleven to the world. Although the New Testament does not contain a fully-developed Trinitarian doctrine, the baptismal formula assumes some form of identity among Father, Son, and Spirit, all of whom share one "name." The earthly career of Emmanuel ends as it began, with the promise of abiding presence (1:23).

Reflecting on the Word

"Why are you standing there looking at the sky?" my friend asked as we traveled across campus. "Look at the clouds!" I exclaimed. The clouds in the summer at Notre Dame are glorious. The moisture from nearby Lake Michigan makes them radiant in the blue sky. I love clouds. I love flying because of the elation of soaring up through cumulus clouds. I like climbing mountains, and the resulting exhausted joy of looking down at the clouds it brings. I remember one bone-weary-beyond-weary, emotionally exhausted day when I looked up at the clouds and yelled, "Come any time now, Lord! What are you waiting for?" I smile inside when the scriptures put the sky and clouds and significant events together—Elijah's chariot; Jesus' baptism, transfiguration, and ascension. It fires the imagination.

The disciples lived solidly on the ground. They never flew in an airplane. Yet the heavens in Israel are also glorious. The shimmer of the moonlight during a night of fishing, the sparkle that bounces up from the Sea of Galilee in the day, the glistening of the sun over the Mediterranean—to "look up" probably fired the disciples' hearts as well.

The Ascension marks Luke's conclusion to Jesus' earthly ministry. If he had stayed, the disciples could still have slapped him on the back with a joke and he would not have minded. He could have continued to heal the sick and the blind. But he would have been limited to contacting those who were geographically close to him.

Jesus is now physically gone. Yet at the same time, Jesus is here. We can taste his presence. We can feel it. We can know it. Though Jesus has gone "into the clouds," he is closer than he would have been if he had physically stayed among us. The Lord is near to us. Always.

Consider/Discuss

❖ It is a paradox of our faith that the God of distance is also the God of nearness. When we put "a face" to the divine, which one more freely arises in our spiritual imagination—distance or nearness? Why does it matter that we envision both?

❖ Think of someone you love dearly who has departed in death. How have you (or have you not) felt closer to that person now that he or she dwells in the communion of saints? Describe what that experience is like.

Living and Praying with the Word

Lord, you are highly exalted, King over all the earth. You rule over nations. You keep the stars in their courses. At the same time, you are here. You are near. How can this be? You have said that you will be with us always, to the end of the age. When we take you for granted, show us the surpassing greatness of your strength. When we shy away from your power, be our divine Tenderness. Come, Lord Jesus! Come at the end of the age. Please come now. We need you. Let us be "filled with the fullness of all things" in every way.

MAY 24, 2020

SEVENTH SUNDAY OF EASTER

Today's Focus: Prepare for the Spirit, Together and in Prayer

One of the things that the Easter season does is lead us toward
and build us up for the coming of the Spirit at Pentecost.
This takes readiness on our part, a community gathered in prayer.

FIRST READING   *Acts 1:12–14*

After Jesus had been taken up to heaven the apostles returned to Jerusalem from the mount called Olivet, which is near Jerusalem, a sabbath day's journey away.

When they entered the city they went to the upper room where they were staying, Peter and John and James and Andrew, Philip and Thomas, Bartholomew and Matthew, James son of Alphaeus, Simon the Zealot, and Judas son of James. All these devoted themselves with one accord to prayer, together with some women, and Mary the mother of Jesus, and his brothers.

PSALM RESPONSE   *Psalm 27:13*

I believe that I shall see the good things of the Lord in the land of the living.

SECOND READING   *1 Peter 4:13–16*

Beloved: Rejoice to the extent that you share in the sufferings of Christ, so that when his glory is revealed you may also rejoice exultantly. If you are insulted for the name of Christ, blessed are you, for the Spirit of glory and of God rests upon you. But let no one among you be made to suffer as a murderer, a thief, an evildoer, or as an intriguer. But whoever is made to suffer as a Christian should not be ashamed but glorify God because of the name.

GOSPEL   *John 17:1–11a*

Jesus raised his eyes to heaven and said, "Father, the hour has come. Give glory to your son, so that your son may glorify you, just as you gave him authority over all people, so that your son may give eternal life to all you gave him. Now this is eternal life, that they should know you, the only true God, and the one whom you sent, Jesus Christ. I glorified you on earth by accomplishing the work that you gave me to do. Now glorify me, Father, with you, with the glory that I had with you before the world began.

"I revealed your name to those whom you gave me out of the world. They belonged to you, and you gave them to me, and they have kept your word. Now they know that everything you gave me is from you, because the words you gave to me I have given to them, and they accepted them and truly understood that I came from you, and they have believed that you sent me. I pray for them. I do not pray for the world but for the ones you have given me, because they are yours, and everything of mine is yours and everything of yours is mine, and I have been glorified in them. And now I will no longer be in the world, but they are in the world, while I am coming to you."

Understanding the Word

At his ascension, Jesus had ordered the apostles to remain in Jerusalem to await their baptism by the Holy Spirit (1:4–5). Now they return to Jerusalem just across the Kidron Valley from Mount Olivet—no further than a Jew was allowed to walk on the Sabbath. It is characteristic of Acts that Jesus' followers pray together at important moments, as they do here. The presence of the women, including the mother of Jesus, underscores the important role that women will continue to play in Luke's account. The list of the eleven apostles (minus Judas Iscariot) sets the stage for his replacement in the following passage (1:15–26).

Peter exhorts his audience to make sure that if they suffer, it is for the right reason. As he has already pointed out several times, Christ himself suffered, and so it is to be expected that his followers will, too. Yet as long as they are being insulted or suffering for the name of Christ, they have cause to rejoice, for his experience of glory will be theirs, too. Not all suffering is cause for rejoicing, of course, but only unjust suffering. Suffering as a result of grievous sin, of course, does not reflect the suffering of Christ, and so does not lead to glory.

In his prayer to the Father at the Last Supper, Jesus states a central theme of John's Gospel: eternal life consists in knowing the Father and the Son he sent. Jesus has given glory to God by making the Father known on earth. Now he asks the Father to give him the glory he already possesses as the Word who came into the world (1:1–14). As the Prologue states, that world did not receive the Word; Jesus affirms here that only those whom God had given him "out of the world" believed in him. The world here means those aspects of human reality that are opposed to God. This is why Jesus does not pray "for the world," which is implacably opposed to him, but only for those who have believed in him and whom he now leaves, for the time being, in the midst of that hostile world.

Reflecting on the Word

Have you ever wondered why we don't have a liturgical season that specifically leads to Pentecost? We have Advent to get ready for Christmas. We have Lent to cleanse our hearts for Easter. Why not a unique time to prepare ourselves for the indwelling of the Spirit and the equipping for mission?

Or do we?

In today's first reading, the apostles and the broader group of Easter witnesses gather to pray. They are getting ready. They may not have consciously realized it, but we can see it clearly in hindsight: they are on another edge of time, the edge of some happening that is about to be personally life-changing and historically world-changing. They are getting ready for Pentecost.

Change experts say that there are stages to prepare to make a significant change that lasts. If you want to lose weight, first take some time to analyze what you eat and when and why. Then plan how to diet accordingly. If you intend to move to a new country, take some time to learn the language and the customs and prepare yourself mentally to make that radical shift. Enduring change requires a time of preparation.

God must be the original change expert. Wisely, Jesus did not throw the disciples into mission right away. Luke says that he taught them how to understand the scriptures. He repeatedly asked them to pray and prepare. It will not be an easy task that he asks of them. They will be persecuted. They will share in his sufferings. In today's Gospel, he prays for them to be one. He wants to make sure that they have the tools needed to carry out the mission—both the empowerment of the Spirit and the strength of community.

Holy saints who have gone before us, pray for that for us as well.

Consider/Discuss

❖ Do we have the tools that we need to carry out Christ's mission? Are we as Holy Spirit–empowered as we need to be? Is our community strong? How can we pray and plan to allow God's revitalization to happen?

❖ The Holy Spirit is often said to be the most "overlooked" member of the Trinity, especially in the western Church. How can we liturgically elevate the feast of Pentecost so that the Spirit's empowerment and mission also get their due?

Living and Praying the Word

Spirit of the Living God, your church on earth needs you. Help us to do our part. We consecrate ourselves to you in whatever walk of life you have called us. Help us to devote ourselves to prayer for the church and your fullness. You rushed in upon the disciples and changed them into holy men and women. Rush upon us this week too as we prepare our hearts for your feast.

MAY 31, 2020

PENTECOST SUNDAY

Today's Focus: The Erupting Spirit

It is easy to be focused on Pentecost's diversity of tongues spoken. Search a bit deeper, though, to discover that the Spirit's joy must erupt into words of faith.

FIRST READING
Acts 2:1–11

When the time for Pentecost was fulfilled, they were all in one place together. And suddenly there came from the sky a noise like a strong driving wind, and it filled the entire house in which they were. Then there appeared to them tongues as of fire, which parted and came to rest on each one of them. And they were all filled with the Holy Spirit and began to speak in different tongues, as the Spirit enabled them to proclaim.

Now there were devout Jews from every nation under heaven staying in Jerusalem. At this sound, they gathered in a large crowd, but they were confused because each one heard them speaking in his own language. They were astounded, and in amazement they asked, "Are not all these people who are speaking Galileans? Then how does each of us hear them in his native language? We are Parthians, Medes, and Elamites, inhabitants of Mesopotamia, Judea and Cappadocia, Pontus and Asia, Phrygia and Pamphylia, Egypt and the districts of Libya near Cyrene, as well as travelers from Rome, both Jews and converts to Judaism, Cretans and Arabs, yet we hear them speaking in our own tongues of the mighty acts of God."

PSALM RESPONSE
Psalm 104:30

Lord, send out your Spirit, and renew the face of the earth.

SECOND READING
1 Corinthians 12:3b–7, 12–13

Brothers and sisters: No one can say, "Jesus is Lord," except by the Holy Spirit. There are different kinds of spiritual gifts but the same Spirit; there are different forms of service but the same Lord; there are different workings but the same God who produces all of them in everyone. To each individual the manifestation of the Spirit is given for some benefit.

As a body is one though it has many parts, and all the parts of the body, though many, are one body, so also Christ. For in one Spirit we were all baptized into one body, whether Jews or Greeks, slaves or free persons, and we were all given to drink of one Spirit.

On the evening of that first day of the week, when the doors were locked, where the disciples were, for fear of the Jews, Jesus came and stood in their midst and said to them, "Peace be with you." When he had said this, he showed them his hands and his side. The disciples rejoiced when they saw the Lord. Jesus said to them again, "Peace be with you. As the Father has sent me, so I send you." And when he had said this, he breathed on them and said to them, "Receive the Holy Spirit. Whose sins you forgive are forgiven them, and whose sins you retain are retained."

Understanding the Word

Pentecost was the Greek name for the summer harvest festival held fifty days after Passover (Deuteronomy 16:9–12). It was one of the three pilgrimage festivals in which "devout Jews from every nation under heaven" were expected to come to Jerusalem. At the sound of a strong driving wind these same Jews rush to the scene to discover Jesus' disciples speaking in their various languages. Ultimately, the Spirit's work will not be limited to the "gift of tongues," but this along with the power to speak of "the mighty acts of God" is the most immediate effect of Pentecost. With the coming of the Spirit, the disciples are equipped to further Jesus' mission to gather "all nations" to God, beginning with Israel.

Socioeconomic divisions in Corinth have been exacerbated by a tendency to interpret different charisms of the Spirit as status indicators. Paul emphasizes that God has endowed the Corinthians with a variety of gifts—different gifts, different forms of service, different workings—that are meant to enrich the community, not divide it. They have not been given to individuals as much as they have been given to the community as a whole, and for the whole community's benefit. The fact that the same Spirit is responsible for the variety of gifts means that, ultimately, they are meant to unify the one body of Christ, which the Spirit is building and unifying through those same gifts.

In John's Gospel the risen Lord bestows the Spirit on his followers not at Pentecost but on the evening of the Resurrection. Compelled by fear to barricade themselves behind doors, they nevertheless suddenly discover that Christ has been able to enter into their midst. Although some of his disciples may have good reason to fear even him, having abandoned him at his darkest hour, Jesus greets them immediately with peace. His wounds are offered not as a reproach, but as evidence that it is he, the wounded Jesus, who greets them with twice peace, a sign of reconciliation. Breathing on them the promised Holy Spirit (14:15–17), Jesus empowers them to offer that same reconciliation through the forgiveness of sins.

135

Reflecting on the Word

She whispered under her breath, "Lord, have mercy." The others in the room echoed, "Lord, have mercy." It was not a church but a hospital room. Gospel music was playing softly on the player on the windowsill. She smiled, "Lord, have mercy God almighty, I am coming home!" Words of faith—the Spirit of God overflowed within her and her joy erupted into words.

The feast of Pentecost is the day to celebrate the gift of speech! Some of us speak for a living. Preachers preach often in the Easter season. Teachers talk the whole school year through. Sometimes we may wonder, where does the power come from to speak effectively? And do words make any difference in this world that is already so full of words?

The experience of the Spirit in the second chapter of Acts came to seemingly dried-up and disheartened disciples. The Spirit rushed upon them like a mighty wind! Out of their emptiness, Acts tells us, three thousand people were converted and the church was born. At that moment, Christian preaching was also born. What if Peter had not spoken? What if he had remained silent? The Spirit so filled him that he had to speak. He had to speak. His joy bubbled up into words, telling the glorious story of Jesus' resurrection. Human speech matters more than we can ever imagine.

Our words matter, too. On this holy day of empowering, do we hunger for those we love to meet the living God? If so, what words do we speak? We have to discern our words carefully. But joy bubbling into words of faith, even when they are hesitant, can have an effect. For if those we love have not heard, how are they going to believe? Come, Holy Spirit, fill the words of your faithful!

Consider/Discuss

❖ Jesus breathed on his future preachers and said, "Receive the Holy Spirit." This tender waft of Jesus' air became the mighty wind of Pentecost. Who has breathed on you words that have transformed your life?

❖ Faith is caught as much as it is taught. Yet words are necessary. We have to speak. Where do you struggle with speaking—talk too little? too much? too unthinkingly? too carefully? Spend a little time in prayer, discerning where your words may have hurt and how very much your words of love matter. What do you need to do to become a more Holy Spirit–inspired speaker?

Living and Praying with the Word

On this holy day of days, Holy Spirit, erupt within us. Send tongues of fire upon us so that we are aflame with your joy. We cannot fulfill our mission on our own strength. You are the Delight of delights, the Wonder of wonders. We are thrilled to exult in you. You are Holy Wisdom; fill us this day so that your inspired words radiate out through us into a world hungry for your glory.

Notes

ORDINARY TIME II

The first readings in Ordinary Time address key biblical themes. The prophet Jeremiah's struggle to fulfill his mission of preaching God's challenging word in the face of a hostile response (Jeremiah 20:7–9, 10–13) shines a light on human rejection of the divine offer of salvation. Ezekiel proclaims that God desires above all that the wicked turn from their ways and thus spare their lives (Ezekiel 33:7–9; 18:25–28). In a number of passages Isaiah announces that God expects good fruit of righteousness and justice (Isaiah 5:1–7), and calls Israel to turn from unsatisfying pursuits to receive from the divine abundance "real bread" that satisfies (Isaiah 55:1–3). Those who struggle to be faithful are offered every opportunity to turn back and be forgiven, so that they might enjoy all the benefits God has in store for them (Isaiah 55:6–9). Overall, the Old Testament readings make it clear that God's saving will—not just for Israel but for all peoples—has been strong from the beginning (Isaiah 56:1, 6–7).

Much in Ordinary Time is taken up with Paul's Letter to the Romans. In this great epistle, Paul depicts the situation *of* humanity as a result of Adam's disobedience: we became bound by sin and subject to death (5:12–15). But Christ's own death and resurrection have released us from this bondage, making the baptized adopted children and heirs of God (6:3–4, 8–11). As we are no longer in bondage to sin, we must stop acting as if we were and put aside the works of the "flesh," of the "old self," and allow God's Spirit to conform us to the likeness of Christ (8:9, 11–13; 8:18–23; 8:35, 37–39; 12:1–2; 13:8–10). In his Letter to the Philippians, Paul also addresses the ethical implications of Christ's humbling himself to save us, calling on his readers to have the same mind as Christ and put aside their own selfishness (2:1–11). Finally, Paul encourages the Thessalonians to face hardship and affliction with enduring hope and joy as they await the *parousia,* in which Christ will welcome both the living and the dead into his kingdom (1:5c–10; 4:13–18).

Amid the various stories, sayings, and parables, some clear themes emerge in the readings for Matthew's Gospel. The first is the saving power of God manifest in Jesus, who provides for hungry stomachs and souls (14:13–33; 15:21–28). The second is the opposition to the Good News by a sinful and still broken world (10:26–33; 10:37–42; 11:25–30; 21:33–43). The third and most developed theme is the challenge of entering the kingdom, which requires us to overcome sinful tendencies, be transformed, and persevere in the face of many challenges (13:1–23; 13:44–52; 16:21–27; 18:21–35; 22:1–14; 25:1–13; 25:31–46).

THE MOST HOLY TRINITY

Today's Focus: The Trinity—A Divine Dance

An ancient understanding of the persons of the Trinity refers to them as dancing together. The good news is, we're invited to join in the dancing!

FIRST READING   *Exodus 34:4b–6, 8–9*

Early in the morning Moses went up Mount Sinai as the LORD had commanded him, taking along the two stone tablets.

Having come down in a cloud, the LORD stood with Moses there and proclaimed his name, "LORD." Thus the LORD passed before him and cried out, "The LORD, the LORD, a merciful and gracious God, slow to anger and rich in kindness and fidelity." Moses at once bowed down to the ground in worship. Then he said, "If I find favor with you, O LORD, do come along in our company. This is indeed a stiff-necked people; yet pardon our wickedness and sins, and receive us as your own."

PSALM RESPONSE   *Daniel 3:52b*

Glory and praise for ever!

SECOND READING   *2 Corinthians 13:11–13*

Brothers and sisters, rejoice. Mend your ways, encourage one another, agree with one another, live in peace, and the God of love and peace will be with you. Greet one another with a holy kiss. All the holy ones greet you.

The grace of the Lord Jesus Christ and the love of God and the fellowship of the Holy Spirit be with all of you.

GOSPEL   *John 3:16–18*

God so loved the world that he gave his only Son, so that everyone who believes in him might not perish but might have eternal life. For God did not send his Son into the world to condemn the world, but that the world might be saved through him. Whoever believes in him will not be condemned, but whoever does not believe has already been condemned, because he has not believed in the name of the only Son of God.

Understanding the Word

Much of the book of Exodus is concerned with answering the question "Who is the LORD?" In the deliverance from Egypt, provision in the wilderness, and establishment of the covenant, God is shown to be faithful, powerful, and wise. The present scene takes place shortly after the affair of the golden calf, which nearly ends the covenant relationship. Thanks to Moses, who reminds the LORD of his fidelity, the covenant has been renewed. It is against this background that the famous phrase must be understood: The God of Israel can be angered by human infidelity, but God's mercy, grace, kindness, and fidelity far outshine that anger. This is who the LORD is.

Throughout his second letter to them, Paul has been admonishing the Corinthians to forsake the division and lack of fidelity to the gospel way of life that he has seen among them. He warns them to examine themselves to see if they are living in faith: "Test yourselves" (13:5). Despite the severe tone, he ends by exhorting them to rejoice—they have been saved by Christ. In that joy they should recognize their fellowship and act accordingly, with mutual encouragement, agreement, and peace. Then their community will be a sign of God's love and peace. The letter ends with an invocation of Christ, God (the Father), and the Holy Spirit, one of the clearest "trinitarian" expressions in the New Testament.

In his conversation with Nicodemus, Jesus has told him that "no one can enter the kingdom of God without being born of water and Spirit" (3:5). That is, one must be (re)born from above. This is a gift from God that can only be accepted by believing that Jesus is God's Son, given by God—both in the sense of the incarnation of the Word and in his death on the cross—so that those who do believe might have eternal life. In John, "eternal life" refers to a "abundant life" (10:10), a quality of life that can be lived on earth and after bodily death, rather than simply a "duration" of life after death.

Reflecting on the Word

We know so little of God. When it comes to describing the Trinity, we can feel that we know even less. The Mystery of Mysteries, the God-Who-Is—Father, Son, and Holy Spirit—is not just a philosophical doctrine to be illustrated with clovers and candles. The Trinity is a Someone, Someone who is deeply involved in our lives.

Saints Basil the Great, Gregory of Nyssa, and Gregory of Nazianzus (known as the Cappadocian Fathers) saw the interrelationship of the Father, Son, and Holy Spirit as a dance. They described a divine give-and-take, a *perichoresis* (dancing together), a mystical solidarity of interdependence, a never-ending "I am here for you" and "I am constant in my care for you" within the oneness of God. That mutual love overflows to us.

In the scriptures, we see that God continually communicates as the Father who never stops seeking out wayward Israel, the Son who becomes flesh and gives up his life for us, and the Holy Spirit who is with us always.

Our Triune God so loves the world that those divine "hands" invite us: Come, join in the dance! What does that look like? Think of Fred Astaire and Ginger Rogers—they whirl and flow across a stage together with just a nudge or a touch. Folk dancers have a similar perpetual motion of bowing and twirling and jumping. With practiced responsiveness, they move as one.

Can we join in the dance? We might choose to live as plodders who stumble through life. Or we could discover holy agility. The Holy Spirit leans toward us, gently touching and nudging us in everyday life, whispering, "Be attentive. Follow my lead!" To move within the life of the Trinity is exciting, exhilarating. God's tender "Take my hand. I am here for you" is offered to us at all times.

Consider/Discuss

❖ We are not God and God is not us. How does that distinction set us free to be dancing partners with the Triune God? In the Gospel (John 3:1–5), how did Jesus offer his hand to Nicodemus to join in the dance?

❖ Sometimes we do plod. We may not sense the movement of the Spirit. Sometimes we don't "get" the Trinity. We may wonder, how can anybody get so excited about Trinity? Think of the little nudges that you have felt. How can we trust that God is constantly at work in our lives and learn to be even more attentive and responsive?

Living and Praying with the Word

God of Trinity, you are so beautiful, so beautiful in motion! All that we see in the created world leads us to you. Holy Spirit, surround us, enthuse us, and sustain us. You are deeply within us, and yet sometimes, we are not deeply within you. We beg for your grace to grow more agile. And when you do give us those tastes of abundant life in the divine dance that surrounds us, how can we keep from singing . . . and dancing!

THE MOST HOLY BODY AND BLOOD OF CHRIST

Today's Focus: Tastes of Beauty in the Body of Christ

Sometimes when the world around us is rejecting Christ, we must recall those moments in our lives when we were touched by Christ, the Bread of Life.

FIRST READING
Deuteronomy 8:2–3, 14b–16a

Moses said to the people: "Remember how for forty years now the LORD, your God, has directed all your journeying in the desert, so as to test you by affliction and find out whether or not it was your intention to keep his commandments. He therefore let you be afflicted with hunger, and then fed you with manna, a food unknown to you and your fathers, in order to show you that not by bread alone does one live, but by every word that comes forth from the mouth of the LORD.

"Do not forget the LORD, your God, who brought you out of the land of Egypt, that place of slavery; who guided you through the vast and terrible desert with its saraph serpents and scorpions, its parched and waterless ground; who brought forth water for you from the flinty rock and fed you in the desert with manna, a food unknown to your fathers."

PSALM RESPONSE
Psalm 147:12

Praise the Lord, Jerusalem.

SECOND READING
1 Corinthians 10:16–17

Brothers and sisters: The cup of blessing that we bless, is it not a participation in the blood of Christ? The bread that we break, is it not a participation in the body of Christ? Because the loaf of bread is one, we, though many, are one body, for we all partake of the one loaf.

GOSPEL
John 6:51–58

Jesus said to the Jewish crowds: "I am the living bread that came down from heaven; whoever eats this bread will live forever; and the bread that I will give is my flesh for the life of the world."

The Jews quarreled among themselves, saying, "How can this man give us his flesh to eat?" Jesus said to them, "Amen, amen, I say to you, unless you eat the flesh of the Son of Man and drink his blood, you do not have life within you. Whoever eats my flesh and drinks my blood has eternal life, and I will raise him on the last day. For my flesh is true food, and my blood is true drink. Whoever eats my flesh and drinks my blood remains in me and I in him. Just as the living Father sent me and I have life because of the Father, so also the one who feeds on me will have life because of me.

This is the bread that came down from heaven. Unlike your ancestors who ate and still died, whoever eats this bread will live forever."

Understanding the Word

Israel has finally arrived on the threshold of the Promised Land. Through the years, they struggled to trust that the God who delivered them from bondage can take care of them and provide for all their needs. This has been, and will continue to be, an important challenge, since distrust leads to the worship of other gods. Moses thus reminds the people of all God has done for them, providing them with food and water, and not just any food, but manna, a special food created by God for them. Through the trials, God has been teaching them that they can and must rely on God, who provides all they need for the journey.

Paul's rhetorical questions regarding the blood and body of Christ occur within the context of an admonition to the Corinthians to avoid buying meat known to have been offered to pagan gods. Eating meat from such sacrifices, even if one does not believe that the gods are real, constitutes a "participation" with them. Just as ancient Israel could have no relationship with any gods but the God of the covenant, so Christians may not "participate" with anyone but Christ. They do this in the sharing of the cup of blessing and the breaking of the bread. This common participation creates a single body, whose members are responsible for each other and therefore should show proper concern for each other.

Jesus' claim to be "the living bread that came down from heaven" occurs within a scene that begins with a question about believing that Jesus has been sent by God. The crowd has asked for a sign ("What can you do?" [6:30]), like the sign of the manna given in the desert. Jesus responds that he himself is the true bread from heaven. Just as the manna nourished the people, Jesus says, so he, who is the true bread from heaven, will nourish those who can accept it. When they eat Jesus' flesh they will be receiving him, establishing or strengthening a mutual indwelling. Through this mutual "abiding" Jesus shares his own eternal life with the recipient.

Reflecting on the Word

She was young. But she remembers that dry day like it was yesterday. "This is ridiculous. How can he give us his flesh to eat?" She listens to the shouting. She sits outside the synagogue. As a woman, she's not permitted to enter. But she can hear them clearly. This is Jesus of Nazareth they are yelling at; Jesus, whose love has transformed her; Jesus, whose words burn like a fire inside of her. Can they not see what he is offering? "Bread of Life—who does he think he is? We know his father from Nazareth. He's a carpenter's son." The door opens and the leaders stomp their feet into the dust of the dry ground and walk away.

She wants to shout after them in the distance, "You never really heard him," but again she hears voices at the doorway, not so loud, but irritated: "This saying is hard; who can accept it? The Bread of Life! How can he say he is the Bread of Life?" Those who had walked closely with him began to walk away also. She knew these ones. She had eaten with them. They were his own. "We will no longer go with him . . . I am going home." She is grief-stricken. She shouts, "How can you leave him? His words are Spirit and life!" "Ah, woman, you are young. Go home also."

The door opens a third time and he comes out, full of sorrow. "Will you also leave me?" Peter says the words she will remember all her life. She has told them to her children and her children's children. Now as her community is struggling with betrayal and desertion, she shares what Peter said: "Master, to whom shall we go? You have the words of eternal life."

Rain began to fall on the dry soil, watering the earth.

Consider/Discuss

❖ Is this teaching of Jesus too hard? Doubt tastes like dust in the mouth. Faith refreshes like the rain. As many walk away, how can we express what Jesus in the Eucharist means to us? How can we describe the taste of glory that comes as we open our hands to receive him?

❖ We believe that the Eucharist is the sacrament of unity in the Church. Yet like this unnamed young woman of the first century, some sit at the peripheries, some voices are not heard, some are rendered invisible. How can we be more conscientious in our sharing, our *koinonia*, in bringing in those at the edges, to solidify the Body of Christ?

Living and Praying with the Word

Lord, you are the Bread of Life. We have tasted your manna. We have been touched by your presence. You unite us so that together we can abide in you. At the same time, we grieve for those who walk away. We love them. How can they go? Even the angels weep.

Holy Spirit, bubble up within us so that we bring your life to the world in which we live.

TWELFTH SUNDAY IN ORDINARY TIME

Today's Focus: Ordinary Time, Extraordinary Courage

*The Spirit can grant us courage every day to accomplish
more than we think we are capable of on our own. Extraordinary!*

FIRST READING
Jeremiah 20:10–13

Jeremiah said:
"I hear the whisperings of many:
'Terror on every side!
Denounce! let us denounce him!'
All those who were my friends
are on the watch for any misstep of mine.
'Perhaps he will be trapped; then we can prevail,
and take our vengeance on him.'
But the LORD is with me, like a mighty champion:
my persecutors will stumble, they will not triumph.
In their failure they will be put to utter shame,
to lasting, unforgettable confusion.
O LORD of hosts, you who test the just,
who probe mind and heart,
let me witness the vengeance you take on them,
for to you I have entrusted my cause.
Sing to the LORD,
praise the LORD,
for he has rescued the life of the poor
from the power of the wicked!"

PSALM RESPONSE
Psalm 69:14c

Lord, in your great love, answer me.

SECOND READING
Romans 5:12–15

Brothers and sisters: Through one man sin entered the world, and through sin, death, and thus death came to all men, inasmuch as all sinned—for up to the time of the law, sin was in the world, though sin is not accounted when there is no law. But death reigned from Adam to Moses, even over those who did not sin after the pattern of the trespass of Adam, who is the type of the one who was to come.

But the gift is not like the transgression. For if by the transgression of the one the many died, how much more did the grace of God and the gracious gift of the one man Jesus Christ overflow for the many.

Jesus said to the Twelve: "Fear no one. Nothing is concealed that will not be revealed, nor secret that will not be known. What I say to you in the darkness, speak in the light; what you hear whispered, proclaim on the housetops. And do not be afraid of those who kill the body but cannot kill the soul; rather, be afraid of the one who can destroy both soul and body in Gehenna. Are not two sparrows sold for a small coin? Yet not one of them falls to the ground without your Father's knowledge. Even all the hairs of your head are counted. So do not be afraid; you are worth more than many sparrows. Everyone who acknowledges me before others I will acknowledge before my heavenly Father. But whoever denies me before others, I will deny before my heavenly Father."

Understanding the Word

Just prior to this week's reading, Jeremiah has complained to God that God has "seduced" him—drawn him into a difficult mission of proclaiming God's word of judgment to a faithless and violent people. In the face of rejection, the prophet has tried to walk away from his calling, but like a fire burning in his heart, the word of God demands to be heard (20:7–9). Yet despite danger and even the treachery of friends, Jeremiah ultimately trusts that God will defend him "like a mighty champion" because he is doing God's work. In Jeremiah we see both the depths of suffering in relationship with God and the heights of trust and hope despite it all.

Paul explains to the Romans how the death of Christ has saved humanity from death and sin. Paul understands sin here not as a human act of the breaking of covenant commands ("law"), but as a malevolent, intractable power that entered the world through human disobedience. This power, which spread through all Adam's descendants, brought with it death. Thus all people, even those who were not under the covenant obligations to God, sinned, even if they were not breaking "the law" (Torah). Thus death "reigned" over all. The obedience of Christ ends this reign by flooding humanity with grace, a gift from God to deliver the descendants of Adam from the bondage of sin and its "wages" of death (6:23).

As Jesus sends the Twelve out to proclaim the kingdom, he warns them of opposition. This warning shades into predictions of what the early church will face after Easter. Out of fear for their lives and livelihoods, they will be tempted to withdraw from the task of proclaiming the gospel, or even to deny Christ. Yet this is what they are being formed to do: to proclaim publicly what they are learning from and about Jesus. In the face of fear, they must remember not only that God cares for them, but also that even physical death is to be preferred to the spiritual death that would follow from apostasy or abandoning the call to proclaim the gospel.

Reflecting on the Word

The prophet Jeremiah captures my imagination. He is called to speak the word of the Lord at a tender age: "I am too young," he objects. Repeatedly he resists his call to preach: "I try to hold it in, but it burns like fire in my heart, imprisoned in my bones." He is brutally honest before God. He is also starkly straightforward with kings. His forthrightness gets him into trouble: he's thrown into the muck of a cistern, imprisoned in the stocks, mocked and made fun of, and ultimately hauled off to Egypt to end his life where he doesn't want to be.

Do you ever wonder if Jeremiah wished that he could simply be an ordinary guy? God's call was sometimes just too challenging. "You duped me, LORD," he says, "and I let myself be duped." He may have prayed today's psalm: "Rescue me from the mire, and do not let me sink . . . for it is on your account that I bear insult." Though he is smacked down over and over, Jeremiah keeps popping back up again.

In today's Gospel, Jesus warns the disciples of that same kind of opposition. He knows that the muck is real. But he says time after time, "Do not be afraid . . . Even the hairs of your head are counted." What are we to be afraid of? Not physical death, but spiritual cowardice.

Fortitude is one of the gifts of the Holy Spirit. There may be times when life calls for swashbuckling bravado. But more often, the Divine Nudge encourages us to roll out of bed with an "it doesn't matter how you feel today, just get up and keep going" kind of everyday courage. Sainthood is in the small things. Heroic virtue grows through giving God one obedient yes at a time.

Consider/Discuss

❖ Fear is part of life. We get burned and we grow cautious. Yet Jesus says repeatedly, "Do not be afraid." In what part of our lives do we need Holy Spirit fortitude so that we can keep rising back up to do what we are called to do, in spite of our fear or weakness?

❖ The saints and prophets were brutally honest in their relationship with God. Are you willing to yell at God, to pour out your heart in prayer and be forthright with the Creator of the universe? Why or why not? What does that look like?

Living and Praying with the Word

Lord, sometimes I'd rather stay in bed and take life easy. Yet Jeremiah and the saints and you yourself show me another way—to keep giving and loving and preaching even when it is personally challenging. Guide my discernment in the balance between self-care and self-gift. I seek you. I offer myself to you. Help me to trust you to use me according to your best lights, for you watch over even the hairs of my head. Cast out my fear and keep me close to you.

THIRTEENTH SUNDAY IN ORDINARY TIME

Today's Focus: A Season of Generosity

Made in the image of God, baptized into the Body of Christ, we are called upon to die to ourselves so that God's generous love might be shared.

FIRST READING *2 Kings 4:8–11, 14–16a*

One day Elisha came to Shunem, where there was a woman of influence, who urged him to dine with her. Afterward, whenever he passed by, he used to stop there to dine. So she said to her husband, "I know that Elisha is a holy man of God. Since he visits us often, let us arrange a little room on the roof and furnish it for him with a bed, table, chair, and lamp, so that when he comes to us he can stay there." Sometime later Elisha arrived and stayed in the room overnight.

Later Elisha asked, "Can something be done for her?" His servant Gehazi answered, "Yes! She has no son, and her husband is getting on in years." Elisha said, "Call her." When the woman had been called and stood at the door, Elisha promised, "This time next year you will be fondling a baby son."

PSALM RESPONSE *Psalm 89:2a*

For ever I will sing the goodness of the Lord.

SECOND READING *Romans 6:3–4, 8–11*

Brothers and sisters: Are you unaware that we who were baptized into Christ Jesus were baptized into his death? We were indeed buried with him through baptism into death, so that, just as Christ was raised from the dead by the glory of the Father, we too might live in newness of life.

If, then, we have died with Christ, we believe that we shall also live with him. We know that Christ, raised from the dead, dies no more; death no longer has power over him. As to his death, he died to sin once and for all; as to his life, he lives for God. Consequently, you too must think of yourselves as dead to sin and living for God in Christ Jesus.

Jesus said to his apostles: "Whoever loves father or mother more than me is not worthy of me, and whoever loves son or daughter more than me is not worthy of me; and whoever does not take up his cross and follow after me is not worthy of me. Whoever finds his life will lose it, and whoever loses his life for my sake will find it. Whoever receives you receives me, and whoever receives me receives the one who sent me. Whoever receives a prophet because he is a prophet will receive a prophet's reward, and whoever receives a righteous man because he is a righteous man will receive a righteous man's reward. And whoever gives only a cup of cold water to one of these little ones to drink because the little one is a disciple—amen, I say to you, he will surely not lose his reward."

Understanding the Word

The stories of Elisha are filled with examples of God saving people in distress. Through the young prophet God purifies water for one city; fills all the empty vessels of a poor widow with oil, saving her from creditors; cures a stew that has been poisoned; heals a foreigner of leprosy. Gratitude to the prophet was thus really gratitude to God. In the reading we see also the prophet's gratitude, expressed through the promise of a child for an elderly couple. The woman does indeed have a son (who will fall ill, die, and be raised by the prophet), once again showing that the God of Israel is a God a life.

Paul has been arguing that the death of Christ brought an end to the reign of sin and death. How does this work? When one is in bondage to someone, Paul says, that bondage naturally ends when we die (6:7). In the same way, if we die with Christ in baptism we are freed from bondage to sin. We are also raised with him and are freed from the power of sin and death. Paul's larger point here is ethical: because Christians have died to sin, and are no longer under its power, they must stop acting as if they were. They must start living for God, not continuing to serve sin.

Jesus warns his disciples that the gospel will not be received in all quarters and that he will prove, both during and after his earthly life, to be a cause of division. His followers should know that being his disciple will be the hardest thing they have ever had to do, requiring more of them than they imagine: losing family, even their lives. They will have to "take up their crosses," the instrument of their deaths. Yet this death will lead to life—a promise only those who have faith in Jesus can believe. Even those who receive the one who proclaims the gospel will gain their reward. Both those who sacrifice for Jesus and those who receive them are assured that their efforts will redound to them in the end.

Reflecting on the Word

It might seem to be a funny time to be talking about death. Right now, much of the northern temperate region is in full flower: roses are blooming, peach trees are setting fruit, and rivers are flowing. Thinking about death belongs to those dark and gloomy days in mid-January when it is so dreary.

But Jesus talks about losing our lives. And it is June: bright, happy, generous June. How are we to make sense of that paradox? Losing life, when we are surrounded by so much life?

Perhaps, though, life is made up of small deaths. To die to self, to make ourselves do what we don't really want to do, actually seems easier in June. It is an almost playfully die-to-self time, time to take the hand of a child and go look at the grasshoppers when you know that the guests are about to pull into the driveway and the dishes are not washed; time to call an elderly friend when it will use up an hour of your life; time to say yes to an adult son or daughter even when it may cost a lot.

June is the time to strive for the greater, the more expansive, the honorable. The way that we choose to live is the way that we will die—with our hands wide open or with our fists tightly closed. Jesus' call to generosity, to give ourselves away, can blossom because of the buoyancy breaking all around us. How can we not be more conscientious today when the bees are working so hard to make honey? Give a cup of water to a little one? Certainly. Take up the cross, Jesus? Surely. Die to sin, St. Paul? Indubitably. It is June. Lord, your glory and your grace are here. We can do that!

Consider/Discuss

❖ God's bounty is all around us. What can we do today to be more generous?

❖ When was the last time that you looked at the grasshoppers? The clouds? The birds in a tree? Take a moment and do something "unimportant" with someone you love.

Living and Praying with the Word

Creator God, sometimes we forget how buoyant your salvation is. Grace us today with time to savor all that you have given us. Sometimes we walk on by something that is so beautiful. Thank you for the stars. Thank you for babies' toenails. Thank you for the smile on my friend's face. Thank you, most of all, for being our lavish God.

FOURTEENTH SUNDAY IN ORDINARY TIME

Today's Focus: Burdens Borne by Love

Love can make our burdens lighter. When we share the burdens of life with Christ in our fellow disciples, burdens are easier to bear.

FIRST READING   *Zechariah 9:9–10*

Thus says the LORD:
    Rejoice heartily, O daughter Zion,
      shout for joy, O daughter Jerusalem!
See, your king shall come to you;
      a just savior is he,
meek, and riding on an ass,
      on a colt, the foal of an ass.
He shall banish the chariot from Ephraim,
      and the horse from Jerusalem;
the warrior's bow shall be banished,
      and he shall proclaim peace to the nations.
His dominion shall be from sea to sea,
      and from the River to the ends of the earth.

PSALM RESPONSE   *Psalm 145:1*

I will praise your name for ever, my king and my God.

SECOND READING   *Romans 8:9, 11–13*

Brothers and sisters: You are not in the flesh; on the contrary, you are in the spirit, if only the Spirit of God dwells in you. Whoever does not have the Spirit of Christ does not belong to him. If the Spirit of the one who raised Jesus from the dead dwells in you, the one who raised Christ from the dead will give life to your mortal bodies also, through his Spirit that dwells in you. Consequently, brothers and sisters, we are not debtors to the flesh, to live according to the flesh. For if you live according to the flesh, you will die, but if by the Spirit you put to death the deeds of the body, you will live.

At that time Jesus exclaimed: "I give praise to you, Father, Lord of heaven and earth, for although you have hidden these things from the wise and the learned you have revealed them to little ones. Yes, Father, such has been your gracious will. All things have been handed over to me by my Father. No one knows the Son except the Father, and no one knows the Father except the Son and anyone to whom the Son wishes to reveal him.

"Come to me, all you who labor and are burdened, and I will give you rest. Take my yoke upon you and learn from me, for I am meek and humble of heart; and you will find rest for yourselves. For my yoke is easy, and my burden light."

Understanding the Word

In this salvation oracle to the post-exilic community, the identity of the royal figure is unstated, but he fulfills the expectations of many prophets of the ideal Davidic king. Donkeys were regularly associated with royal figures in the ancient Near East and the fact that he arrives on a donkey rather than on a horse, with all the military connotations of that animal, suggests this "just savior" will be humble and peaceful. He ends warfare in both the former kingdom of Israel (Ephraim) and in Jerusalem. The mention of Israel, destroyed centuries before the oracle was probably uttered, points toward the divine will to bring all of God's people, currently scattered around the world, back to the land.

Paul continues his exploration of how the death of Christ has released those in bondage to sin. He now introduces the idea of flesh versus spirit. Flesh refers to that aspect of the human person that opposes God, that remains under the thumb of sin and inclined toward it. For the baptized, this "flesh" constitutes the "old self," which is opposed to the spirit, that aspect of the human person that is not under the reign of sin but under the reign of the Spirit of God in Christ. He reminds the Romans that those in whom the Spirit dwells are no longer under the bondage of sin and therefore are not "debtors to the flesh."

Jesus has just proclaimed that Chorazin, Bethsaida, and Capernaum will face judgment for not repenting after witnessing his mighty deeds; they have not recognized who Jesus is and what he is about. They represent "the wise and the learned," whose sophistication prevents them from accepting Jesus and his message. Only the "little ones," capable of "childlike" faith, are able to see that Jesus does the work of the Father and reveals him. Those willing to take on the yoke of discipleship will discover it to be a source of refreshment, not only because of the subject matter (God), but also because their teacher (who reveals God) is gentle and kind to those who wish to learn from him.

Reflecting on the Word

I lie in bed half awake and half asleep, thinking about "my yoke is easy and my burden is light." In this blurred mental state, scenes flash through my head.

The burden is light? Ponderous chords from the musical *Les Misérables* say not. Prisoners sweat in the sun. Their backs are hopelessly bent. How can the yoke be easy? Oppression and misery and pain; there is so much bondage in the world.

In the darkness behind my eyelids, my mind zooms to yesterday. I see my friend. I recall the hospital bed in her living room: a time she will never forget. Her husband died in that bed while they were saying the rosary.

I see a young mother and her six-month-old son. Rocking and feeding, playing and interacting—all day and all night, she is yoked to that boy. Babies are hard work.

So why are some yokes easier to bear? There was a deep love between my friend and her dying husband. There was warmth in my daughter-in-law's eyes yesterday when she looked into the eyes of my grandson. We will do difficult things for love. Love makes the burden light.

Sin makes the burden heavy. We cannot act as though everything is not so bad after all. Oppression is wrong. Misery harms. Prisoners matter. We carry the burdens of others—not nameless faces in a movie, but the needy folks who surround us. Yet the joy of discipleship is that we do not carry that weight alone.

Now I am ready to wake up. The love of this world is strong. The burden of the world is heavy. This is a paradox bigger than I can shoulder. I get out of bed, grateful that this world has a Savior, and more grateful that it is not me.

Consider/Discuss

❖ God is the one who wants to save us, to carry our burdens, to set us free. How do we resist that? How do we burden ourselves down?

❖ The joy of love makes life lighter. Who has helped you to carry your cross?

Living and Praying with the Word

Jesus, you ask us to be childlike, to trust you to carry our burdens. Love has lifted us up. Sin has torn us down. You know that we have experienced both. Lord, give us the strength this day to do all that we can today for whomever you put in our path. We are willing to work hard to make a difference in this world, but you are going to have to carry it, for we cannot. Come, Savior of the world, come!

FIFTEENTH SUNDAY IN ORDINARY TIME

Today's Focus: Sowing Seed—Attentively

Anyone who plants or grows anything knows how much is dependent on the quality of the soil. Let us—sowers of the seed of God's word— be attentive to the soil!

FIRST READING
Isaiah 55:10–11

Thus says the LORD:
Just as from the heavens
   the rain and snow come down
and do not return there
   till they have watered the earth,
   making it fertile and fruitful,
giving seed to the one who sows
   and bread to the one who eats,
so shall my word be
   that goes forth from my mouth;
my word shall not return to me void,
   but shall do my will,
   achieving the end for which I sent it.

PSALM RESPONSE
Luke 8:8

The seed that falls on good ground will yield a fruitful harvest.

SECOND READING
Romans 8:18–23

Brothers and sisters: I consider that the sufferings of this present time are as nothing compared with the glory to be revealed for us. For creation awaits with eager expectation the revelation of the children of God; for creation was made subject to futility, not of its own accord but because of the one who subjected it, in hope that creation itself would be set free from slavery to corruption and share in the glorious freedom of the children of God. We know that all creation is groaning in labor pains even until now; and not only that, but we ourselves, who have the firstfruits of the Spirit, we also groan within ourselves as we wait for adoption, the redemption of our bodies.

In the shorter form of the reading, the passages in brackets are omitted.

On that day, Jesus went out of the house and sat down by the sea. Such large crowds gathered around him that he got into a boat and sat down, and the whole crowd stood along the shore. And he spoke to them at length in parables, saying: "A sower went out to sow. And as he sowed, some seed fell on the path, and birds came and ate it up. Some fell on rocky ground, where it had little soil. It sprang up at once because the soil was not deep, and when the sun rose it was scorched, and it withered for lack of roots. Some seed fell among thorns, and the thorns grew up and choked it. But some seed fell on rich soil, and produced fruit, a hundred or sixty or thirtyfold. Whoever has ears ought to hear."

[The disciples approached him and said, "Why do you speak to them in parables?" He said to them in reply, "Because knowledge of the mysteries of the kingdom of heaven has been granted to you, but to them it has not been granted. To anyone who has, more will be given and he will grow rich; from anyone who has not, even what he has will be taken away. This is why I speak to them in parables, because

they look but do not see and hear but do not listen or understand.

Isaiah's prophecy is fulfilled in them, which says:
You shall indeed hear but not understand,
  you shall indeed look but never see.
Gross is the heart of this people,
  they will hardly hear with their ears,
  they have closed their eyes,
  lest they see with their eyes
  and hear with their ears
and understand with their hearts and be converted,
  and I heal them.

"But blessed are your eyes, because they see, and your ears, because they hear. Amen, I say to you, many prophets and righteous people longed to see what you see but did not see it, and to hear what you hear but did not hear it.

"Hear then the parable of the sower. The seed sown on the path is the one who hears the word of the kingdom without understanding it, and the evil one comes and steals away what was sown in his heart. The seed sown on rocky ground is the one who hears the word and receives it at once with joy. But he has no root and lasts only for a time. When some tribulation or persecution comes because of the word, he immediately falls away. The seed sown among thorns is the one who hears the word, but then worldly anxiety and the lure of riches choke the word and it bears no fruit. But the seed sown on rich soil is the one who hears the word and understands it, who indeed bears fruit and yields a hundred or sixty or thirtyfold."]

Understanding the Word

The first reading concludes chapters 40–55 of Isaiah, most of which come from the end of the exilic period. This section of Isaiah, which focuses on God's intention to restore a people under judgment, begins with attention to God's "word" as sure and effective (40:5, 8). What God announces will happen simply because it is the word of God. Now God promises that repentant sinners will find mercy because, unlike human beings, God does not nurse grudges but is instead "generous in forgiving" (55:7). Those who cannot believe in God's mercy or in the divine intention to save are exhorted to trust in the always-efficacious word of God.

Continuing his line of argument from the last couple of weeks, Paul reflects on what it means to have died with Christ. Not only have the baptized, now "in Christ," been released from slavery to sin and death, they have also been adopted as God's children and heirs along with Christ. But this inheritance, which is their glorification, comes with a price, suffering (8:14–17), which is nevertheless a small price to pay for what awaits them. And not only them, but all of creation, which right now is also subject to death. Just as "the children of God," who in their physical bodies share in the corruption of the created world, will one day experience the "redemption of our bodies," so too will all creation be redeemed.

Jesus' parable describes the three classic obstacles to doing the will of God: the evil one, who prevents the word from being truly heard; the flesh, that part of the human person that will abandon God's will if it means struggle or trouble; and the world, those aspects of human society that are opposed to God, yet appealing to the flesh. Jesus speaks in enigmatic parables because the kingdom is only for those who are willing to put in the time and struggle to understand its proclamation, which cannot be appreciated on a single, simple hearing. The medium, then, is the message: the kingdom of God, in which the will of God is known and lived, is for those who are willing to sacrifice to enter it. This has been Jesus' message from the beginning.

Reflecting on the Word

Farming has changed. Imagine, just for a moment, how Jesus might have told this parable differently today:

A sower went out to sow. The seed was the Word of God, precious and life-giving, too good to be scattered about without careful preparation. Therefore, the Sower paid careful attention to the soil: where it was rocky, he dug out the rocks; where it was too acidic or too alkaline, he adjusted the pH. Late in the autumn, he added three inches of manure and planted a cover crop, which he then turned under in early March. When planting season came, he set the seeds one by one in rows spaced six inches apart. Where the seeds dropped on the rocky path, he placed them back into the rich loam. He sent the sun to shine. He watered the seeds carefully. He asked the Holy Spirit to breathe on them each day. And before the weeds got too big, he hoed the soil, being careful not to damage the roots of the Word of God plants. With such personal care, the seeds grew tall and bore fruit, a hundred-fold to the glory of God.

What do you think? In Jesus' original version, the message is that our receptivity to the Word of God is what matters. In the modern version, as God's hands, we share in sowing the Word of God. Do we "scatter the Word of God" without attending to the soil? As much devotion needs to go into what is being received as to what we are saying. Sometimes we have to be willing to sacrifice our own assumptions to nurture the growth of others. More nourishment, a little less acidic, a bit of weeding . . . the care with which we plant the Word of God: it matters.

Consider/Discuss

❖ We cannot make seeds grow; that is God's job. But we can attend to the conditions within which growth is most likely to occur. What have you yourself seen? What "soil conditions" have most helped your faith to grow?

❖ The reign of God is worth our best efforts. Yet throughout Christian history, because of this parable, "they're not good soil" has excused ministry that has not borne fruit. (To be fair, some soil is so acidic that nothing will grow.) Rather than pointing a finger at others' unreceptivity, how can we ourselves become more adept at preparing soil?

Living and Praying with the Word

Lord, you give us rain from heaven to water the earth. Your showers keep the earth soft. You want your word to bear fruit; you want it to achieve what you sent it for. We, in turn, want to serve you and your Word. Teach us what we need to know so that the words that we say will be living and effective. Holy Spirit, come to the aid of our weakness so that we bear fruit that will last.

SIXTEENTH SUNDAY IN ORDINARY TIME

Today's Focus: Who Knows?

---

*We often do not know what we do not know when it comes
to making judgments about others. God alone knows us and others,
so we rely on God's vision, not our own.*

FIRST READING

Wisdom 12:13, 16–19

There is no god besides you who have the care of all,
  that you need show you have not unjustly condemned.
For your might is the source of justice;
  your mastery over all things makes you lenient to all.
For you show your might when the perfection of your power is disbelieved;
  and in those who know you, you rebuke temerity.
But though you are master of might, you judge with clemency,
  and with much lenience you govern us;
  for power, whenever you will, attends you.
And you taught your people, by these deeds,
  that those who are just must be kind;
and you gave your children good ground for hope
  that you would permit repentance for their sins.

PSALM RESPONSE

Psalm 86:5a

Lord, you are good and forgiving.

SECOND READING

Romans 8:26–27

Brothers and sisters: The Spirit comes to the aid of our weakness; for we do not know how to pray as we ought, but the Spirit himself intercedes with inexpressible groanings. And the one who searches hearts knows what is the intention of the Spirit, because he intercedes for the holy ones according to God's will.

In the shorter form of the reading, the passages in brackets are omitted.

Jesus proposed another parable to the crowds, saying: "The kingdom of heaven may be likened to a man who sowed good seed in his field. While everyone was asleep his enemy came and sowed weeds all through the wheat, and then went off. When the crop grew and bore fruit, the weeds appeared as well. The slaves of the householder came to him and said, 'Master, did you not sow good seed in your field? Where have the weeds come from?' He answered, 'An enemy has done this.' His slaves said to him, 'Do you want us to go and pull them up?' He replied, 'No, if you pull up the weeds you might uproot the wheat along with them. Let them grow together until harvest; then at harvest time I will say to the harvesters, "First collect the weeds and tie them in bundles for burning; but gather the wheat into my barn." ' "

[He proposed another parable to them. "The kingdom of heaven is like a mustard seed that a person took and sowed in a field. It is the smallest of all the seeds, yet when full-grown it is the largest of plants. It becomes a large bush, and the 'birds of the sky come and dwell in its branches.' "

He spoke to them another parable. "The kingdom of heaven is like yeast that a woman took and mixed with three measures of wheat flour until the whole batch was leavened."

All these things Jesus spoke to the crowds in parables. He spoke to them only in parables, to fulfill what had been said through the prophet:

I will open my mouth in parables,
I will announce what has lain hidden from the foundation of the world.

Then, dismissing the crowds, he went into the house. His disciples approached him and said, "Explain to us the parable of the weeds in the field." He said in reply, "He who sows good seed is the Son of Man, the field is the world, the good seed the children of the kingdom. The weeds are the children of the evil one, and the enemy who sows them is the devil. The harvest is the end of the age, and the harvesters are angels. Just as weeds are collected and burned up with fire, so will it be at the end of the age. The Son of Man will send his angels, and they will collect out of his kingdom all who cause others to sin and all evildoers. They will throw them into the fiery furnace, where there will be wailing and grinding of teeth. Then the righteous will shine like the sun in the kingdom of their Father. Whoever has ears ought to hear."]

Understanding the Word

Because of God's unparalleled and unchallenged power, the wicked are given opportunity to repent; divine forgiveness is not coerced ("Neither out of fear for anyone did you grant release for their sins" [Wisdom 12:11]). God's sovereign power ensures that God does not need to explain or justify either condemnation or forgiveness, and is "lenient to all." There is no divine ego at stake, giving God freedom to act generously. This divine mercy is a lesson to God's people, who learn that God's justice is not opposed to kindness, but actually manifests itself in kindness. God's absolutely free justice is ground for hope in God's mercy.

Paul reminds the Romans that through the Spirit they have been adopted as God's children and now "groan within ourselves as we wait for adoption, the redemption of our bodies" (Romans 8:23). The guarantee of this hope is the gift of the Spirit, who not only leads and transforms the faithful, but also helps them pray. Human beings, as the agents of God's redemption of all of creation, are called to intercede with God, but as they are (for the time being) subject to corruption and death, they are weak and do not know exactly how to intercede. The Spirit dwelling in each believer makes up for this weakness by expressing the groaning of creation and "the holy ones," and is heard by God.

Three parables illustrate the kingdom of heaven. At least on this side of eternity, it is a mix of the good and the bad. Readers have taken the weeds and the wheat to represent either individuals or the tendencies within each heart. In the first case, the warning is to let God sort out the sinners from the saints; judgment is God's prerogative (Matthew 7:1–5). In the second case, the assurance is that while there are within us both the good and the bad, God is patient and, in God's way, removes that which needs to be removed. The other two parables reflect the biblical insistence that God's greatest works have small, hidden, unlikely beginnings. The kingdom (God) works in ways that we often cannot appreciate.

Reflecting on the Word

It was early spring. The master gardener was really busy. A kind friend offered to weed her perennial garden while the weeds were still small. She was very grateful. He was an expert on tulips. He knew what tulip leaves looked like. So he diligently weeded that garden clean. When he was done, the tulip leaves proudly stood out from the bare soil that surrounded them. As spring unfolded in the garden, though, there were no forget-me-nots. The coreopsis was gone. There were no more buttercups. The tulips grew strong and died back. The next year, that same friend offered to help. "Let me do the weeding," the master gardener said.

We really don't know what we don't know. Sometimes we assume that we know ourselves and others. The research, however, reveals that we create stories in our minds based on partial pieces of information. We do not have all the evidence on anything. If you and I had the job of weeding out the good and the bad in a group of people, we may see the acts that a person does and judge accordingly. But moral theologians tell us that moral blame is based on act, circumstance, and intention. We can and must judge acts as morally wrong or right, but we do not have enough information to pass further judgment on a person. Only God knows the circumstance and intentions behind an act.

Why doesn't God ask us to do the weeding? Little leaves that come up in early spring do not look like the flowers they will be when they are mature. We would often pluck out the wrong things if it were up to us. We don't know what we don't know. Jesus offers today's parable so that we will practice mercy, not judgment.

"Let me do the weeding," the Master Gardener says.

Consider/Discuss

❖ The most beautiful flower in a garden may look like a dead stick in early spring. Think back to some of the ugly things you may have done in your life. How has God helped you to grow so that you mature and blossom?

❖ We tell stories about people in our minds. Have you ever had an "aha!" moment when you've said, "How could I have been so wrong about that person?"

Living and Praying with the Word

Good Gardener of us all, sometimes we look just like dead sticks or tiny weeds. But you have a vision of what we can become. Affirm our strengths. Challenge our weaknesses. Never let us stop growing. And today, assist us in revising our story about someone. Reveal to us where we are impatient or unmerciful or unkind or uncharitable, for we want to see others as you do.

SEVENTEENTH SUNDAY IN ORDINARY TIME

Today's Focus: What Really Matters?

What "pearl of great price" does God have in store for you today? It most likely isn't a winning lottery ticket or an actual pearl, but an opportunity to bring the reign of God into the world.

FIRST READING
1 Kings 3:5, 7–12

The LORD appeared to Solomon in a dream at night. God said, "Ask something of me and I will give it to you." Solomon answered: "O LORD, my God, you have made me, your servant, king to succeed my father David; but I am a mere youth, not knowing at all how to act. I serve you in the midst of the people whom you have chosen, a people so vast that it cannot be numbered or counted. Give your servant, therefore, an understanding heart to judge your people and to distinguish right from wrong. For who is able to govern this vast people of yours?"

The LORD was pleased that Solomon made this request. So God said to him: "Because you have asked for this—not for a long life for yourself, nor for riches, nor for the life of your enemies, but for understanding so that you may know what is right—I do as you requested. I give you a heart so wise and understanding that there has never been anyone like you up to now, and after you there will come no one to equal you."

PSALM RESPONSE
Psalm119:97a

Lord, I love your commands.

SECOND READING
Romans 8:28–30

Brothers and sisters: We know that all things work for good for those who love God, who are called according to his purpose. For those he foreknew he also predestined to be conformed to the image of his Son, so that he might be the firstborn among many brothers and sisters. And those he predestined he also called; and those he called he also justified; and those he justified he also glorified.

In the shorter form of the reading, the passages in brackets are omitted.

Jesus said to his disciples: "The kingdom of heaven is like a treasure buried in a field, which a person finds and hides again, and out of joy goes and sells all that he has and buys that field. Again, the kingdom of heaven is like a merchant searching for fine pearls. When he finds a pearl of great price, he goes and sells all that he has and buys it. [Again, the kingdom of heaven is like a net thrown into the sea, which collects fish of every kind. When it is full they haul it ashore and sit down to put what is good into buckets. What is bad they throw away. Thus it will be at the end of the age. The angels will go out and separate the wicked from the righteous and throw them into the fiery furnace, where there will be wailing and grinding of teeth.

"Do you understand all these things?" They answered, "Yes." And he replied, "Then every scribe who has been instructed in the kingdom of heaven is like the head of a household who brings from his storeroom both the new and the old."]

Understanding the Word

King Solomon is known in the tradition for having unparalleled wisdom. The Bible affirms that wisdom comes from God, it is not a human creation. Accordingly, Solomon became wise because he asked for the divine gift of wisdom. God, who might have expected a human king to grasp for wealth or long life, instead receives a request from Solomon for the wisdom to rule justly. Nothing could be more pleasing to the divine will than a desire to serve God and God's people well and with integrity. Thus God readily accedes to Solomon's pious request. (And because Solomon did not ask for it, God throws in wealth and the promise of long life.)

Paul has been writing to the Romans about the hope of glory they have as adopted children of God in Christ. This destiny has been part of the divine plan from the beginning, and is achieved through conformity to Christ, the exemplary human being. Those who are called to this glory are first justified, the divine accomplishment in Christ that has been the subject of much of the earlier part of the letter. The point of this short section is to emphasize that God has had things securely in hand from the beginning. All things work for good for those who respond to the divine call to be conformed to Christ, and thus justified, one day glorified.

Throughout Matthew's Gospel Jesus has warned that entering the kingdom of heaven is a challenging undertaking, and few persevere. Yet persevere they must. Like a great treasure or a valuable pearl, the kingdom is worth giving up everything else to "obtain." The invitation is open to everyone. Like a great net, it sweeps through the world capturing everyone. Only those who refuse to conform their lives to it will find themselves cast out. The kingdom is a gift but, paradoxically, one that comes at a price. Those who understand this are able to accept both his "new" teaching and recognize that it is a reflection of the "old" teaching of the law and prophets (Matthew 5:17–20).

Reflecting on the Word

What does it mean to you, on this day, to hear Jesus say to sell all that you have for the kingdom of heaven? Does it might mean that you empty your bank account, give your resources to the poor, and go become a missionary in a far-off place? Does it mean that you once more offer breakfast (kindly) to an unappreciative teenager when every bone in your body wants to do otherwise? Does it might mean that you put all your cans of green beans and crushed pineapple into a box and drive down to the St. Vincent DePaul Center and leave it on their doorstep before they open?

Not as a pious platitude, but in a concrete-and-practical-everyday-sort-of-way, what does "sell all you have for the kingdom of heaven" actually mean? I am guessing, since you are reading this reflection on a hot day at the end of July (when you could be doing so many other things), that this is a question that matters to you.

For that's what it boils down to, doesn't it: What matters? Jesus calls us to be single-minded about what matters. If you find a treasure in a field, buy the field; if you find a pearl of great price, buy the pearl. Distractions swirl around us; clutter kills clarity. Focus clarifies. Single-mindedness simplifies. Figure out what matters. Solomon asked God for a listening heart so that he could discern carefully. We ask for that, too. Before we even get out of bed in the morning, we pray, "Lord, make it clear what matters today." Then in the power of the Holy Spirit, when you discover today's treasure, with unstinting resolve, go for it! Lay down your life, in matters great and small. Passionately. Totally. For the glory of God.

Consider/Discuss

❖ The morning offering is a prayer in which we give God our upcoming day so that we are conformed into the image of Christ. What most richly brings about our daily transformation?

❖ Where is the clutter? Look at time, thoughts, emotions, activities, possessions, relationships. What can you clean today?

Living and Praying with the Word

Holy Spirit, come and rule the ordinary days of our lives. Give us the grace of discernment to see what really matters. We want to follow where you guide us. Transform our clutter into focus. We don't always see clearly, but in our heart of hearts, we want to follow you wholeheartedly. Wonderful are your ways! Show us. Lead us. Transform us to be the people you want us to be.

EIGHTEENTH SUNDAY IN ORDINARY TIME

Today's Focus: Waiting in Joyful Hope

Our day-to-day lives are filled with various hungers and thirsts. Deepest among these is our hunger and thirst for God, who alone can satisfy that need.

FIRST READING

Isaiah 55:1–3

Thus says the LORD:
All you who are thirsty,
   come to the water!
You who have no money,
   come, receive grain and eat;
Come, without paying and without cost,
   drink wine and milk!
Why spend your money for what is not bread;
   your wages for what fails to satisfy?
Heed me, and you shall eat well,
   you shall delight in rich fare.
Come to me heedfully,
   listen, that you may have life.
I will renew with you the everlasting covenant,
   the benefits assured to David.

PSALM RESPONSE

Psalm 145:16

The hand of the Lord feeds us; he answers all our needs.

SECOND READING

Romans 8:35, 37–39

Brothers and sisters: What will separate us from the love of Christ? Will anguish, or distress, or persecution, or famine, or nakedness, or peril, or the sword? No, in all these things we conquer overwhelmingly through him who loved us. For I am convinced that neither death, nor life, nor angels, nor principalities, nor present things, nor future things, nor powers, nor height, nor depth, nor any other creature will be able to separate us from the love of God in Christ Jesus our Lord.

GOSPEL

Matthew 14:13–21

When Jesus heard of the death of John the Baptist, he withdrew in a boat to a deserted place by himself. The crowds heard of this and followed him on foot from their towns. When he disembarked and saw the vast crowd, his heart was moved with pity for them, and he cured their sick. When it was evening, the disciples approached him and said, "This is a deserted place and it is already late; dismiss the crowds so that they can go to the villages and buy food for themselves." Jesus said to them, "There is no need for them to go away; give them some food yourselves." But they said to him, "Five loaves and two fish are all we have here." Then he said, "Bring them here to me," and he ordered the crowds to sit down on the grass. Taking the five loaves and the two fish, and looking up to heaven, he said the blessing, broke the loaves, and gave them to the disciples, who in turn gave them to the crowds. They all ate and were satisfied, and they picked up the fragments left over—twelve wicker baskets full. Those who ate were about five thousand men, not counting women and children.

Understanding the Word

Chapters 40–55 of Isaiah, which emerged out of the late exilic period, insist that God is bringing an end to the period of judgment and will restore Israel beyond its former glory. This judgment came about because of Israel's persistent refusal to believe that God alone, and not other gods, could provide all that Israel needed. In other words, they offered to other gods worship and sacrifice and received nothing in return. Now they are being offered a chance at real bread, at true satisfaction. All that is required is trust and fidelity that God, and God alone, is the source of life for Israel.

Paul has assured the Romans that they are the recipients of God's gracious plan to bring them into conformity with the image of Christ, fulfilling their destiny to be God's adopted children and heirs with Christ to glory. Knowing this, and that "all things work for good for those who love God," they have nothing to fear. They have been baptized in Christ because of God's own plan, and God will not allow that plan to go awry. They are secure in Christ and thus in Christ's love. Absolutely nothing on earth, not angelic or other powers, not death itself can separate Christians from God. (Height and depth, as creatures, may refer to hostile forces associated with zodiacal signs.)

When Jesus hears that Herod's impulsiveness and pride have led to the death of John the Baptist, his response is to withdraw in solitude. Yet when the crowds pursue him his pity for them recalls him to ministry. This is, after all, what he has come to do. The miracle of the fish and loaves reflects the abundance of God's care and provision for the people, seen in Israel's history and often imagined as a banquet in the eschaton (end of time). God's abundant generosity is seen in the fact that they have more left over than they began with. Scholars note that the word for "fragments" here is the same as the word used in early Christian sources for the broken bread in eucharistic celebrations.

Reflecting on the Word

It's a look in the eyes—simple, trusting, innocent, almost pleading. The psalmist must have known it: "The eyes of all look hopefully to you." Do you know that look?

I recall one day when I was trimming the fat off of a ham. I opened the door to the garage with a plateful of scraps. Our dog, Heikki, sat waiting. His big brown eyes looked hopefully at me. His tail wagged. Something tasty was coming!

Another day, the smell of brownies fills the kitchen. The timer rings. Ten-year-old Samadhi dashes around the corner and her big brown eyes look hopefully at me: are they done yet? Something delicious is coming!

What about the ten thousand hungry eyes in that deserted place in the Gospel? Might they have had that same pleading, hopeful look as Jesus looked up to heaven, said the blessing and broke the loaves of bread? Something good was coming!

I remember my mom standing in the front hall at the storm door watching for family to arrive for Christmas. Her blue eyes brimmed with expectation. She waited in joyful hope. Someone beloved was arriving!

Have you seen that look? Do you have that look?

Like the people in that deserted place, we get hungry. We get thirsty. The sun is hot and the wait is long and we are not satisfied. When troubles come, sometimes we turn our eyes inward, clench our fists, and get stuck in anxiety and worry that swirls round and round inside.

In our thirst, we could instead look up, wag our tails, and dash around the corner with a look in our eyes that something more is coming. We wait in joyful hope. Someone beloved is coming!

"You open wide your hand and satisfy the desire of every living thing." We are fed, deliciously.

Consider/Discuss

❖ At our Sunday liturgy, we open wide our hands to receive Jesus in the Eucharist. What "look" do we have in our eyes at that time?

❖ We live in a culture inundated with self-absorbed anxiety. How do "being thirsty or hungry" for God and "being anxious" differ? What does our response to trouble reveal about where (and from whom) we expect to find answers?

Living and Praying with the Word

Lord, you are near to all who call upon you. You ask us to pay attention, to be aware, to come to you, source of living water. Open our clenched fists, for why should we hang on to the anxiety and worry that do not bring us life? Help us to lift our eyes to you and wait in joyful hope. You give us more than we could ever ask for: overflowing baskets full of abundance.

NINETEENTH SUNDAY IN ORDINARY TIME

Today's Focus: "Come!"

We are surrounded by the mighty power of God, who also beckons to us, summoning us with a vibrant invitation. In times of trial and storm, we need to listen carefully for that voice.

FIRST READING
1 Kings 19:9a, 11–13a

At the mountain of God, Horeb, Elijah came to a cave where he took shelter. Then the LORD said to him, "Go outside and stand on the mountain before the LORD; the LORD will be passing by." A strong and heavy wind was rending the mountains and crushing rocks before the LORD—but the LORD was not in the wind. After the wind there was an earthquake—but the LORD was not in the earthquake. After the earthquake there was fire—but the LORD was not in the fire. After the fire there was a tiny whispering sound. When he heard this, Elijah hid his face in his cloak and went and stood at the entrance of the cave.

PSALM RESPONSE
Psalm 85:8

Lord, let us see your kindness, and grant us your salvation.

SECOND READING
Romans 9:1–5

Brothers and sisters: I speak the truth in Christ, I do not lie; my conscience joins with the Holy Spirit in bearing me witness that I have great sorrow and constant anguish in my heart. For I could wish that I myself were accursed and cut off from Christ for the sake of my own people, my kindred according to the flesh. They are Israelites; theirs the adoption, the glory, the covenants, the giving of the law, the worship, and the promises; theirs the patriarchs, and from them, according to the flesh, is the Christ, who is over all, God blessed forever. Amen.

GOSPEL
Matthew 14:22–33

After he had fed the people, Jesus made the disciples get into a boat and precede him to the other side, while he dismissed the crowds. After doing so, he went up on the mountain by himself to pray. When it was evening he was there alone. Meanwhile the boat, already a few miles offshore, was being tossed about by the waves, for the wind was against it. During the fourth watch of the night, he came toward them walking on the sea. When the disciples saw him walking on the sea they were terrified. "It is a ghost," they said, and they cried out in fear. At once Jesus spoke to them, "Take courage, it is I; do not be afraid." Peter said to him in reply, "Lord, if it is you, command me to come to you on the water." He said,

"Come." Peter got out of the boat and began to walk on the water toward Jesus. But when he saw how strong the wind was he became frightened; and, beginning to sink, he cried out, "Lord, save me!" Immediately Jesus stretched out his hand and caught Peter, and said to him, "O you of little faith, why did you doubt?" After they got into the boat, the wind died down. Those who were in the boat did him homage, saying, "Truly, you are the Son of God."

Understanding the Word

After besting Jezebel's prophets, Elijah runs away to Horeb, where God appears, accusingly asking him why he is there. He responds that his life has been threatened. The command to "stand before the LORD" means to serve God; Elijah is in effect being told to get back to work. Yet before he returns to the task, God has a lesson for him. Visible phenomena that regularly accompany God are not God, who is found in silence, barely perceptible, but nonetheless present. God again asks, so why are you here? Although Elijah's role as God's prophet endangers him, God's protecting presence is with him, even when he cannot see it. He must learn to trust in it.

Paul has proclaimed that God has predestined and foreknown those who would be conformed to Christ and become heirs with him to glory. Thus a difficult question: what to make of the fact that so many Jews have not accepted that Jesus is the Messiah? To speak of the divine plan is to speak of God's history with Israel, beginning with God's "adoption" of Israel and culminating in the promised Messiah. Accordingly, they should be receiving the adoption, the inheritance, and the glory now coming to those who have been conformed to Christ through baptism. It would appear that something has gone horribly wrong with God's plan. Paul will go on to develop his argument that this does not mean that "the word of God has failed" (9:6).

The multiplication of the fish and loaves showed that in Jesus God was providing, something God regularly does in the scriptures. Today's reading, which immediately follows, features another action associated with God: salvation from chaos, often portrayed as dangerous waters. Just as in the Old Testament God proclaims that in the divine presence there is nothing to fear from chaos, so does Jesus. But it requires faith to believe that

Jesus can save from chaos. Thus it is not so much that Jesus has walked on water that causes those in the boat to exclaim that he is the Son of God, as their witness that he has saved Peter from the chaotic waters (despite his lack of faith).

Reflecting on the Word

In the Gospel, the disciples battle a headwind. The sea is rough. Their boat struggles. In the first reading, Elijah has clashed with King Ahab and Queen Jezebel and has run from their death threats. Now he experiences an earthquake and crushing rocks and violent wind. What a lot of trouble in both stories! Do you ever feel pandemonium swirling around you?

In the turbulence, Elijah hears a "silent sound." He knows the whisper of his God and comes to meet God at the entrance of the cave. From the surface of the stormy sea, Jesus says one word to Peter: "Come." Peter recognizes the call of his Master. He steps out of the boat.

"Come!" Often, we think about what that means to us. But what does this vibrant beckoning say about the reality of who our God is? The Almighty has the raw power to rock mountains. The Son has the authority to still violent seas. The Spirit hovers over creation. Yet at the core of that Triune sovereignty is the resounding call: "Come!"

We hear "Come!" in the call of the disciples. We hear it in "Let all who thirst, come!" We hear it in "The Spirit and the bride say, 'Come!' " Jesus reveals to us how deeply we are desired: "Come to me." Augustine says that our hearts are restless until they rest in God. How much more restless is God's heart for us?

God's "Come!" enfolds our entire being. We are wanted. That same divine command triggered the process of our birth—we are desired on earth. A heavenly "Come!" will set the process of our death in motion: we are sought after in heaven. No matter what, the chaos will not win. We have nothing to fear. Radiant delight surrounds us at all times.

Consider/Discuss

❖ The eternal "Come!" can be so quiet that we have to tune our spiritual senses to perceive it, for in the bedlam of life, we may miss it. What of the chaos can we "turn down" in order to hear more carefully the still small voice of our Beloved?

❖ Peter steps out of the boat after he recognizes the call of Jesus, the Master. The rest of the disciples do not. Which of the characters in the story do you identify with? Would you stay in the boat? Would you step out onto the water? Why or why not?

Living and Praying with the Word

Jesus, you summon us in prayer, "Come to me!" You beckon us when we are heavily laden. You call to us when we are afraid. You want to give us your peace. At the same time, you know that we push back. You even know why, when we do not. Lord, strengthen our spiritual powers so that we grow more sensitive to hearing you. You are restless for us. Open our hands and help us come to you.

THE ASSUMPTION OF THE BLESSED VIRGIN MARY

Today's Focus: God to the Rescue!

Like the woman in Revelation, we can find ourselves facing fear and terror. The Lord rescues us and brings us to safety and peace, surrounding us with love.

FIRST READING
Revelation 11:19a; 12:1–6a, 10ab

God's temple in heaven was opened, and the ark of his covenant could be seen in the temple.

A great sign appeared in the sky, a woman clothed with the sun, with the moon beneath her feet, and on her head a crown of twelve stars. She was with child and wailed aloud in pain as she labored to give birth. Then another sign appeared in the sky; it was a huge red dragon, with seven heads and ten horns, and on its heads were seven diadems. Its tail swept away a third of the stars in the sky and hurled them down to the earth. Then the dragon stood before the woman about to give birth, to devour her child when she gave birth. She gave birth to a son, a male child, destined to rule all the nations with an iron rod. Her child was caught up to God and his throne. The woman herself fled into the desert where she had a place prepared by God.

Then I heard a loud voice in heaven say:
"Now have salvation and power come,
   and the Kingdom of our God
   and the authority of his Anointed One."

PSALM RESPONSE
Psalm 45:10bc

The queen stands at your right hand, arrayed in gold.

SECOND READING
1 Corinthians 15:20–27

Brothers and sisters: Christ has been raised from the dead, the firstfruits of those who have fallen asleep. For since death came through man, the resurrection of the dead came also through man. For just as in Adam all die, so too in Christ shall all be brought to life, but each one in proper order: Christ the firstfruits; then, at his coming, those who belong to Christ; then comes the end, when he hands over the kingdom to his God and Father, when he has destroyed every sovereignty and every authority and power. For he must reign until he has put all his enemies under his feet. The last enemy to be destroyed is death, for "he subjected everything under his feet."

Mary set out and traveled to the hill country in haste to a town of Judah, where she entered the house of Zechariah and greeted Elizabeth. When Elizabeth heard Mary's greeting, the infant leaped in her womb, and Elizabeth, filled with the Holy Spirit, cried out in a loud voice and said, "Blessed are you among women, and blessed is the fruit of your womb. And how does this happen to me, that the mother of my Lord should come to me? For at the moment the sound of your greeting reached my ears, the infant in my womb leaped for joy. Blessed are you who believed that what was spoken to you by the Lord would be fulfilled."

And Mary said:
"My soul proclaims the greatness of the Lord;
my spirit rejoices in God my Savior
for he has looked upon his lowly servant.
From this day all generations will call me blessed:
the Almighty has done great things for me
and holy is his Name.
He has mercy on those who fear him
in every generation.
He has shown the strength of his arm,
and has scattered the proud in their conceit.
He has cast down the mighty from their thrones,
and has lifted up the lowly.
He has filled the hungry with good things,
and the rich he has sent away empty.
He has come to the help of his servant Israel
for he has remembered his promise of mercy,
the promise he made to our fathers,
to Abraham and his children for ever."

Mary remained with her about three months and then returned to her home.

Understanding the Word

After the seventh trumpet has blown, signaling God's triumph over diabolic powers, the temple opens and the ark of the covenant is revealed. This scene of divine victory immediately shifts to an image of Israel giving birth to the Messiah. The child is saved from Satan, the huge red dragon attempting to destroy him. One sees here a reference to the attempt of the powers of hell to destroy Jesus through his death on the cross, only to be foiled when he is raised from the dead and ascends to heaven. The woman, who now represents the persecuted church, is protected by God just as Israel was protected in the wilderness after the Exodus.

Some Christians in Corinth apparently denied the resurrection of the dead, to which Paul responded that if there is no resurrection, then obviously Christ was not raised from the dead, making their faith in him pointless. They are still in their sins, have no hope beyond this life, and those who have already "fallen asleep in Christ have perished." But Christ was raised from the dead, and his resurrection was not just for him but for all who have received life in and through him. At his second coming, those who are "in Christ" will be resurrected, too. Christ alone will be sovereign, the only authority, and all powers will be subject to him, including and especially the power of death.

Mary expresses prophetically in her Magnificat the meaning of the coming of the Messiah. True to character, God has shown mercy not just to her, but to all who have remained faithful and waited in hope for the longed-for salvation, making good on the ancient promises. The fulfillment of God's promise of salvation, however, will not be good news for everyone. Those who do not fear God, the proud and the rich, those who are satisfied with a world just the way it is, in which some have and others do not—for these, the coming of the Messiah will be a time of judgment on them and on their way of life.

Reflecting on the Word

I had a dream on the feast of the Assumption many years ago. It was one of those dark and scary dreams in which I was running through the streets of a town, dodging evil creatures and malevolent attackers. Suddenly I found myself in an abandoned lot. No trees. No buildings to hide me. No, no, no! I was totally exposed.

Have you ever had a nightmare like that? Or lived through a horror like that? Today's reading from Revelation starts with a similar terror. A woman wails aloud. A serpent stands ready to devour her child about to be born, a horrifying reptile whose tail can sweep away the stars!

Yet the child is caught up to God. The woman is secured in the radiance of the desert. She and her baby are safe. As we celebrate the Assumption, we read this account because of its parallels. We believe that at the moment of death, however it happened, Mary was not devoured by death, but caught up to God.

Is death like that distress? Is it followed by an abiding sense of tranquility? We do not know. We may think that we grasp God, but in reality, no. The Redeemer is here for us. The Lord is our Rescuer, the one who snatches us from terror and brings us to peace.

In my dream, as I stood so frightened in that open field, peaceable people encircled me, powerful people who loved me and were pleased with me. The horror could not come near. I was safe. I was secure. Brightness surrounded me. Now when I think of Mary and the communion of saints, I swell with courage. I feel that I have been surrounded by them.

No matter what, we are safe. We dwell secure. All will be well.

Consider/Discuss

❖ When you were younger, was there a place where you dwelt secure or a person with whom you were thoroughly "at home"? Where do you find safety now?

❖ What is it like to feel alone and in terror? How is that different from being surrounded by love? Think of times when the Lord has been your Rescuer.

Living and Praying with the Word

Holy Spirit, you are the divine tie who binds us with those who are in heaven. Illumine our hearts to see that we are not alone, that those who have gone before us are cheering us onward toward peace and everlasting life. Be with us in moments of earthly terror and fear. Rather than seeing things from our earthly perspective, grant us knowledge to see things from a heavenly viewpoint, that ultimately, when this is over, all will be well. Snatch us up, carry us away to you!

TWENTIETH SUNDAY IN ORDINARY TIME

Today's Focus: A Tale of a Healer

Whenever life needs healing, it is our love for those in need, our hope for a different and better future that propels our faith forward, leading us to search for healing until we find it.

FIRST READING
Isaiah 56:1, 6–7

Thus says the LORD:
Observe what is right, do what is just;
    for my salvation is about to come,
    my justice, about to be revealed.

The foreigners who join themselves to the LORD,
    ministering to him,
loving the name of the LORD,
    and becoming his servants—
all who keep the sabbath free from profanation
    and hold to my covenant,
them I will bring to my holy mountain
    and make joyful in my house of prayer;
their burnt offerings and sacrifices
    will be acceptable on my altar,
for my house shall be called
    a house of prayer for all peoples.

PSALM RESPONSE
Psalm 67:4

O God, let all the nations praise you!

SECOND READING
Romans 11:13–15, 29–32

Brothers and sisters: I am speaking to you Gentiles. Inasmuch as I am the apostle to the Gentiles, I glory in my ministry in order to make my race jealous and thus save some of them. For if their rejection is the reconciliation of the world, what will their acceptance be but life from the dead?

For the gifts and the call of God are irrevocable. Just as you once disobeyed God but have now received mercy because of their disobedience, so they have now disobeyed in order that, by virtue of the mercy shown to you, they too may now receive mercy. For God delivered all to disobedience, that he might have mercy upon all.

At that time, Jesus withdrew to the region of Tyre and Sidon. And behold, a Canaanite woman of that district came and called out, "Have pity on me, Lord, Son of David! My daughter is tormented by a demon." But Jesus did not say a word in answer to her. Jesus' disciples came and asked him, "Send her away, for she keeps calling out after us." He said in reply, "I was sent only to the lost sheep of the house of Israel." But the woman came and did Jesus homage, saying, "Lord, help me." He said in reply, "It is not right to take the food of the children and throw it to the dogs." She said, "Please, Lord, for even the dogs eat the scraps that fall from the table of their masters." Then Jesus said to her in reply, "O woman, great is your faith! Let it be done for you as you wish." And the woman's daughter was healed from that hour.

Understanding the Word

The final chapters of Isaiah come from the post-exilic period, a time of struggle, in which God's promises of restoration were slow in coming to fruition. The prophetic exhortation encourages continued hope in God's salvation and justice. The promises now extend not just to ethnic Israel, but to all who come to God's "holy mountain" (the temple in Jerusalem) to worship God and to abide by the covenant. This passage is one of several that appear in the post-exilic period that refer to God's larger plan to bring "all peoples" into relationship through Israel. Those who would join themselves to God will also be expected to love, serve, and obey.

Paul has been grappling with the question of Israel's role within God's plan, in light of the fact that so many Jews have not accepted Jesus as the Messiah (Romans 9–11). Knowing that God has not rejected the chosen (11:1), he suggests this (temporary) rejection was part of the plan to carry salvation beyond Israel. Those Gentiles who have accepted Christ should not judge Jews who have not, for their own salvation is only possible because they have been "grafted" onto Israel and received the benefits of their covenant relationship with God. Paul's hope is that Israel has been allowed to disobey so that, like the Gentiles, they too can receive God's mercy.

While in Gentile territory, Jesus encounters a woman who calls him "Lord" and "Son of David," terms one would expect only from Jews who recognized him as Messiah. Uncharacteristically, Jesus ignores her. Yet when his disciples ask him to send her away, he doesn't; he simply says he was not sent to the Gentiles. Perhaps recognizing that this objection does not constitute an outright refusal, the woman persists. Once again Jesus merely offers an objection: what is meant for the children (Israel) should not be given to the dogs (Gentiles). She persists, pointing out that there is enough of his salvific power to go around. This insightful retort wins the day. Jesus rewards her persistence, a sign of her faith.

185

Reflecting on the Word

The sun shone as she sat stroking a puppy on the step. The others gathered around. They wanted to hear her story again. "Tell us about when the Master came here to Tyre." The growing Christian community hungered for stories about Jesus.

"The difficulty started when I was four—my arms and legs began to twitch. Sometimes, I blacked out. My mother began to moan, 'Oh no, the demon wants her!' My older brother had writhed and died when that same demon had arrived. I was scared.

"One day, my mother saw a group of Jewish men visiting the city. She glimpsed Jesus the healer. She called out to him, 'Have pity on me, Lord, Son of David! My daughter is tormented by a demon.' The men ignored her. She knew that she didn't belong there. But she really loved me. Her heart ached from the grief that she might lose me, too. 'Send her away,' a man grunted. Jesus didn't. At that moment, my mother said her heart swelled with hope. Maybe? Could the mercy of the God of Israel extend even north of the border?

"Hope and love made my mother persist. She would not give up. She fell to her knees and cried out, 'Help me, sir!'

She said that she'll never forget how gently Jesus said, 'It is not right to take the children's bread and give it to the puppies.' She felt the Holy Spirit swell up within her: "Even the little dogs eat the scraps under the table!" Jesus was astonished. His face shone as he looked her in the eye. At that moment I was healed! Until the day she died, she told everyone about God's mercy toward me. And she seemed to take in every stray puppy in the city."

Consider/Discuss

❖ Think of a time when you persisted in prayer. What was it that made you keep asking?

❖ How is the mercy of God greater than any of our expectations? Where have you experienced that mercy?

Living and Praying with the Word

God of mercy, be gracious to us. We know that none of us deserve your love. Yet we hope in you. You gather people from all over the world to rejoice in you. In solidarity with the scared and the forlorn, the outcast and the refugee, we praise you for always loving us. Together, bring us to your holy mountain and reconcile this world that you have made.

TWENTY-FIRST SUNDAY IN ORDINARY TIME

Today's Focus: Jesus Christ Is Lord!

The phrase "Jesus Christ is Lord!" comes off the tongue easily enough,
but have we stopped to examine the many implications inside it,
the truly radical nature of that claim?

FIRST READING
Isaiah 22:19–23

Thus says the LORD to Shebna, master of the palace:
"I will thrust you from your office
 and pull you down from your station.
On that day I will summon my servant
 Eliakim, son of Hilkiah;
I will clothe him with your robe,
 and gird him with your sash,
 and give over to him your authority.
He shall be a father to the inhabitants of Jerusalem,
 and to the house of Judah.
I will place the key of the House of David on Eliakim's shoulder;
 when he opens, no one shall shut
 when he shuts, no one shall open.
I will fix him like a peg in a sure spot,
 to be a place of honor for his family."

PSALM RESPONSE
Psalm 138:8bc

Lord, your love is eternal; do not forsake the work of your hands.

SECOND READING
Romans 11:33–36

Oh, the depth of the riches and wisdom and knowledge of God! How inscrutable are his judgments and how unsearchable his ways!

For who has known the mind of the Lord
 or who has been his counselor?
Or who has given the Lord anything
 that he may be repaid?

For from him and through him and for him are all things. To him be glory forever. Amen.

Jesus went into the region of Caesarea Philippi and he asked his disciples, "Who do people say that the Son of Man is?" They replied, "Some say John the Baptist, others Elijah, still others Jeremiah or one of the prophets." He said to them, "But who do you say that I am?" Simon Peter said in reply, "You are the Christ, the Son of the living God." Jesus said to him in reply, "Blessed are you, Simon son of Jonah. For flesh and blood has not revealed this to you, but my heavenly Father. And so I say to you, you are Peter, and upon this rock I will build my church, and the gates of the netherworld shall not prevail against it. I will give you the keys to the kingdom of heaven. Whatever you bind on earth shall be bound in heaven; and whatever you loose on earth shall be loosed in heaven." Then he strictly ordered his disciples to tell no one that he was the Christ.

Understanding the Word

The context of Isaiah's oracle is the siege of Jerusalem by Assyria around 701 B.C. Shebna, a scribe, holds the office of "master of the palace" or "royal steward," a position of high authority. Apparently at some point he brought scandal to the royal household and was replaced by Eliakim, a move here attributed to the judgment of God on Shebna. As royal steward, Eliakim will now hold "the key of the House of David," a symbol of his high authority. Such is the honor of this post that his family's glory will depend on him ("hang" from him), who is fixed like a peg in the wall, holding "descendants and offspring" like "little dishes" (22:24).

Paul knows that God's word has not failed, so Israel's refusal to accept Jesus as Messiah must be part of God's intention from the beginning. It has allowed for the extension of salvation to the Gentiles. This plan for the salvation of the world reveals God's wisdom, which remains inscrutable and unsearchable, even as the outlines come slowly into view. Ultimately, Paul cannot know exactly what God is up to in all the details, but believes that what God is doing is good and it ultimately means mercy for all, including the currently "disobedient" Israel. This is cause for wonder and reasons to give glory to God, whose ways may not be known, but can be trusted.

When Jesus asks his disciples who people say he is, they give the standard conjectures that he is a forerunner, but not the Messiah himself. Because Simon has received from God the insight that Jesus is in fact the Christ and Son of God, he receives the name by which he has been known to the reader, but never called by anyone in the Gospel until now: Petros, or "rock." As elsewhere in the Bible, the new name reflects both a change of status and the meaning of that change. The notion that the gates of the netherworld will not prevail against the church can mean that the dark powers thought to emerge from them will not be able to defeat the church, or that they will not be able to prevent the church from defeating them.

Reflecting on the Word

Imagine that you are Judas Iscariot in this scene. You stand beneath the cliffs at Caesarea Philippi. Streams of water flow past lush growths of fig trees. This is one of Jesus' favorite places of peace, a retreat from the stark heat and the politics of Jerusalem. Yet in the midst of this Roman city of pagan worship, your heart is not at peace. Jesus asks you all, "Who do you say that I am?" You've been pondering that question yourself. You hope for a rich intellectual discussion now.

Who does Peter think that he is? The big fisherman butters up the carpenter from Galilee by blurting out, "You are the Messiah, the Son of the living God." Come on, Peter. That is pretty radical stuff—how can you say that? It has been an incredible journey, true. We've seen bent limbs made straight, the blind see, crazy people restored to their right minds . . . Jesus is a good guy, no mistake, but the Messiah? He might lead a revolution and set our nation free. Or he might not. He's hard to read. He might be useful. But he's unpredictable. Not easy to manipulate.

Look at the way Jesus is exalting Peter, the lumbering lout. "Keys to the kingdom? Rock?" No way. Judas has been trying to get the others to follow his lead, but they keep looking to Simon for leadership. He's the least qualified to lead this group—impulsive, inconsistent, a big mouth, runs when things get tough. Nothing firm about him, certainly no "rock." Why doesn't Jesus turn to you—you've got a good head for figures, you plan ahead, you have a passion to get things done. Peter? None of those qualities. Jesus turns and looks at you. His eyes search yours, "Who do you say that I am, Judas?"

Consider/Discuss

❖ Is God "useful" to us? Do we feel we have to stand on our own or is Jesus our "Lord"? Or is it sometimes both? What does it mean to say with our whole heart that someone else, not us, is in charge of our lives and our parish communities, that "Jesus is Lord"?

❖ In the Gospels, Peter is sometimes portrayed as inept. But when the Holy Spirit descended upon him at Pentecost, he became highly qualified to do what he had to do. Do we ever use Peter's example to excuse our weaknesses, permitting ourselves to slack off from being effective in human endeavors? Or do we allow the Holy Spirit to strengthen us so that we grow skilled in our discipleship?

Living and Praying with the Word

God of the Church, unless we see things from your perspective, we don't always know the difference between wisdom and foolishness, especially in institutions. You see our brokenness. You know the times when we have used the things of faith only for our own advantage. Forgive us for that. Purify us so that your Spirit can flow through us more virtuously. We pray for the Church. Holy Spirit, unite what is fragmented and bring us together. Thank you for that hope of a new day when all will be one.

TWENTY-SECOND SUNDAY IN ORDINARY TIME

Today's Focus: Moving On, Even in Pain

We all think we understand how things should proceed, have an instinct about how life should go. There are times, however, when the unexpected calls on us to release our grasping and our certainty.

FIRST READING

Jeremiah 20:7–9

You duped me, O LORD, and I let myself be duped;
  you were too strong for me, and you triumphed.
All the day I am an object of laughter;
  everyone mocks me.

Whenever I speak, I must cry out,
  violence and outrage is my message;
the word of the LORD has brought me
  derision and reproach all the day.

I say to myself, I will not mention him,
  I will speak in his name no more.
But then it becomes like fire burning in my heart,
  imprisoned in my bones;
I grow weary holding it in, I cannot endure it.

PSALM RESPONSE

Psalm 63:2b

My soul is thirsting for you, O Lord my God.

SECOND READING

Romans 12:1–2

I urge you, brothers and sisters, by the mercies of God, to offer your bodies as a living sacrifice, holy and pleasing to God, your spiritual worship. Do not conform yourselves to this age but be transformed by the renewal of your mind, that you may discern what is the will of God, what is good and pleasing and perfect.

GOSPEL

Matthew 16:21–27

Jesus began to show his disciples that he must go to Jerusalem and suffer greatly from the elders, the chief priests, and the scribes, and be killed and on the third day be raised. Then Peter took Jesus aside and began to rebuke him, "God forbid, Lord! No such thing shall ever happen to you." He turned and said to Peter, "Get behind me, Satan! You are an obstacle to me. You are thinking not as God does, but as human beings do."

Then Jesus said to his disciples, "Whoever wishes to come after me must deny himself, take up his cross, and follow me. For whoever wishes to save his life will lose it, but whoever loses his life for my sake will find it. What profit would there be for one to gain the whole world and forfeit his life? Or what can one give in exchange for his life? For the Son of Man will come with his angels in his Father's glory, and then he will repay all according to his conduct."

Understanding the Word

Jeremiah has struggled not only with the mission to proclaim God's word, but also with the way God had gone about practically coercing him into the task from the beginning (1:5). Jeremiah's attitude comes out most clearly in this famous passage in which he accuses God of "duping" (or "seducing") him. The prophet feels God has put something over on him, and he has allowed it to happen. The result has been nothing but pain. Yet Jeremiah is unable to simply walk away. God has gotten into Jeremiah's bones and the call to proclaim God's word is unrelenting. This is what Jeremiah was born for and there is no walking away from it.

Having concluded that no matter how mysterious are God's ways, they are for the good of everyone, Paul turns to the response his audience should have to this divine mercy, which is to offer themselves to God. This requires them to reject the tendency of the "old self" (or the "flesh") to conform to the values and expectations of the world. Having died to sin in Christ, and with the Spirit dwelling within them, they must be re-formed and have their minds, wills, perspectives renewed. Being conformed to Christ means becoming like him, who was devoted to nothing but the will of God, and thus sought always to do what God—not "the age"—considered good, pleasing, and perfect.

Immediately after being proclaimed the rock upon which Jesus will build his church, Peter reveals the limits of his understanding of the Christ. When Jesus announces that he will suffer and be killed, Peter responds according to quite human ways of thinking: The Messiah and Son of God could not possibly suffer and die. Jesus immediately recognizes this reasoning as a satanic temptation to abandon the course and insists that the kingdom of heaven is costly. This is not a new teaching—Jesus has been proclaiming it along. What is new is the realization that the Son of God himself will pay the highest price. As he has previously assured them, the price will be worth it. They will gain the very thing they think they are losing, and more.

Reflecting on the Word

My oldest daughter climbed at a young age. At seven months, she didn't understand caution. So my husband and I scooted on the floor behind her to ensure that she didn't fall. One day, she climbed up on the coffee table, threw out her arms, and sparkled with a smile. As she tumbled off, Dan caught her. No child of ours would ever get hurt while on our watch!

It is in our nature to safeguard those we love. Going to kindergarten, heading to high school, departing for college—sometimes we'd rather that children just stay little. Animals instinctively protect.

Peter swore to protect Jesus. He was certain that his friend was not going to die. No buddy of his would ever get hurt while on his watch!

But Jesus valued the enduring will of God over Peter's short-lived preservation. He exclaimed, "You are not thinking as God does!" To die on the cross was something that the Savior had to do, even though it would be agonizing.

Jeremiah was tired of getting into trouble on God's behalf. Self-protectively, he cried out, "Just let me be! Let me hold this message inside—I will not speak it." But speaking was something he had to do, even though it hurt. The will of God burned like a fire within him.

Children grow up. Spouses die. Friends move. Grandmas go to eternity. We may be tempted to hold our loved ones back, but we cannot save them. Are we being prudently protective or self-servingly possessive? To release others is something we have to do, even though it may hurt.

The Lord guards them for eternity; no one will snatch them away. Therefore we relinquish to God our own certainty about how things should go. Sometimes we resist doing that—so did Jeremiah—so did Peter.

Consider/Discuss

❖ Who do you try to protect? How much of his or her future can you truly control? There is a fine line in discernment between trusting God to take care of those we love and chasing after our own ideas of how things should go. Think of a current situation that worries you—what is the most prudent path to take?

❖ The Holy Spirit teaches us to think as God does rather than as human beings do. When does the surrender to the will of God feel almost too hard to bear? How have we experienced the Lord's grace in carrying that cross?

Living and Praying with the Word

Jesus, you were not happy with Peter for wanting to avoid pain. We too may not want to let go of children or a spouse or friends or others who are close to us. It hurts. We don't want to be hurt. Create in us a desire to follow you so closely that we are willing to surrender all for the love of you. Burn in our hearts; put fire in our bones, so that we put you first in our lives.

Take care of _____ (name[s]). We entrust those we love into your hands, for you hold them even more tenderly than we do. Thank you.

TWENTY-THIRD SUNDAY IN ORDINARY TIME

Today's Focus: Go and Tell—Carefully!

Resolving conflicts is always difficult; in the context of the church it can be downright tricky. Disciples are called to continual discernment through the Spirit, for the well-being of the community.

FIRST READING
Ezekiel 33:7–9

Thus says the LORD: You, son of man, I have appointed watchman for the house of Israel; when you hear me say anything, you shall warn them for me. If I tell the wicked, "O wicked one, you shall surely die," and you do not speak out to dissuade the wicked from his way, the wicked shall die for his guilt, but I will hold you responsible for his death. But if you warn the wicked, trying to turn him from his way, and he refuses to turn from his way, he shall die for his guilt, but you shall save yourself.

PSALM RESPONSE
Psalm 95:8

If today you hear his voice, harden not your hearts.

SECOND READING
Romans 13:8–10

Brothers and sisters: Owe nothing to anyone, except to love one another; for the one who loves another has fulfilled the law. The commandments, "You shall not commit adultery; you shall not kill; you shall not steal; you shall not covet," and whatever other commandment there may be, are summed up in this saying, namely, "You shall love your neighbor as yourself." Love does no evil to the neighbor; hence, love is the fulfillment of the law.

GOSPEL
Matthew 18:15–20

Jesus said to his disciples: "If your brother sins against you, go and tell him his fault between you and him alone. If he listens to you, you have won over your brother. If he does not listen, take one or two others along with you, so that 'every fact may be established on the testimony of two or three witnesses.' If he refuses to listen to them, tell the church. If he refuses to listen even to the church, then treat him as you would a Gentile or a tax collector. Amen, I say to you, whatever you bind on earth shall be bound in heaven, and whatever you loose on earth shall be loosed in heaven. Again, amen, I say to you, if two of you agree on earth about anything for which they are to pray, it shall be granted to them by my heavenly Father. For where two or three are gathered together in my name, there am I in the midst of them."

Understanding the Word

Drawing on the analogy of a watchman, God reminds Ezekiel how crucial his prophetic task is. If a sentinel sees an enemy advancing against a city and warns the people, but they do nothing, the people only have themselves to blame when they succumb to the enemy. But if the sentinel fails to warn the people, when disaster strikes he is guilty of a great crime. A crucial element of the analogy is the correlation between physical death and the death of sin, which is no less real for being "spiritual." Not to warn the wicked of their sinfulness is as disastrous a dereliction of duty as failing to warn them of impending (but preventable) physical destruction.

As he continues to exhort the Romans to conform themselves to Christ rather than to the age, Paul focuses on the call to love as a manifestation of the Christian's conformity to Christ. A little earlier in the letter, he had urged the Romans to avoid repaying evil with evil, but instead to bless, live at peace, "conquer evil with good" (12:21). Since loving others is the fulfillment of the law, which the Christian must heed as the will of God, we are obliged to love others—it is a debt we owe them. The earlier exhortation makes clear that this "debt" extends even to those who persecute or harm us; it is not an option.

Jesus' instructions make it clear that when the church must address sin, it should be done in a way that minimizes publicity and shame. The intention is to right the wrong, not to punish. The process thus begins between the two individuals involved, expanding beyond them only if necessary. Only those who, after repeated attempts, refuse to listen should be treated "as a Gentile or tax collector," in other words, "excommunicated." It's helpful here to recall Jesus' attitude toward Gentiles and tax collectors in this Gospel (9:10–11), which is to invite them into the kingdom, suggesting that his desire is that the "excommunication" be not only a last resort, but also not the last word.

Reflecting on the Word

A watchman's duty is well-defined: if an enemy ship is seen in the harbor, sound the alarm; if you don't disclose the danger, then you are the one responsible for your city's destruction. Jesus' mandate to call out "a brother" is also clear: when there is a shining love between you and a fellow child of God, by all means, go and talk to him or her about the misdeed and try to set things straight.

But what if the relationship involves power? As we strive toward a climate of transparency in our church and in our culture, how to enact this Gospel grows murkier. Should you surface management mistakes to your boss? Must you speak to a parent about dishonesty? Do you disclose a superior's misdeeds? Power stays in power by fear. When do you speak up? If you reveal "wickedness," because of the power imbalance you may have to put up with anger, retribution, and the loss of your good name. "Go and tell" is a tricky directive in an environment of dominance. Those on the underside of power have been silent for centuries.

How do we determine what the Lord is calling us to say and do? John the Baptist spoke truth to power and was beheaded. Jesus remained silent before Herod and was crucified anyway. How much risk can we take? How do we find clear direction when we feel as though we're walking in a fog?

In prayer and discernment with others, we ask: What does God want me to do? What is my motive for opening this conversation? Will speaking up worsen the situation? Like Ezekiel, if God is unmistakably calling you to "be a sentinel," then proceed carefully, but in courage do proceed. Jesus himself suggests that we have a back-up plan ready.

Consider/Discuss

❖ Think of situations when you have said nothing about wrongs that you have endured. What was the reason for your silence? In hindsight, what could you have done differently? As you talk this through with others, how might that discussion help you to handle a sticky situation that you are in right now?

❖ St. Paul says to "owe nothing to anyone, except to love one another." That is a real challenge. How can we grow into that inner freedom, that degree of boundlessness when we totally release our fear of others? How can we grow to be indebted only to God?

Living and Praying with the Word

Lord Jesus, you found yourself in many sticky situations. You know how tangled human life can be. As we gather together in your name, be here in our midst and give us clarity. Over and over again, you said in the Gospels, "Do not be afraid." But sometimes we are afraid to speak up. Sometimes it is right to be cautious about speaking up. Send us your Holy Spirit in abundance to reveal to us the best direction to take. Mother Mary, untangler of knots, pray for us!

TWENTY-FOURTH SUNDAY IN ORDINARY TIME

Today's Focus: Reflecting God's Abundance

---

*God has generously provided for us, and continues to shower us
with merciful love. We are called to share God's generosity with everyone.*

FIRST READING

Sirach 27:30 — 28:7

Wrath and anger are hateful things,
  yet the sinner hugs them tight.
The vengeful will suffer the LORD's vengeance,
  for he remembers their sins in detail.
Forgive your neighbor's injustice;
  then when you pray, your own sins will be forgiven.
Could anyone nourish anger against another
  and expect healing from the LORD?
Could anyone refuse mercy to another like himself,
  can he seek pardon for his own sins?
If one who is but flesh cherishes wrath,
  who will forgive his sins?
Remember your last days, set enmity aside;
  remember death and decay, and cease from sin!
Think of the commandments, hate not your neighbor;
  remember the Most High's covenant, and overlook faults.

PSALM RESPONSE

Psalm 103:8

The Lord is kind and merciful, slow to anger, and rich in compassion.

SECOND READING

Romans 14:7–9

Brothers and sisters: None of us lives for oneself, and no one dies for oneself. For if we live, we live for the Lord, and if we die, we die for the Lord; so then, whether we live or die, we are the Lord's. For this is why Christ died and came to life, that he might be Lord of both the dead and the living.

GOSPEL

Matthew 18:21–35

Peter approached Jesus and asked him, "Lord, if my brother sins against me, how often must I forgive? As many as seven times?" Jesus answered, "I say to you, not seven times but seventy-seven times. That is why the kingdom of heaven may be likened to a king who decided to settle accounts with his servants. When he began the accounting, a debtor was brought before him who owed him a huge amount. Since he had no way of paying it back, his master ordered him to be sold, along with his wife, his children, and all his property, in payment of the debt. At that, the servant fell down, did him homage, and said, 'Be patient with me, and I will pay you back in full.' Moved with compassion the master of that servant let him go and forgave him the loan. When that servant had left, he found one of his fellow servants who owed him a much smaller amount. He seized him and started to choke him, demanding, 'Pay back what you owe.' Falling to his knees, his fellow servant begged him, 'Be patient with me, and I will pay you back.' But he refused. Instead, he had the fellow servant put in prison until he paid back the debt. Now when his fellow servants saw what had happened, they were deeply disturbed, and went to their master and reported the whole affair. His master summoned him and said to him, 'You wicked servant! I forgave you your entire debt because you begged me to. Should you not have had pity on your fellow servant, as I had pity on you?' Then in anger his master handed him over to the torturers until he should pay back the whole debt. So will my heavenly Father do to you, unless each of you forgives your brother from your heart."

Understanding the Word

In a passage that mentions "sin" six times, Sirach focuses on refusal to forgive. Here the sinner is not so much the one who causes wrath and anger, as the one who "hugs them tight," like a security blanket; not the one who offends, but the one who avenges the offense. It is preposterous to hope to be forgiven for one's own sins if one is not willing to forgive others. It is presumptuous to expect the sinless deity to forgive our sins when, as sinful human beings, we are unwilling to do the same thing. Refusal to forgive is a form of hate, which is antithetical to the ethical perspective of the covenant between God and Israel.

Paul's insistence that Christians live and die for the Lord occurs within an exhortation against judging others. Those whose consciences lead them to abstain from certain foods must not be despised by those with different scruples, and vice versa. The point, Paul says, is that each should be eating (or not eating) for the Lord. If we are doing it for the Lord, and it is not evil, then it is good. In fact, everything, even up to one's own death, should be done for the Lord. It is the Lord, he goes on to say, who will judge us. We will give an account to the one for whom we have done everything, and that is the Lord, not each other.

Immediately after Jesus gives instructions on the church's proper response to obstinate sinners (Matthew 18:15–20), Peter inquires about the limits of forgiveness. Jesus' answer—there are no limits—must have astounded those who thought that seven times was already quite generous. The parable gives a straightforward rationale for the demand that humans place no limits on their willingness to forgive: because God places no limits on the divine willingness to forgive. To act as if we have the right to limit forgiveness when we ourselves must ask for it repeatedly constitutes gross hypocrisy and ingratitude. We ourselves are the ones who place limits on God's forgiveness of us when we insist on placing limits on our forgiveness of others.

Reflecting on the Word

There is a creek behind the house where my daughter Maria used to live in the foothills of the Sierra Nevada Mountains in California. In spring, water generously cascades down from the mountaintops; the river sparkles and crashes and seems almost alive. Huge cedar logs float downstream upon that rush of water. You could hear the bubbling of flowing water when her kitchen window was open.

The mercy of God flows upon us like that river of generosity. The psalmist sings of that bounty: The Lord "redeems your life from destruction, and crowns you with kindness and compassion." Jesus tells of the lavishness of a king who forgives his servant a huge debt. You can hear the bubbling of flowing water.

But today's Gospel story doesn't stay with abundance. It devolves rapidly to the servant's forgetfulness of generosity, which leads him to such meanness and malice that he chokes his fellow servant, demanding immediate repayment. Instead of passing on that generosity, he nourishes anger and holds onto wrath. That is an abomination to the Giver of the river of life!

I was surprised when I'd visit Maria again in September. Her creek had shrunk to a silent trickle. Big logs were stuck in the rocks. Sticks and leaves were trapped behind the logs. Masses of gunk choked off the water. What had flowed in such a lively way in the spring was clogged in the fall.

When we refuse mercy to another, how can we expect to be healed ourselves? We choke off God's generosity. Jesus teaches us to pray, "Forgive us our trespasses as we forgive those who trespass against us." There are no limits to the cascading of God's mercy. Jesus tells us that there should be no limits to our forgiveness as well. Flow, river, flow!

Consider/Discuss

❖ In this season of harvest, take some time to look around and be grateful for God's abundance. How does immersing ourselves in God's generosity set us free to pour out mercy to others?

❖ The resentments of earth may pull us down, but the Holy Spirit wants to bubble up and sparkle within you and me. What is blocking us? Where do we find pollution in our lives, the cedar logs of unforgiveness that dam(n) up our souls?

Living and Praying with the Word

Holy Spirit, we open our hearts to you. Fill us with your courage to love so that time after time, even when we've been hurt, we forgive. We pain you often. You have forgiven us so many times. Don't let hard-heartedness choke us. We offer you those people and those issues that bother us. Please put them on a log and let them float down your river. Then bubble up within us and restore our joy.

TWENTY-FIFTH SUNDAY IN ORDINARY TIME

Today's Focus: Expectations Turned Upside Down

Jesus' stories often feature an inverting of the expectations of the world.
When he does this, it shows us that the reign of God was, is,
and will be an upside-down reality.

FIRST READING

Isaiah 55:6–9

Seek the LORD while he may be found,
  call him while he is near.
Let the scoundrel forsake his way,
  and the wicked his thoughts;
let him turn to the LORD for mercy;
  to our God, who is generous in forgiving.
For my thoughts are not your thoughts,
  nor are your ways my ways, says the LORD.
As high as the heavens are above the earth,
  so high are my ways above your ways
  and my thoughts above your thoughts.

PSALM RESPONSE

Psalm 145:18a

The Lord is near to all who call upon him.

SECOND READING

Philippians 1:20c–24, 27a

Brothers and sisters: Christ will be magnified in my body, whether by life or by death. For to me life is Christ, and death is gain. If I go on living in the flesh, that means fruitful labor for me. And I do not know which I shall choose. I am caught between the two. I long to depart this life and be with Christ, for that is far better. Yet that I remain in the flesh is more necessary for your benefit.

Only, conduct yourselves in a way worthy of the gospel of Christ.

GOSPEL

Matthew 20:1–16a

Jesus told his disciples this parable: "The kingdom of heaven is like a landowner who went out at dawn to hire laborers for his vineyard. After agreeing with them for the usual daily wage, he sent them into his vineyard. Going out about nine o'clock, the landowner saw others standing idle in the marketplace, and he said to them, 'You too go into my vineyard, and I will give you what is just.' So they went off. And he went out again around noon, and around three o'clock, and did likewise. Going out about five o'clock, the landowner found others standing around, and said to them, 'Why do you stand here idle all day?' They answered, 'Because no one has hired us.' He said to them, 'You too go into my vineyard.' When it was evening the owner of the vineyard said to his foreman, 'Summon the laborers and give them their pay, beginning with the last and ending with the first.' When those who had started about five o'clock came, each received the usual daily wage. So when the first came, they thought that they would receive more, but each of them also got the usual wage. And on receiving it they grumbled against the landowner, saying, 'These last ones worked only one hour, and you have made them equal to us, who bore the day's burden and the heat.' He said to one of them in reply, 'My friend, I am not cheating you. Did you not agree with me for the usual daily wage? Take what is yours and go. What if I wish to give this last one the same as you? Or am I not free to do as I wish with my own money? Are you envious because I am generous?' Thus, the last will be first, and the first will be last."

Understanding the Word

The reading from Isaiah suggests that even after the Babylonian exile had ended, Israel (or some of it) still struggled to be faithful to God. While there are no limits to the mercy of God, who is generous in forgiving, that forgiveness must be sought through repentance. God does respond to evil and one must not delay in repenting. Thus the insistence that one must "seek the LORD while he may be found" (Isaiah 55:6). Yet hope lies in the fact that God does not calculate forgiveness as we do. As merciful as sinful human beings are capable of being, God is more merciful. And in situations that human beings would find completely unforgivable, God's forgiveness for those who repent is unbounded.

Paul is writing to the Philippians from prison, stating that his imprisonment and suffering have "turned out rather to advance the gospel" (1:12). His fervent hope is that no matter what happens, Christ will continue to be glorified in him. He would like to die, so that he can be with Christ (and end his suffering). On the other hand, if he lives he will be able to spread the gospel, teach, and support other Christians. He has learned to be content either way. The exhortation to conduct themselves in a way worthy of the gospel leads into the next section of the letter, in which he will address some divisions within the community.

Contemporary audiences of the parable of the workers sometimes fail to notice that those who did not work until the end of the day had not deliberately avoided labor; no one had hired them. All of the workers in this parable lead a precarious existence, not knowing from day to day if they will make any money to feed their families. The owner of the vineyard, in paying all of the workers a day's wage, is paying them not according to how much they have worked, but according to how much they need. The parable emphasizes the generosity of God's kingdom, in which everyone's needs are met, regardless of their ability or good fortune. God cares more about mercy than fairness.

Reflecting on the Word

In a tight job market, ideal candidates may be handpicked—those with the best grade point average or the most personable smile, those who carry themselves as though they came from money, those with perfect teeth. The others don't even get called for an interview, as if implicitly sending the message, "Don't bother; we're not hiring your kind."

Who got picked early in the morning in Jesus' vineyard story? A savvy winegrower would probably have told his foreman to choose the younger men first: the tall, the sturdy, and the strong—that is who we want to work in our fields. Who waited all day and got picked last? Maybe it was the old. Maybe it was the one-armed or the crippled. Property owners who sought for success might suggest to these workers, "Don't bother; we don't need your kind."

This parable reminds me of gym class. We used to pick teams. (Do schools still do that?) I hate to admit it, but as a super-athletic kid, it was a buzz to be selected first. Maybe these guys who had worked all day in the vineyard carried that same swagger: "I'm good, I'm tough, I was picked first to work. And who are these losers? And why are you paying them the same wage as me?"

Jesus flips our expectations of success upside down in this parable. When the Lord rewards his team, he values more than outer appearance. He prizes the heart. He is open-handed with the late-bloomers. Certainly God's ways are not our ways. Imagine God saying, "You, you, and you—you are wanted. You, you, and you—you are chosen." Can you hear it? "Who, me? You want me?" God says, "Yes, yes, and yes! Good salary. Great benefits. I do want your kind. Come!"

Consider/Discuss

❖ When have you been picked last (or first) for something? What did that feel like? How did that affect how you saw yourself? How does that influence the way that you feel about the marginalized?

❖ "God wants you. God has chosen you." Does that statement land differently depending on the successes that life has dealt you? Do the privileges that have come your way or the hardships you have endured affect how you see God's innermost desire for you?

Living and Praying with the Word

Jesus, you continually chose surprising friends. The broken, the outcast, the unwanted—they all found a home in you. Your way of seeing people turns our imagination upside down, for your ways of measuring are not what we are used to. When we are stuck in certain patterns of thinking about the values of success and power, change our hearts. Help us to be merciful as you are merciful.

SEPTEMBER 27, 2020

TWENTY-SIXTH SUNDAY IN ORDINARY TIME

Today's Focus: Can You Be Coached?

God doesn't seek out the perfect, but looks for those who are willing, who are humble, who will try, and—when and if they fail—will try again to do God's will.

FIRST READING   *Ezekiel 18:25–28*

Thus says the LORD: You say, "The LORD's way is not fair!" Hear now, house of Israel: Is it my way that is unfair, or rather, are not your ways unfair? When someone virtuous turns away from virtue to commit iniquity, and dies, it is because of the iniquity he committed that he must die. But if he turns from the wickedness he has committed, and does what is right and just, he shall preserve his life; since he has turned away from all the sins that he has committed, he shall surely live, he shall not die.

PSALM RESPONSE   *Psalm 25:6a*

Remember your mercies, O Lord.

SECOND READING   *Philippians 2:1–11 or 2:1–5*

In the shorter form of the reading, the passage in brackets is omitted.

Brothers and sisters: If there is any encouragement in Christ, any solace in love, any participation in the Spirit, any compassion and mercy, complete my joy by being of the same mind, with the same love, united in heart, thinking one thing. Do nothing out of selfishness or out of vainglory; rather, humbly regard others as more important than yourselves, each looking out not for his own interests, but also for those of others.

Have in you the same attitude
  that is also in Christ Jesus,

    [Who, though he was in the form of God,
    did not regard equality with God
    something to be grasped.
  Rather, he emptied himself,
    taking the form of a slave,
    coming in human likeness;
    and found human in appearance,
    he humbled himself,
    becoming obedient to the point of death,

even death on a cross.
Because of this, God greatly exalted him
and bestowed on him the name
which is above every name,
that at the name of Jesus
every knee should bend,
of those in heaven and on earth and under the earth,
and every tongue confess that
Jesus Christ is Lord,
to the glory of God the Father.]

GOSPEL *Matthew 21:28–32*

Jesus said to the chief priests and elders of the people: "What is your opinion? A man had two sons. He came to the first and said, 'Son, go out and work in the vineyard today.' He said in reply, 'I will not,' but afterwards changed his mind and went. The man came to the other son and gave the same order. He said in reply, 'Yes, sir,' but did not go. Which of the two did his father's will?" They answered, "The first." Jesus said to them, "Amen, I say to you, tax collectors and prostitutes are entering the kingdom of God before you. When John came to you in the way of righteousness, you did not believe him; but tax collectors and prostitutes did. Yet even when you saw that, you did not later change your minds and believe him."

Understanding the Word

The reading from Ezekiel emphasizes that the divine will is for the wicked to turn from sin and toward God. What God sees is the direction in which one is currently headed, rather than where one has been. This sounds good when we have turned from evil to good, but the principle is less congenial when we have turned from good to evil. In response to the accusation of unfairness, God notes that what is in fact "unfair" is the human desire to have God always forget past sin but never forget past virtue. God's "fairness" consists in holding us responsible for the life we have chosen rather than the one we have forsaken.

We surmise from Paul's letter to the Philippians that there were divisions within the community, exacerbated by outside opposition. So Paul strongly encourages unity: same mind, same love, united in heart, thinking one thing. This unity is found by sharing the same attitude that Christ had, which was sacrificial *kenosis* ("emptying"), setting aside his own interests for those of others. The force of the exhortation is sympathy or empathy, regarding others as "one with oneself," just as Christ united himself with humanity even to the point of death. Just as there was in Christ no selfishness, no holding back, no concern with "rights" or "prerogatives," so it should be for the Philippians.

The parable of the two sons presents a clear analogy: only those who actually do the will of God, even if they refuse at first, will enter the kingdom. The parable involves two sons, highlighting the fact that even the tax collectors and prostitutes are children of God—disobedient at first, and maybe for a long time, but children nonetheless. The chief priests and the elders, who thought they were following the will of God, were given the opportunity to reassess that belief when John came preaching repentance. They refused to listen to him, even when they observed the conversion of sinners at his preaching. Those who thought they had no need to repent were mistaken.

Reflecting on the Word

I recall a blue sky, a hot grassy field at Sand Run field, and a dozen twelve- to thirteen-year-old boys in their red WASA soccer jerseys. "Out on the field," I called to the team. "Sure, Coach," a short-haired athletic boy yelled out as he jogged toward the goal. A bigger lad stood by the sideline with his arms crossed. He didn't move. He didn't look at me. His body language exuded "No." What was I supposed to do? "Please? We want you out there." He looked me in the eye, shrugged, and lumbered onto the field.

As the season went on, the first "willing" player was skilled and he let the other twelve-year-olds know that he was good—and that he didn't feel that he could learn anything from me about soccer. He didn't get any better.

The second "unwilling" player endured ridicule for being a little chunky and a little slow, but he paid attention. He had never played soccer before. But he learned. He got better. He never became a soccer legend, but he was a delight to coach.

Sometimes we may be tempted to get a little spiritually cocky. We know that we are loved. We know that we matter. We may be the first to jog out onto the field.

But sometimes we avoid looking God in the eye because we don't think that we quite measure up. "Nah, I don't really think so," may be our response when someone tells us, "God loves you." How could God be pleased with us? Want a relationship with us? Care about us?

Coachability—it makes all the difference. Jesus told the Pharisees that "tax collectors and prostitutes are entering the kingdom of God before you." The Lord wasn't looking for the perfect. He was looking for the coachable.

Consider/Discuss

❖ When is it hard to "look God in the eye"? In what ways do you (or do you not) feel that you have to be perfect in order to measure up to God?

❖ Have you ever felt like you told God, "No"? What happened when that turned around to "Yes"? In what ways would you hope to be more coachable?

Living and Praying with the Word

Lord, I'm tired. I don't want to pray. I want to go to bed. I want to curl up under the comforter and shut the world out. What's that you say? You want my "no" to be "yes"? You'll be listening to my breathing? Counting the hairs on my head? Moving within me even when I sleep? Oh. Okay. Well, come on then, let's pray.

TWENTY-SEVENTH SUNDAY IN ORDINARY TIME

Today's Focus: God the Gardener

Even in our largely non-agrarian society, the images of planting, tending, and reaping the benefits of what we've grown is something we understand. All God wants is to reap from us, the vineyard of the Lord.

FIRST READING

Isaiah 5:1–7

Let me now sing of my friend,
    my friend's song concerning his vineyard.
My friend had a vineyard
    on a fertile hillside;
he spaded it, cleared it of stones,
    and planted the choicest vines;
within it he built a watchtower,
    and hewed out a wine press.
Then he looked for the crop of grapes,
    but what it yielded was wild grapes.

Now, inhabitants of Jerusalem and people of Judah,
    judge between me and my vineyard:
What more was there to do for my vineyard
    that I had not done?
Why, when I looked for the crop of grapes,
    did it bring forth wild grapes?
Now, I will let you know
    what I mean to do with my vineyard:
take away its hedge, give it to grazing,
    break through its wall, let it be trampled!
Yes, I will make it a ruin:
    it shall not be pruned or hoed,
    but overgrown with thorns and briers;
I will command the clouds
    not to send rain upon it.
The vineyard of the LORD of hosts is the house of Israel,
    and the people of Judah are his cherished plant;
he looked for judgment, but see, bloodshed!
    for justice, but hark, the outcry!

PSALM RESPONSE

Isaiah 5:7a

The vineyard of the Lord is the house of Israel.

Brothers and sisters: Have no anxiety at all, but in everything, by prayer and petition, with thanksgiving, make your requests known to God. Then the peace of God that surpasses all understanding will guard your hearts and minds in Christ Jesus.

Finally, brothers and sisters, whatever is true, whatever is honorable, whatever is just, whatever is pure, whatever is lovely, whatever is gracious, if there is any excellence and if there is anything worthy of praise, think about these things. Keep on doing what you have learned and received and heard and seen in me. Then the God of peace will be with you.

GOSPEL *Matthew 21:33–43*

Jesus said to the chief priests and the elders of the people: "Hear another parable. There was a landowner who planted a vineyard, put a hedge around it, dug a wine press in it, and built a tower. Then he leased it to tenants and went on a journey. When vintage time drew near, he sent his servants to the tenants to obtain his produce. But the tenants seized the servants and one they beat, another they killed, and a third they stoned. Again he sent other servants, more numerous than the first ones, but they treated them in the same way. Finally, he sent his son to them, thinking, 'They will respect my son.' But when the tenants saw the son, they said to one another, 'This is the heir. Come, let us kill him and acquire his inheritance.' They seized him, threw him out of the vineyard, and killed him. What will the owner of the vineyard do to those tenants when he comes?" They answered him, "He will put those wretched men to a wretched death and lease his vineyard to other tenants who will give him the produce at the proper times." Jesus said to them, "Did you never read in the Scriptures:

The stone that the builders rejected
has become the cornerstone;
by the Lord has this been done,
and it is wonderful in our eyes?

Therefore, I say to you, the kingdom of God will be taken away from you and given to a people that will produce its fruit."

Understanding the Word

The prophet Isaiah sings of "my friend" who had a vineyard. Israel is often spoken of in the Bible as the vine God has planted or the vineyard God has cultivated. God has put a great amount of work and care into the vineyard, giving it everything it needs to produce a "crop" of righteousness and fidelity to God, only to find the wild and useless grapes of injustice and bloodshed. Just as a vineyard owner might rightly and prudently abandon the vineyard, so God might do the same to Israel. The oracle, then, is meant to justify the divine decision to bring judgment and exile to Judah, absent the desired repentance.

It is clear from Paul's letter that the Philippians struggled with internal tensions as well as outside opposition. Although the Christian path is difficult—Paul himself has likened it to a prize toward which one constantly strives—it is in fact a joyous struggle because it involves becoming more like Christ and it occurs "in Christ." This transformation is slow, and perhaps painful, but it manifests itself in peace, kindness, calm. The struggle the Philippians are undergoing tests their resolve to follow Christ, but they must know that it is a path marked out by what is true, honorable, just, pure, lovely, and gracious. In a word, it is the path to excellence on which they travel with their God and Messiah.

In this third vineyard-owner parable, the tenants rebel and take over the vineyard as if it belonged to them, refusing to recognize the rights of both the vineyard owner (God) and his son (Jesus). The curious feature is the statement that they killed the son in order to acquire the inheritance, which suggests a desire to appropriate to themselves his authority. The chief priests and the scribes, then, are being accused not of failing to recognize the authority of Jesus but seeking to destroy him precisely because they do recognize him as the son. Jesus accuses them of profound malice in seeking to appropriate to themselves his authority over the vineyard (Israel).

Reflecting on the Word

On this day of honor for St. Francis of Assisi, the prophet Isaiah describes how much God the gardener cherishes the vineyard—such care, such choice vines the divine hand has planted! That image naturally turns my thoughts to my relationship with my garden. I too get attached to my plants. I start my lavender and tomatoes from seed. I place them into soil that I have composted and manured. But my attachment is only a semblance of the devotion that God has for the human vineyard.

Last summer when I came back from vacation, the bunnies had chewed all my pole beans at ground level. The deer had chomped the tops off the sunflowers. Oh, I was exasperated. Imagine the angst when the stone fence around your vineyard is allowed to crumble so that wild beasts trample and eat all your grapevines. When you deeply care about something, you are more deeply hurt when it is not cared for.

Jesus' parable mirrors the Old Testament prophets' solemn warnings to the leaders of Israel. The "Great-I-Am" is looking for fruit. But there is no fruit. God's distress is with caregivers who do not give care. Leadership means to cherish and tend the vineyard, to do everything necessary to bring it to fruition.

As we read this series of vineyard parables in Matthew, we might question whether God is very "nice." We hear death and destruction, the wrath of the landowner and handing the stewardship to another—Jesus' ending is not "nice." Though American culture places a high value on "niceness," there is no "nice" in the Bible. God is merciful. God is kind. God also wants justice. God intends for this vineyard to be treated right. Woe to those who do not.

Consider/Discuss

❖ We throw our whole heart into many things in life—gardens, children, relationships, parish, school, job, business, and so on. What does it feel like when something we care about yields "rotten grapes"? What role does (or doesn't) "righteous indignation" play in the Christian life?

❖ In my early days of gardening, I was too "nice" to thin overgrown perennials and throw out diseased tomatoes. As a result, the whole garden suffered. What are the challenges to "just letting things go"? How do we balance that with pruning for the "greater good"?

Living and Praying with the Word

Lord our God, you are true. You are honorable. You are good. Thank you for caring for each of us and all of us so deeply. In whatever role you give us in life, send us your grace to discern how we are to lead and care for those whom you entrust to us. Help us to listen carefully to your warnings and not be so self-assured that we do not hear your correction. Not to us, but to you, is the glory when our efforts bear good fruit.

TWENTY-EIGHTH SUNDAY IN ORDINARY TIME

Today's Focus: Opening Your Invitation

Who doesn't like to be invited to a party? The best part of the celebration God invites us to is that even if we don't feel we are worthy or ready, God's desire that we attend overwhelms our imagined shortcomings.

FIRST READING

Isaiah 25:6–10a

On this mountain the Lord of hosts
   will provide for all peoples
a feast of rich food and choice wines,
   juicy, rich food and pure, choice wines.
On this mountain he will destroy
   the veil that veils all peoples,
the web that is woven over all nations;
   he will destroy death forever.
The Lord God will wipe away
   the tears from every face;
the reproach of his people he will remove
   from the whole earth; for the Lord has spoken.
   On that day it will be said:
"Behold our God, to whom we looked to save us!
   This is the Lord for whom we looked;
   let us rejoice and be glad that he has saved us!"
For the hand of the Lord will rest on this mountain.

PSALM RESPONSE

Psalm 23:6cd

I shall live in the house of the Lord all the days of my life.

SECOND READING

Philippians 4:12–14, 19–20

Brothers and sisters: I know how to live in humble circumstances; I know also how to live with abundance. In every circumstance and in all things I have learned the secret of being well fed and of going hungry, of living in abundance and of being in need. I can do all things in him who strengthens me. Still, it was kind of you to share in my distress.

My God will fully supply whatever you need, in accord with his glorious riches in Christ Jesus. To our God and Father, glory forever and ever. Amen.

In the shorter form of the reading, the passage in brackets is omitted.

Jesus again in reply spoke to the chief priests and elders of the people in parables, saying, "The kingdom of heaven may be likened to a king who gave a wedding feast for his son. He dispatched his servants to summon the invited guests to the feast, but they refused to come. A second time he sent other servants, saying, 'Tell those invited: "Behold, I have prepared my banquet, my calves and fattened cattle are killed, and everything is ready; come to the feast." ' Some ignored the invitation and went away, one to his farm, another to his business. The rest laid hold of his servants, mistreated them, and killed them. The king was enraged and sent his troops, destroyed those murderers, and burned their city. Then he said to his servants, 'The feast is ready, but those who were invited were not worthy to come. Go out, therefore, into the main roads and invite to the feast whomever you find.' The servants went out into the streets and gathered all they found, bad and good alike, and the hall was filled with guests. [But when the king came in to meet the guests, he saw a man there not dressed in a wedding garment. The king said to him, 'My friend, how is it that you came in here without a wedding garment?' But he was reduced to silence. Then the king said to his attendants, 'Bind his hands and feet, and cast him into the darkness outside, where there will be wailing and grinding of teeth.' Many are invited, but few are chosen."]

Understanding the Word

Chapters 25–27 of Isaiah contain certain elements found in later apocalyptic literature: worldwide judgment, cosmic upheaval, God's defeat of dark powers and deliverance from them, and the enthronement of God in the temple on the holy mountain in Jerusalem. The image of a banquet, which God hosts on this mountain, conveys the abundance and joy that the rescued faithful will experience once God has defeated the dark forces. The most powerful of these, death itself, will also fall, leaving nothing to mar the joy of God's reign over "all nations" as the devastated world is renewed. Those who have been brought to God's mountain will be safe from all harm, for the divine protection ("hand") will rest on the mountain.

Paul has apparently received some money from the Philippians, prompting him to comment on the vicissitudes of his apostleship, which has its material as well as spiritual high and low points. At times he has been comfortable and at other times his circumstances have been more "humble." From this he has learned how to "go with the flow," accepting whatever comes along. As always, the strength to persevere comes from Christ, who supplies everything Paul could possibly need. This confidence in the providential care of God allows Paul to be open to whatever comes. Throughout the letter, in various ways, this theme of radical selflessness has appeared, rooted not only in the example of Christ but also trust in God.

215

Jesus teaches consistently in Matthew's Gospel that while absolutely everyone is invited to enter the kingdom of heaven, the price of admission is high. The gate is narrow and the road is difficult, and few find it (7:13–14). The guest in the parable represents those who have failed to understand this fundamental teaching. He has taken up the king's generous invitation, but by failing to dress appropriately (even though, we must assume, he could have), he has demonstrated an overly casual attitude, treating the event as if it were simply a matter of "come as you are," an insult to the generosity of the king. The kingdom of God, the parable reminds us, is not something we should take for granted.

Reflecting on the Word

"What a day this has been!" I sighed to my new wife as the last of the clouds turned orange over the sea. This morning as the sun rose in the eastern sky, my heart had beaten with excitement: the wedding is coming! We will feast for seven days! The clamor in the kitchens proclaims the abundance to come. My father the king is so kind. My cup will overflow with joy. All will be good.

Then all was not good. The guests would not come. They rejected his invitation. They mistreated and killed our servants. It felt as though a web of darkness had descended, like a veil covering their eyes. How could they so scorn his generosity? They twisted his open-handed invitation into a disaster. I was devastated.

My father was not going to let me down. He sent out servants to bring in anyone, anyone at all, shouting into the streets, "Come to the feast, you will all be well fed!" He knew the new guests wouldn't have wedding clothes, for they didn't know that they would be invited. I watched the servants carry armloads of garments to the doors. All would be taken care of. And they started pouring in. The crippled and the beggars, the hungry and the weary—they all threw on the fine clothes that my father provided. Rich food and choice wine—oh, they had never tasted such goodness! They lacked for nothing. (There was one who tried to ruin the day, but enough talk of calamity.)

I turn my face to my bride. The look in her eyes and her eager "yes, yes, and yes!" more than make up for the numerous exclamations of "no!" this day. The night is here. A blessed new day will dawn.

Consider/Discuss

❖ In what ways do we look into the Bridegroom's eyes and bring him joy with our "yes, yes, and yes"? What do we look forward to in the new day that will dawn?

❖ How has the lavishness of God fed us even when we have not expected it? What is our responsibility in response to that generosity?

Living and Praying with the Word

Lord, you are our God! You have been a refuge to the poor, a haven to the needy in times of distress. We are the poor. We are the needy. Sometimes we reject you and push you away and do not let you clothe us. Strengthen our "yes" so that it becomes eager and consistent, for we do not ever want to disappoint you. Lavish your Spirit upon us, for we hunger to partake of your feast.

TWENTY-NINTH SUNDAY IN ORDINARY TIME

Today's Focus: Walking on the Edge

---

*Today, as usual, when an attempt is made to trick Jesus into answering
a question that seems to have no right answers, he nimbly skips up
that precarious edge to point us beyond—and above.*

FIRST READING   Isaiah 45:1, 4–6

Thus says the LORD to his anointed, Cyrus,
   whose right hand I grasp,
subduing nations before him,
   and making kings run in his service,
opening doors before him
   and leaving the gates unbarred:
For the sake of Jacob, my servant,
   of Israel, my chosen one,
I have called you by your name,
   giving you a title, though you knew me not.
I am the LORD and there is no other,
   there is no God besides me.
It is I who arm you, though you know me not,
   so that toward the rising and the setting of the sun
   people may know that there is none besides me.
I am the LORD, there is no other.

PSALM RESPONSE   Psalm 96:7b

Give the Lord glory and honor.

SECOND READING   1 Thessalonians 1:1–5b

Paul, Silvanus, and Timothy to the church of the Thessalonians in God the
Father and the Lord Jesus Christ: grace to you and peace. We give thanks to God
always for all of you, remembering you in our prayers, unceasingly calling to mind
your work of faith and labor of love and endurance in hope of our Lord Jesus
Christ, before our God and Father, knowing, brothers and sisters loved by God,
how you were chosen. For our gospel did not come to you in word alone, but also
in power and in the Holy Spirit and with much conviction.

The Pharisees went off and plotted how they might entrap Jesus in speech. They sent their disciples to him, with the Herodians, saying, "Teacher, we know that you are a truthful man and that you teach the way of God in accordance with the truth. And you are not concerned with anyone's opinion, for you do not regard a person's status. Tell us, then, what is your opinion: Is it lawful to pay the census tax to Caesar or not?" Knowing their malice, Jesus said, "Why are you testing me, you hypocrites? Show me the coin that pays the census tax." Then they handed him the Roman coin. He said to them, "Whose image is this and whose inscription?" They replied, "Caesar's." At that he said to them, "Then repay to Caesar what belongs to Caesar and to God what belongs to God."

Understanding the Word

In the Bible, Cyrus of Persia is credited with ending the Babylonian exile. Yet Isaiah is careful to note that Cyrus, unknowingly, is an agent of the God of Israel, who is using him to defeat Babylon and restore the Chosen People to their land. This is why Cyrus is called here the Lord's "anointed" (Messiah). Cyrus might be expected to believe that one of his own national gods was responsible for assuring his victories, but this is not the case. In fact, God insists, there are no other gods. The larger implication is that the sovereign reach of God extends well beyond Israel to include all of earth's rulers, most of whom do not even know this God (yet).

When Paul left Thessalonica his companions Timothy and Silvanus stayed behind, joining him later in Corinth with a report of conditions in the northern city. The good report prompts Paul's thanksgiving. Throughout the letter Paul will attend to the question of Christ's return, a theme signaled here by the reference to "endurance in hope of our Lord Jesus Christ." The basis for their faith, love, and hope is the gospel, whose truth was made evident in power. Evidently the Thessalonians had experienced something that allowed them to believe the gospel was more than just another philosophy or religious system. The truth of the gospel was made evident to them, in some way, by its fruits.

The trap set for Jesus places him in a bind. If he refuses to pay the Roman tax, he's a rebel. If he pays the tax too eagerly, some would consider him a traitor to his people. Jesus cleverly avoids the trap by contrasting the image of Caesar with the image of God. The coin is stamped with the image of Caesar; humans are stamped with the image of God (Genesis 1:27; 9:6). The coin belongs to Caesar, so it's just a piece of metal; if he wants his coin back, give it to him. Jesus is far more concerned about making sure that God gets back what belongs to God; that is what Jesus' mission is about.

Reflecting on the Word

I had to pay close attention. The rocks were covered with lichen and slippery from the morning dew. Boulders slanted and tipped. On that early June morning when we hiked "The Knife Edge" at the top of the world on Mount Katahdin in Maine, cliffs dropped a thousand feet on both sides. I wasn't scared, but the potential peril made me careful about where I placed my feet. I wanted to get safely to the summit.

Jesus walks his own "Knife Edge" in today's Gospel. The Pharisees offer two precipices for him to tumble down: be popular with the Jewish crowds by thumbing your nose at the Roman emperor or preach sedition by not giving authority its due. There is danger in whichever answer he chooses. They hope to lure him to his demise.

But the wisdom of God is more astute than tricky tempters. Jesus is attentive to where he sets his feet, hyper-alert to the peril the posturers are posing. Instead of veering toward one of their cliffs, he redirects them toward the summit: Look up! Look higher! You belong to God. Everything belongs to God, even the Caesar who appears to be so mighty and so grand. "Repay to Caesar what belongs to Caesar and to God what belongs to God."

The Pharisees are amazed. Maybe it is Jesus' cunning. Maybe it was more than that. Perhaps his response stirred their hearts? His words sent them higher, echoing their own psalm: "Give to the LORD the glory due his name!"

I did get through that boulder field safely. That fourteen-year-old summer, I was only beginning to learn wisdom about the cliffs of life. The trek was painstaking, yes. But the view from the mountaintop? That was amazing.

Consider/Discuss

❖ What are the "cliffs" in your life? How does the Tempter try to lure you toward your spiritual demise? When has the Holy Spirit brought you back onto the path toward the Summit?

❖ When you have been in a position of authority (as a parent or pastor; babysitter, teacher or boss), how have you had to walk that narrow path between pleasing "the crowd" and following the rules? How did you find God's wisdom in what to do or say?

Living and Praying with the Word

Lord, the effort to be true to you requires continual effort. Thank you that we do not walk alone. Thank you, Holy Spirit, for the times when you have strengthened our weak knees and redirected our gaze on this hard road of pilgrimage. God of glory, when we see you face to face, the sweat and the struggle will fade away. Sovereign Lord, you alone are our Source and our Summit, for all the earth belongs to you.

THIRTIETH SUNDAY IN ORDINARY TIME

Today's Focus: Taking God's Love for Granted

Rather than thinking of our love for God in terms of quantities, perhaps understanding it as having dimensions will allow God to beckon us more deeply into love, into greater constancy of love.

FIRST READING

Exodus 22:20–26

Thus says the LORD: "You shall not molest or oppress an alien, for you were once aliens yourselves in the land of Egypt. You shall not wrong any widow or orphan. If ever you wrong them and they cry out to me, I will surely hear their cry. My wrath will flare up, and I will kill you with the sword; then your own wives will be widows, and your children orphans.

"If you lend money to one of your poor neighbors among my people, you shall not act like an extortioner toward him by demanding interest from him. If you take your neighbor's cloak as a pledge, you shall return it to him before sunset; for this cloak of his is the only covering he has for his body. What else has he to sleep in? If he cries out to me, I will hear him; for I am compassionate."

PSALM RESPONSE

Psalm 18:2

I love you, Lord, my strength.

SECOND READING

1 Thessalonians 1:5c–10

Brothers and sisters: You know what sort of people we were among you for your sake. And you became imitators of us and of the Lord, receiving the word in great affliction, with joy from the Holy Spirit, so that you became a model for all the believers in Macedonia and in Achaia. For from you the word of the Lord has sounded forth not only in Macedonia and in Achaia, but in every place your faith in God has gone forth, so that we have no need to say anything. For they themselves openly declare about us what sort of reception we had among you, and how you turned to God from idols to serve the living and true God and to await his Son from heaven, whom he raised from the dead, Jesus, who delivers us from the coming wrath.

When the Pharisees heard that Jesus had silenced the Sadducees, they gathered together, and one of them, a scholar of the law, tested him by asking, "Teacher, which commandment in the law is the greatest?" He said to him, "You shall love the Lord, your God, with all your heart, with all your soul, and with all your mind. This is the greatest and the first commandment. The second is like it: You shall love your neighbor as yourself. The whole law and the prophets depend on these two commandments."

Understanding the Word

Having delivered Israel from Egypt, God now sets forth the expectations of the covenantal relationship. Chief among them is a concern for the vulnerable, especially, but not only, aliens (non-Israelites residing on Israelite land), widows, and orphans (that is, children without fathers). Without an adult male Israelite relation to defend them, these people were particularly vulnerable to injustice and fraud. The poor in general were also subject to manipulation and exploitation. In Israel God is creating a just, compassionate society that reflects the divine character by ensuring that the defenseless are protected. The disturbing threat of sword and "poetic justice" for those who abuse widows and orphans emphasizes the strength of divine concern for them.

Despite "great affliction" the Thessalonians have persevered in imitating Paul, who in turn has imitated Christ. The gospel has transformed their entire worldview, and their new lives of faith have been such that others have observed and been edified as they spread the gospel not only in words but through their example. The gospel, which had been received "in power . . . with much conviction" has brought joy, hope, and conversion to the Thessalonians. This transformation is part of the content of their witness to the gospel; they have become "a model for all believers." This, despite, or perhaps because of, the "great affliction" that they have nevertheless endured with "joy from the Holy Spirit."

The question put to Jesus about the greatest commandment is presented as a test, although we are not told in what the test consists. We know that there was a tradition of pointing toward certain commandments as in effect summing up all of the Law and the prophets. Therefore Jesus' response by quoting first Deuteronomy 6:5 and then Leviticus 19:18 would probably not have been controversial, and indeed he receives no rebuttal from the Pharisees. It is interesting to note that the second commandment is "like" the first in that they both command "love," understood in the biblical sense not as an emotion so much as a committed stance. For God, it means devotion and wholehearted commitment. For neighbor, it means commitment to their good, and seeking to help them when they need it.

Reflecting on the Word

As I work with good-hearted preachers, I hear in homilies repeatedly that God loves us and that we are to love God and our neighbor. Do you hear (or say) that, too? Some of us use "churchy words" over and over again. Might we not have a hard time transcending the superficial to say something fresh and new about love today when we have talked about love so many times? Love, love, love, blah, blah, blah . . .

How can we go deeper? For inspiration, we turn to a medieval Carmelite monk whose affection for God was so warm that his kindliness overflowed to others. Brother Lawrence of the Resurrection wrote in *The Practice of the Presence of God* that all counts for lost in the time that is not spent in loving God. Wherever he was, he practiced the presence of God. Whatever he did, he did with Jesus. He flipped an omelet with God; he repaired shoes with the Lord; he spoke with others while remaining attentive to the Holy Spirit within his heart. Three hundred years later, his little maxims about love of God and love of neighbor are still invigorating.

You and I, how can we love more deeply? We can be more constant in our communion with God. We can pray more often. Today's psalmist offers us little words of love to pray all day, modeling for us how to cherish the living God: "I love you, O Lord, my strength, O Lord, my rock, my fortress, my deliverer!" Lifting up our hearts for thirty seconds, we can send our adorations to God. Loving tenderness then wells up within us and overflows to others.

We have little control over "how good" we are in prayer or in love. But we can be more constant with them both.

Consider/Discuss

❖ With Brother Lawrence, we can gain the habit of being constant in practicing the presence of God. Partner with one other person to try that for one whole day. Share with one another what that experience was like.

❖ Think about times when you have taken expressions of love for granted: at the end of a phone call, as one is going out the door, etc. What jogs you out of that fog to better appreciate who and what you have?

Living and Praying with the Word

O Lord our rock, our redeemer, our stronghold, do not let us take your love for granted! When we absorb the immensity of your care for us, then we want to love you with all our heart and soul and mind and strength. Deepen us this day. Well up in our hearts and help us to radiate your love to others. For through you and with you and in you, we have our being. We love you. We love you. We love you.

ALL SAINTS

Today's Focus: *The Aroma of the Heavenly Feast*

Do we imagine the heavenly banquet as having an aroma?
One that wafts toward us, lifting us up in the manner of a blissful cartoon
character? Oh, what a fragrance the celestial delights must have!

FIRST READING

Revelation 7:2–4, 9–14

I, John, saw another angel come up from the East, holding the seal of the living God. He cried out in a loud voice to the four angels who were given power to damage the land and the sea, "Do not damage the land or the sea or the trees until we put the seal on the foreheads of the servants of our God." I heard the number of those who had been marked with the seal, one hundred and forty-four thousand marked from every tribe of the Israelites.

After this I had a vision of a great multitude, which no one could count, from every nation, race, people, and tongue. They stood before the throne and before the Lamb, wearing white robes and holding palm branches in their hands. They cried out in a loud voice:

"Salvation comes from our God, who is seated on the throne,
and from the Lamb."

All the angels stood around the throne and around the elders and the four living creatures. They prostrated themselves before the throne, worshiped God, and exclaimed:

"Amen. Blessing and glory, wisdom and thanksgiving,
honor, power, and might
be to our God forever and ever. Amen."

Then one of the elders spoke up and said to me, "Who are these wearing white robes, and where did they come from?" I said to him, "My lord, you are the one who knows." He said to me, "These are the ones who have survived the time of great distress; they have washed their robes and made them white in the Blood of the Lamb."

PSALM RESPONSE

Psalm 24:6

Lord, this is the people that longs to see your face.

SECOND READING   *1 John 3:1–3*

Beloved: See what love the Father has bestowed on us that we may be called the children of God. Yet so we are. The reason the world does not know us is that it did not know him. Beloved, we are God's children now; what we shall be has not yet been revealed. We do know that when it is revealed we shall be like him, for we shall see him as he is. Everyone who has this hope based on him makes himself pure, as he is pure.

GOSPEL   *Matthew 5:1–12a*

When Jesus saw the crowds, he went up the mountain, and after he had sat down, his disciples came to him. He began to teach them, saying:
"Blessed are the poor in spirit,
    for theirs is the Kingdom of heaven.
Blessed are they who mourn,
    for they will be comforted.
Blessed are the meek,
    for they will inherit the land.
Blessed are they who hunger and thirst for righteousness,
    for they will be satisfied.
Blessed are the merciful,
    for they will be shown mercy.
Blessed are the clean of heart,
    for they will see God.
Blessed are the peacemakers,
    for they will be called children of God.
Blessed are they who are persecuted for the sake of righteousness,
    for theirs is the kingdom of heaven.
Blessed are you when they insult you and persecute you and utter every kind of evil against you falsely because of me. Rejoice and be glad, for your reward will be great in heaven."

Understanding the Word

The scene in Revelation, which occurs as an interlude in the depiction of apocalyptic judgment, focuses on those who will be protected because of their fidelity to God. The "seal of the living God" is like a signet ring used to claim ownership; those who have been marked with the seal belong to God and are therefore safe. They are among the "great multitude" that includes Christians from beyond ethnic Israel who have "won the victory" and remained faithful during the time of persecution. The robes washed white in the blood of Christ signify renewal, joy, and resurrection; the palms signify victory. Now safe, the faithful worship God with the Lamb, a fitting response to the salvation won from them both.

The First Letter of John has, up to the point of our reading, been developing the theme of "fellowship with God," which means a sharing in God's eternal life through Christ. This fellowship is manifested in loving others, repentance, and avoiding sin. To be in fellowship with God means to be a child of God. This places us in the light, in truth and goodness, not in the darkness of moral depravity. The relationship is in place and is safe as long as we remain in fellowship with Christ. Those who have hope in the future glory that they will share with Christ ensure that they are pure, avoiding turning away from Christ and his commandment, which in the Johannine literature is summed up in the phrase "love one another."

The Beatitudes are, on the one hand, good news of "blessedness." On the other hand, they make clear that following Jesus is difficult. Poverty of spirit means renunciation of both material and other "possessions." Meekness, mercy, and peacemaking often go against our desire to strike back or get even. We must work diligently to develop the kind of single-minded devotion to God implied in purity of heart and hunger and thirst for righteousness. And of course, no one seeks persecution and insult. Those who are able, throughout their lives, to finally meet the challenge of the Beatitudes are perhaps few, as Jesus will later warn, but they will indeed be blessed.

Reflecting on the Word

The last time I made popcorn the smell reminded me of my mom. The kernels exploded out of the hot-air popper into her green and white mixing bowl. I melted butter as she had. I sprinkled the buttered kernels with salt and stirred it all up. I popped three kernels into my mouth. Delicious! (She ate her popcorn one kernel at a time, so she was a bit more proper than I was.) It may make me old-fashioned, but I don't microwave popcorn in a bag. Why? It does not evoke memories. It does not smell right. It does not bring my mom back to life.

On this feast of All Saints, we celebrate the dead and bring their memory back to life. Yet, when we think about those who have departed, those who have gone to heaven before us . . . well, I think that we have it backwards. But, really, truly, they are the living. We are the dying. From the flash when we were conceived, through our first whiff of lilacs, until that moment when our breathing stops, we are dying for the aroma of eternity. Something heavenly awaits us.

Can you sense that? My mom is alive! My grandma is alive! Your mom or brother or child or sister or aunt or dad is alive! Within the limits of our earthly snuffling, we only sense barrenness where we used to inhale their fragrance. We cannot perceive them. That hollowness can hurt. But they are partaking of the feast of heaven—the most sweet-smelling chocolate cake on earth cannot compare. They have gone before us into the banquet of life. The God of glory is the Fragrance of fragrances, the Delight of delights. Today, with all the church, militant and glorified, may we get a whiff of that glory!

Consider/Discuss

❖ What is your initial reaction when you read that we are the dying and those who have gone before us are the living? Does that feel morbid or glorious? How does it change your worldview when you shift that perspective?

❖ Who do you most want to celebrate today on All Saints Day? Which of the Beatitudes does he or she best exemplify?

Living and Praying with the Word

God of glory, you give us so many heroes and heroines of the faith! They toiled for what was right. They fought for justice. Thank you for giving us so many examples of people of holy virtue. They lived and died for you. They knew you and loved you. We want to be saints, too. Lift us higher! Empower our faith! Take us with you to the banquet! Ah, the joy of All Saints!

THIRTY-SECOND SUNDAY IN ORDINARY TIME

Today's Focus: Trembling, But Confident

The life of faith often holds us in a paradox between a fear of what is to come and assurance that in Christ all will be well. Christians must learn to live within that tension.

FIRST READING
Wisdom 6:12–16

Resplendent and unfading is wisdom,
    and she is readily perceived by those who love her,
    and found by those who seek her.
She hastens to make herself known in anticipation of their desire;
    whoever watches for her at dawn shall not be disappointed,
    for he shall find her sitting by his gate.
For taking thought of wisdom is the perfection of prudence,
    and whoever for her sake keeps vigil
    shall quickly be free from care;
because she makes her own rounds, seeking those worthy of her,
    and graciously appears to them in the ways,
    and meets them with all solicitude.

PSALM RESPONSE
Psalm 63:2b

My soul is thirsting for you, O Lord my God.

SECOND READING
1 Thessalonians 4:13–18 or 4:13–14

In the shorter form of the reading, the passage in brackets is omitted.

We do not want you to be unaware, brothers and sisters, about those who have fallen asleep, so that you may not grieve like the rest, who have no hope. For if we believe that Jesus died and rose, so too will God, through Jesus, bring with him those who have fallen asleep. [Indeed, we tell you this, on the word of the Lord, that we who are alive, who are left until the coming of the Lord, will surely not precede those who have fallen asleep. For the Lord himself, with a word of command, with the voice of an archangel and with the trumpet of God, will come down from heaven, and the dead in Christ will rise first. Then we who are alive, who are left, will be caught up together with them in the clouds to meet the Lord in the air. Thus we shall always be with the Lord. Therefore, console one another with these words.]

Jesus told his disciples this parable: "The kingdom of heaven will be like ten virgins who took their lamps and went out to meet the bridegroom. Five of them were foolish and five were wise. The foolish ones, when taking their lamps, brought no oil with them, but the wise brought flasks of oil with their lamps. Since the bridegroom was long delayed, they all became drowsy and fell asleep. At midnight, there was a cry, 'Behold, the bridegroom! Come out to meet him!' Then all those virgins got up and trimmed their lamps. The foolish ones said to the wise, 'Give us some of your oil, for our lamps are going out.' But the wise ones replied, 'No, for there may not be enough for us and you. Go instead to the merchants and buy some for yourselves.' While they went off to buy it, the bridegroom came and those who were ready went into the wedding feast with him. Then the door was locked. Afterwards the other virgins came and said, 'Lord, Lord, open the door for us!' But he said in reply, 'Amen, I say to you, I do not know you.' Therefore, stay awake, for you know neither the day nor the hour."

Understanding the Word

The figure of Woman (or Lady) Wisdom constantly seeks to instruct anyone who will listen. As "the spotless mirror of the power of God, the image of his goodness" (7:26), she is the perfect teacher. She is not aloof or inaccessible, but is available to anyone who seeks her out, watching for her, keeping vigil, as she moves through life making her presence known. But only those who work to master her teachings and conform their lives to them are "worthy of her." Those who do so will gain prudence and wisdom and thus become "righteous." Those who forsake her teaching, on the other hand, will be remain "foolish" and therefore "unrighteous."

The Thessalonians were apparently concerned that those who had died before the return of Christ had perished. Paul reminds them that the resurrection of Christ was only the beginning, that all the baptized would be raised as Christ was. This is why Paul can refer to the dead as having merely "fallen asleep." In fact, at the glorious coming of Christ, the dead, having been raised, will be the first to join Christ in his glory. Drawing on standard apocalyptic images (angels, trumpets, Christ coming on clouds), Paul paints an image of the *parousia*, the hinge-point between the present age and the coming age. Paul's audience is assured that, dead or alive, those who are in Christ will be with him forever.

The parable of the ten virgins draws on the biblical wisdom motif of the distinction between the wise and the foolish. The wise are those who seek to understand the will of God and to live accordingly; they are the righteous. The foolish are not necessarily intellectually stupid, but they are "spiritually" stupid, often wicked, and certainly on the wrong path. In the parable, the foolish virgins represent those who are unprepared because they have failed to heed Jesus' teaching. Readers sometimes fault the wise virgins for being stingy, but the point is that the wise are able to do nothing for the foolish when they wait until it is too late to order their lives properly.

Reflecting on the Word

A friend told me that this parable frightened her when she was little. What if she was foolish and forgot her oil and Jesus abandoned her and she was cast out into the darkness?

A teenager told me about a time when she was five years old. She had come in from playing, and found the curtains drawn and her darkened house empty. Her parents and siblings were nowhere. She sat down and sobbed, thinking that the end-times had come. Jesus had taken them and she had been left behind.

As the sun grows dimmer and the church calendar draws toward its close, we hear much about the final judgment. The Jews of Jesus' day expected Almighty God to declare war on evil at any moment and hold all people accountable for their deeds. Some of Jesus' apocalyptic words feel foreboding. Be ready. The end is coming. If there is "a test," will I pass it? Am I Christian enough? Might I be among the foolish, one who has messed up just too many times?

On the other hand, we might identify with the smart virgins: I am pious. I say my prayers. I am Christian enough. Perhaps everyone will "pass" at the end of time, for God is merciful. Might God choose to hand everyone an "A"?

Which is it? Well—both—and neither.

Yes, the end is coming, whether at our own death or at the conclusion of time. But panic only paralyzes, and presumption makes us imprudent. In wisdom, how are we to approach the Blessed One at judgment? Holy fear and a bit of awestruck trembling are needed. So is the graced conviction that we are profoundly loved and radically forgiven. Awe and confidence walk together hand in hand.

Consider/Discuss

❖ Christian faith is full of paradox. As we prepare for "the end," how do we keep a healthy balance between holy fear and graced confidence? Toward which side do you tend to lean?

❖ Should the "wise" virgins give some of their oil to the "foolish" ones? Should God give everyone an "A" on the final exam? Why or why not?

Living and Praying with the Word

Jesus our Bridegroom, you don't only come in a rush at the end of time. Sometimes you tiptoe in quietly and beckon to us in the depths of our conscience. We know that our end is coming. Give us a touch of holy fear to help us heed you now so we are ready then. Do not let our love grow cold as we wait for you. Come to us, Spirit of warmth, and keep our lamps burning brightly.

THIRTY-THIRD SUNDAY IN ORDINARY TIME

Today's Focus: Return on Investment

God invests in us; we, in turn, invest our lives in God.
The danger comes in making our spiritual lives too transactional.
Rather, we invest—and are invested in—through our relationship with the divine.

FIRST READING
Proverbs 31:10–13, 19–20, 30–31

When one finds a worthy wife,
　her value is far beyond pearls.
Her husband, entrusting his heart to her,
　has an unfailing prize.
She brings him good, and not evil,
　all the days of her life.
She obtains wool and flax
　and works with loving hands.
She puts her hands to the distaff,
　and her fingers ply the spindle.
She reaches out her hands to the poor,
　and extends her arms to the needy.
Charm is deceptive and beauty fleeting;
　the woman who fears the Lord is to be praised.
Give her a reward for her labors,
　and let her works praise her at the city gates.

PSALM RESPONSE
Psalm 128:1a

Blessed are those who fear the Lord.

SECOND READING
1 Thessalonians 5:1–6

Concerning times and seasons, brothers and sisters, you have no need for anything to be written to you. For you yourselves know very well that the day of the Lord will come like a thief at night. When people are saying, "Peace and security," then sudden disaster comes upon them, like labor pains upon a pregnant woman, and they will not escape.

But you, brothers and sisters, are not in darkness, for that day to overtake you like a thief. For all of you are children of the light and children of the day. We are not of the night or of darkness. Therefore, let us not sleep as the rest do, but let us stay alert and sober.

In the shorter form of the reading, the passage in brackets is omitted.

Jesus told his disciples this parable: "A man going on a journey called in his servants and entrusted his possessions to them. To one he gave five talents; to another, two; to a third, one—to each according to his ability. Then he went away. [Immediately the one who received five talents went and traded with them, and made another five. Likewise, the one who received two made another two. But the man who received one went off and dug a hole in the ground and buried his master's money.]

"After a long time the master of those servants came back and settled accounts with them. The one who had received five talents came forward bringing the additional five. He said, 'Master, you gave me five talents. See, I have made five more.' His master said to him, 'Well done, my good and faithful servant. Since you were faithful in small matters, I will give you great responsibilities. Come, share your master's joy.' [Then the one who had received two talents also came forward and said, 'Master, you gave me two talents. See, I have made two more.' His master said to him, 'Well done, my good and faithful servant. Since you were faithful in small matters, I will give you great responsibilities. Come, share your master's joy.' Then the one who had received the one talent came forward and said, 'Master, I knew you were a demanding person, harvesting where you did not plant and gathering where you did not scatter; so out of fear I went off and buried your talent in the ground. Here it is back.' His master said to him in reply, 'You wicked, lazy servant! So you knew that I harvest where I did not plant and gather where I did not scatter? Should you not then have put my money in the bank so that I could have got it back with interest on my return? Now then! Take the talent from him and give it to the one with ten. For to everyone who has, more will be given and he will grow rich; but from the one who has not, even what he has will be taken away. And throw this useless servant into the darkness outside, where there will be wailing and grinding of teeth.'"]

Understanding the Word

The woman in this poem from Proverbs may be understood literally, as the "ideal wife," or symbolically, as Wisdom. The Bible regularly extols wisdom as a great prize, worth more than gold or precious jewels, more than long life or power. As a personification of God's will and reason, Wisdom imparts to those who befriend her all they need to be successful in the world and in their relationship with God. A human wife would have learned from Wisdom and thus manifested her teachings, which extend across the whole human experience, from practical household management to concern for the poor (what Wisdom would call "righteousness") to fear of the Lord (the prerequisite for learning wisdom [Proverbs 9:10]).

The phrase "peace and security" was part of the propaganda of the Roman Empire, so Paul's use of it here points toward those who are content with and profiting from the present age of human rule. These are unprepared, living as it were "at night" and in darkness, for the coming of the Lord. But for those who live in the light, who are hopefully waiting for the Lord and living accordingly, his advent will not come as an unpleasant surprise. Living in the day, they will not be asleep, but awake and ready. In other words, no one knows the "times or seasons," but those who are living the Christian life will be prepared to meet the Lord whenever he comes.

The focus of the parable of the talents is on the unfortunate servant who failed to gain any profit for his master because he was afraid. The Lectionary translation has the servant characterizing his master as "demanding," but the Greek word *(skleiros)* really means hard, harsh, or severe. The servant, afraid to trade because he might lose the money and incur the master's wrath, failed to realize that the master showed confidence in him by giving him the talent and was willing to take a chance on him. The fault lay not in failing to gain any money, but in not even trying out of lack of trust in the master and his wisdom in giving the talent in the first place.

Reflecting on the Word

Another test! This time, it looks like the final in the evangelist Matthew's finance class. Is there an eternal spreadsheet in heaven? Do the angels daily tabulate how much God has invested in us and how much we give back? When we get to the pearly gates, will St. Peter be holding out our heavenly balance sheet?

In today's parable, "talents" were worth a thousand dollars each. In ancient times, the master who gave five talents, or five thousand dollars, invested a lot of money. Even one thousand dollars would have been a generous risk. Did he find the return on investment (ROI) worth it?

A mom gets up at 2:46 a.m. to tend to a vomiting four-year-old. A programmer sips his fourth cup of coffee to get the energy to put the final edits on a project. A coach invests long hours to improve her shooting forward's free throws. Is the ROI worth it?

What are we to make of this parable? Is Jesus urging us toward a responsible lifestyle in which we carefully use (and not bury in the ground) the talents we have been given to build a better world? Is he telling us to dutifully invest the goods of faith toward lifting the lost? Yes and yes.

But even more than that, Christian life is not a bargaining "You gave me this, God, so I'll give you that." The mom may (or may not) make a return on the time she gives to her child in the middle of the night. She loves anyway. The Creator of the world will never make a balanced return on us. God loves anyway. God takes a risk on us. The Giver of gifts asks us to invest our lives in the boldest of schemes: follow Jesus wherever and however he leads. That is a grand venture. The ROI is out of this world.

Consider/Discuss

❖ Have you ever cried out in frustration, "God, you owe me!" or "I deserve more!" How does the bargaining of a "balance-sheet Christianity" disparage the generosity of the risk-taking God? Are we willing to invest our lives and take a risk on the divine giver?

❖ In abuse situations, children hide. When a boss's temper is erratic, employees pull inward. If you had a hard taskmaster, would you feel like hiding your talents in the ground? What would help you to be willing to step out and take a risk?

Living and Praying with the Word

God of love, there is no way that I can give you back as much as I have been given. Do not let me see myself as a number on a heavenly balance sheet. Whatever you call me to do, help me to spend my life with love and generosity. I believe that this life is worth my best effort. Refresh my energy, for sometimes I feel it wearing out. You did not count the cost. Help me to do the same. For you, eternal God, have not just promised a "reward." You have promised me yourself as my future.

OUR LORD JESUS CHRIST, KING OF THE UNIVERSE

Today's Focus: Transformed by Glory

The Glory of Jesus Christ our king isn't something we merely sit back and admire. It envelops us, and its majesty transforms us, until we become Christ-like through its presence and power.

FIRST READING
Ezekiel 34:11–12, 15–17

Thus says the Lord GOD: I myself will look after and tend my sheep. As a shepherd tends his flock when he finds himself among his scattered sheep, so will I tend my sheep. I will rescue them from every place where they were scattered when it was cloudy and dark. I myself will pasture my sheep; I myself will give them rest, says the Lord GOD. The lost I will seek out, the strayed I will bring back, the injured I will bind up, the sick I will heal, but the sleek and the strong I will destroy, shepherding them rightly.

As for you, my sheep, says the Lord GOD, I will judge between one sheep and another, between rams and goats.

PSALM RESPONSE
Psalm 23:1

The Lord is my shepherd; there is nothing I shall want.

SECOND READING
1 Corinthians 15:20–26, 28

Brothers and sisters: Christ has been raised from the dead, the firstfruits of those who have fallen asleep. For since death came through man, the resurrection of the dead came also through man. For just as in Adam all die, so too in Christ shall all be brought to life, but each one in proper order: Christ the firstfruits; then, at his coming, those who belong to Christ; then comes the end, when he hands over the kingdom to his God and Father, when he has destroyed every sovereignty and every authority and power. For he must reign until he has put all his enemies under his feet. The last enemy to be destroyed is death. When everything is subjected to him, then the Son himself will also be subjected to the one who subjected everything to him, so that God may be all in all.

GOSPEL
Matthew 25:31–46

Jesus said to his disciples: "When the Son of Man comes in his glory, and all the angels with him, he will sit upon his glorious throne, and all the nations will be assembled before him. And he will separate them one from another, as a shepherd separates the sheep from the goats. He will place the sheep on his right and the goats on his left. Then the king will say to those on his right, 'Come, you who are blessed by my Father. Inherit the kingdom prepared for you from the foundation of the world. For I was hungry and you gave me food, I was thirsty and you gave me drink, a stranger and you welcomed me, naked and you clothed me, ill and you cared for me, in prison and you visited me.' Then the righteous will answer him and say, 'Lord, when did we see you hungry and feed you, or thirsty and give you drink? When did we see you a stranger and welcome you, or naked and clothe you? When did we see you ill or in prison, and visit you?' And the king will say to them in reply, 'Amen, I say to you, whatever you did for one of the least brothers of mine, you did for me.' Then he will say to those on his left, 'Depart from me, you accursed, into the eternal fire prepared for the devil and his angels. For I was hungry and you gave me no food, I was thirsty and you gave me no drink, a stranger and you gave me no welcome, naked and you gave me no clothing, ill and in prison, and you did not care for me.' Then they will answer and say, 'Lord, when did we see you hungry or thirsty or a stranger or naked or ill or in prison, and not minister to your needs?' He will answer them, 'Amen, I say to you, what you did not do for one of these least ones, you did not do for me.' And these will go off to eternal punishment, but the righteous to eternal life."

Understanding the Word

The reading from Ezekiel comes from a passage that focuses on the failure of Israel's leaders, who have not shown solicitude for the socially and spiritually vulnerable but instead have been negligent or even taken advantage of God's flock for their own gain. Now, God says, I will do myself what you did not do. In God's care, the neglected, abused, or those who were allowed to "go astray" will be cared for properly; "the sleek and the strong" who took advantage of them will receive their judgment. Yet even among the flock will be found the faithless, whom God will seek out. But some of them will resist, proving themselves not part of God's flock, but goats and rams.

At least some of the Corinthian Christians denied the resurrection of the dead, yet had apparently accepted Paul's teaching on Christ's role in God's redemption. Paul points out that if there is no resurrection, and Christ was not raised from the dead, the gospel message is meaningless and false because they are still in their sins and have no hope beyond this life. The gospel is that Christ was raised from the dead, and because of this the baptized have received life in and through him and will be resurrected too at his second coming. Christ alone will be sovereign, the only authority, and all powers will be subject to him, including and especially the power of death.

The final judgment scene must be understood against the background of Jesus' consistent teaching, found throughout Matthew's Gospel, on the great difficulty of entering "the kingdom prepared for you from the foundation of the world." One must completely reform one's life, starting at the level of thought, attitude, and interpretation of reality. Thus the sheep have not made their way easily into the kingdom simply by a few "works of mercy." Their actions represent a fundamental disposition toward God that is manifested in their actions on behalf of others. These are the members of the flock who denied themselves, took up their crosses, and thus became followers of Christ. The goats represent those who never did deny themselves or take up their crosses, and thus never really lived for anyone but themselves.

Reflecting on the Word

On this the last Sunday of the liturgical year, many tongues will sing, "Christ Jesus Victor, Christ Jesus Ruler, Christ Jesus Lord and Redeemer." For the Son of Man is coming in his glory and all his angels will be with him. He will sit on his glorious throne, and all peoples will come before him. Let the trumpets sound!

On this day, we do not look at the little ways in which the Holy Spirit speaks—through the smell of popcorn, the labor of climbing a mountain, or the planting of onions. This feast lifts us to the majestic, toward the awesomeness of God. All those who await us in heaven have vibrated with this glory. They have seen Christ the King.

Have you gotten a taste of that glory—in a dream? On the edge of a song? In the radiance of a sunset? In the joy of a meal? We don't believe based on nothing. God has spoken. God has spoken to us.

The One we celebrate was so tiny at the beginning of this adventure. Today, he is grand as Christ the King. It is as though the coo of a newborn baby has swelled into the Hallelujah Chorus; the silence of a grain of sand has become the roar of the Pacific Ocean; the whisper of a gentle breeze has become the rumble of an earthquake. Rejoice!

In gathering the nations, the King wants our wholehearted "yes!" Have we been so completely changed into the person of Christ that we act as he acts, forgive as he forgives, and reach out as he reaches out? Have we given a cup of water to a little one? Have we fed the hungry? These actions are not just a garment thrown over our grubbiness. The trumpet blasts to transform our whole being.

Consider/Discuss

❖ Teresa of Ávila called her beloved in prayer "Your Majesty." Try using that invocation as you enter into a moment of silence and contemplate the grandeur of God. Have you seen God's glory? Tasted it? Heard it? Felt it? Share the story of that glory with a fellow traveler on the pilgrim road.

❖ As we ponder the sovereignty of Christ, it is an act of our will to obey and follow, to serve as he serves, to love as he loves, and to give as he gives. What one grace can I ask for today to solidify my will to serve my King?

Living and Praying with the Word

Father, Son, and Holy Spirit, thank you that we are not alone. Thank you for the fellow pilgrims who have walked with us this year. Thank you that we walk with the saints on earth and the hosts of heaven. Secure in that solidarity, we turn ourselves toward the light of the new liturgical year. We do not know what lies ahead. We do not know what will be. But we do know that the alleluias of the heavens will hold us, for with them, we too will to glorify you with our lives.

Br. John R. Barker, OFM, is a Franciscan friar with the Province of Saint John the Baptist (Cincinnati). He is currently Associate Professor of Old Testament Studies at Catholic Theological Union in Chicago, where he has taught since 2012. His main areas of biblical research relate to the formation and function of biblical texts, particularly the prophetic literature, and biblical theology. He is the book reviewer for the Old Testament and related topics for The Bible Today, contributes regularly to pastoral publications such as Emmanuel Magazine, and gives biblically-related lectures, presentations, and retreats throughout the US. He recently published the monograph Disputed Temple: A Rhetorical Analysis of the Book of Haggai.

Author: Understanding the Word

Dr. Karla J. Bellinger is the Associate Director of the John S. Marten Program for Homiletics at the University of Notre Dame. Her focus is to help bishops, priests, deacons, and MDiv students to connect their preaching with their listeners. She also teaches a popular prayer class to undergraduates entitled "Belonging to God: How to Dig Deeper in Prayer." Dr. Bellinger presents convocations, workshops and retreats all over the country. Before getting her doctorate in preaching, she was a parish pastoral associate, youth minister, high school theology teacher, hospital chaplain, CYO coach, and non-profit director. Closest to her heart, she and her husband Daniel are the parents of five young adult children and four grandchildren. With a bachelor's degree in forestry, she spends her free time in the natural world. She is a master gardener, so a question about soil is the way to get her talking.

Author: Reflecting on the Word
　　　　　Consider/Discuss
　　　　　Living and Praying with the Word

Notes

Notes

Notes

Notes

Notes